OUR VISION AND VALUES   WOMEN
SHAPING THE 21ST CENTURY

HUTNER, FRANCES CORNWALL

OUR VISION
AND VALUES

OUR VISION
AND VALUES

Women Shaping the 21st Century

Edited by
FRANCES C. HUTNER

 PRAEGER

Westport, Connecticut
London

Library of Congress Cataloging-in-Publication Data

Our vision and values : women shaping the 21st century / edited by
  Frances C. Hutner.
     p.   cm.
  Includes bibliographical references and index.
  ISBN 0–275–94032–2 (alk. paper)
  ISBN 0–275–94932–X (pbk.)
  1. Women—United States—Social conditions.   2. Feminism—United
States.   I. Hutner, Frances Cornwall.
  HQ1426.0958   1994
  305.42′0973—dc20   93–11863

British Library Cataloguing in Publication Data is available.

Library of Congress Catalog Card Number: 93–11863
ISBN: 0–275–94032–2
       0–275–94932–X (pbk.)

First published in 1994

Praeger Publishers, 88 Post Road West, Westport, CT 06881
An imprint of Greenwood Publishing Group, Inc.

Printed in the United States of America

The paper used in this book complies with the
Permanent Paper Standard issued by the National
Information Standards Organization (Z39.48–1984).

10 9 8 7 6 5 4 3 2 1

Copyright Acknowledgments

The authors and publisher gratefully acknowledge permission to reprint the following
previously published items:

Chapter 4 was originally a paper presented at the American Council on Education's
December 1990 Women Presidents' Summit. It has been reprinted with permission from the
American Council on Education. The tables in Chapter 4 are reprinted with permission
from the Center for the American Woman and Politics, Eagleton Institute of Politics,
Rutgers University.

"The Ultimate Mother" was an editorial in the May 12, 1991 *New York Times*. Copyright
© 1991 by The New York Times Company. Reprinted by permission.

The old question was pragmatic—how to get women inside. The enduring questions address vision and values—how to remake the inside, transform it into a better place for everyone.

Ruth Mandel, *Doing It Whose Way? Women in Leadership*

Contents

Acknowledgments

When Mildred Goldberger organized a Princeton Research Forum study group to discuss the outlook for women "after the revolution," she started a process that became this book about women shaping the future. As the book developed she helped frame it and encouraged its authors by providing enthusiasm, advice, and an appropriate place to meet. We give her our many thanks and hope she will be pleased with the results of her efforts and ours.

As editor, I would like to say how much I have appreciated the friendship and support of all of the contributors. I hope that they have found the experience of working together on the book as rewarding as I have.

I would like to thank Anne Keifer, our editor at Praeger Publishers, for her generously given help and for her encouragement when I most needed it.

And finally, I would like to thank my daughter, Louise, for her wise suggestions, her helpful editing, and particularly for her enthusiastic interest in the project. Her positive attitude made our undertaking seem eminently worthwhile.

Frances C. Hutner

OUR VISION
AND VALUES

1

Introduction

Frances C. Hutner

It is the year 2050. Looking backward over the first half of the 21st century what will women see? Will the "Year of the Woman," enthusiastically touted in the 1992 elections, have become the "Century of the Woman"? If so, what will that mean? An end to widespread child poverty? No homelessness? Health care for everyone? Pay equity, regardless of sex or race? Equal educational opportunity? Equal access to occupations and jobs within occupations? Equal emphasis in the health care system on the needs of women, children, and the elderly? Legislatures, courts, churches, corporations, law firms, engineering firms, government bureaucracies, academic institutions, health and social services where women and minorities work and advance without hitting glass walls or ceilings or being glued to sticky floors? Institutions like these with structures fitted to the needs of families? A century when women and men, minorities and majorities, respect each other's differences and abilities, work together as equals, and have the common good as their goal?

Looking forward from the last decade of the 20th century, the women writing this book focus on the future—on what the women looking backward in the year 2050 will see. An unprecedented twenty years of social change have altered almost every aspect of women's lives. What seemed not so long ago to be immutable patterns of work, courtship, family, and community life have all but disappeared. So thorough and rapid has been the pace of change that even the immediate future—next year, the year after—

is hard to see. This time of great change in familiar social structures is upsetting and stressful for everyone—women and men and children. In this book, as thoughtful women scholars, we consider the nature of these changes and their probable outcomes. We are concerned about what is happening to the quality of all of our lives and how women can affect the outcomes in positive ways.

In our lives and professions we have each been part of shaping the feminist history of the past few decades—we are feminist pioneers. We know what life was like before the "revolution," what we were trying to create, and what the successes and pitfalls have been. Our hope is that we can each use our particular knowledge and experience to help women take control of their lives in their several roles as paid workers, and unpaid mothers, wives, caretakers of the elderly, and volunteers.

This book developed from a series of meetings first held under the aegis of the Princeton Research Forum, a multidisciplinary organization of independent scholars. The meetings were entitled "After the Revolution." Having become deeply engaged in these discussions, a core group of interested women met periodically to explore further the issues about the future that we saw as critical. Our talks heightened our concern about the difficult choices and many problems that all women, and particularly young women—our daughters—face today and tomorrow. We decided to write about these issues.

We do not believe in the *que sera, sera* philosophy, that "it"—whatever "it" is—is inevitable. We do believe, and optimistically hope, that as intelligent humans we can all learn from the past and build a better new world in the 21st century. These are some of our thoughts on how to do it.

DISPARATE TOPICS WITH A COMMON THEME

Our topics are diverse; ranging from women in the corporation to women in the church, from how women make a living to how they evaluate risks, from women in politics to women in literature, and from feminist therapy to women's spirituality to women's sexuality. But from all of these seemingly disparate topics a common theme emerges: Women live in a world whose every aspect has been defined by men. Yet, as the writers point out, women's concerns and power differ from men's in important ways that affect how they view risk, sexuality, work, spirituality, the use of language, the role of psychotherapy, politics, and the corporate world. In each of these spheres women have had to adjust to men's definition of women's proper place and their correct behavior.

These adjustments have been enforced by a variety of sanctions, ranging from exclusion to ridicule, from ostracism to the threat (and reality) of poverty, and, in the most egregious cases, from battering and disfigurement to murder. Marc Lépine, the disaffected young man who, on December 6,

1989, killed fourteen women engineering students in the University of Montreal's École Polytechnique—women who had dared to enter a man's field—epitomized the overwhelming need to keep women in their place. He came into a classroom shouting, "you're all a bunch of feminists and I hate feminists," told the men to leave, and opened fire on the women with his semiautomatic rifle, killing six. He then "stalked the cafeteria, classrooms and the corridors of the school, leaving a trail of death and injury in his wake." He left a suicide note blaming feminists for spoiling his life—an aspiring scientist, he had dropped out of junior college shortly before graduation.[1] Yet so commonplace that, unlike the "Montreal Massacre," it goes almost unnoticed, violence in the domestic setting happens every day, apparently a socially acceptable type of control. More than 21,000 domestic crimes against women were reported each week in 1991.[2]

On the bright side, however, our authors point out that American women have made real advances despite still pervasive systemic problems and a virulent backlash. Affirmative action coupled with economic, social, and political pressures have opened doors in education, in work, in politics, in sports, in religion, in the arts, in psychotherapy, and in sexual expression. Seeming defeats, like that of Anita Hill's in the Senate's Clarence Thomas hearings, have turned into victories as many women and men have responded with anger and action, and the issue of sexual harassment has come alive.

More recently, the failed Zoë Baird nomination for attorney general has put the spotlight on the nature and seriousness of the child care problem for all women in the United States. This facet of the roadblocks aspiring women face was further emphasized when the White House dismissed its second female attorney general candidate, Judge Kimba Wood, because it considered her child care arrangements, while legal, to be too controversial. With marvelous irony the administration concluded this saga of working women's difficulties by putting forward another highly qualified woman who, this time, was conveniently single, childless, and unburdened by the need for domestic help. In these and other cases women have been hung out to dry. But gradually, as women move two steps ahead and one step back, it is becoming inarguably clear that the system, not women, is the problem that needs to be fixed.

Women's Lives at Home and at Work

In Chapter 2, Frances Hutner looks at women's role in the economy. She discusses the dual nature of women's work as unpaid domestic workers and as paid members of the labor force. She notes that women's household work of bearing children, nurturing a family, and administering consumption is essential, yet our economy's accounting treats it as a natural function of woman and gives it no value. She investigates how the devaluation of women and their work arose, first using Thorstein Veblen's anthropological analysis of what he termed "the barbarian status of women." Then she describes the history of the devalued and, in fact, usually invisible woman in classical and neoclassical economic theory. Countering this, John Kenneth Galbraith's institutional analysis of women's unsung but critical role as administrators of consumption is, like Veblen's, a pointed critique of our society's values and our economy's way of operating.

As constantly growing numbers of women have become paid workers in the labor force, this devaluation of their work has stuck to them like a burr. They have typically been segregated into women's jobs and paid less than (white) men would be paid for doing work of equal value. Despite their much-increased presence in the labor force, few reach the top ranks of their businesses or professions. Because women need paid work to support themselves and their families, these problems are critical.

Hutner cites the evidence of these problems and their costs to women, men, and their children. She points out that, to borrow from computer jargon, our economy needs to make its institutions woman- and family-friendly. To do this it must first acknowledge and affirm the value of women's work, both at home and in the workplace. Progress is being made but much more must be done to recognize the economic and human realities of the lives of women. If women's vision and values are to shape a better 21st century, they must take control of their own lives in new ways—in government, business, unions, politics, schools, and advocacy groups.

Women in the Corporation

The corporate culture is a striking example of the institutional problems women face at paid work in our economy. In Chapter 3, organizational psychologist Jennifer Macleod uses her extensive experience in conducting self-empowerment workshops for corporations to discuss women's problems in achieving equal opportunity in corporate management. Can progress for women be accelerated by stronger legal, political, economic, and social pressures? Is the long-discussed "fear of success" syndrome really a special women's problem and the cause of their career difficulties? Are women at fault when they hit the "glass ceiling" or find themselves in the "mommy track"?

Macleod says that the effort to achieve full equity has been slow because it has been mainly aimed at symptoms rather than causes. She asserts that without major structural changes "the great remaining barrier to women's progress as managers" in the corporation will persist. She uses a simple but telling workshop scenario, entitled "The Short-Tall Scenario," to illustrate that barrier, showing why few women reach the top levels of a corporate world constructed to serve the biological and cultural characteristics of men.

She concludes with an analysis of the new requirements for effective organizations and advice on how we get there from here.

Doing It Whose Way? Women in Leadership

In the world of politics and government as in business, the media, and higher education, political analyst Ruth Mandel finds that women have achieved new access and social acceptance over what she terms "a remarkable generation." But the research on women in politics, done by the Center for the American Woman and Politics at Rutgers University, which Mandel heads, indicates that this progress is both incremental and marginal. In Chapter 4 Mandel supports this argument with revealing figures on women running for, and elected to, local, state, and congressional office. Marginalized women, she asserts, lack the power to influence policy in a domestic and global world facing overwhelming challenges.

Why, she asks, have so few women reached the top levels of leadership and power? What will it take to get more women into political office? She stresses women's troubling problem: that getting ahead seems to require playing the game by men's rules. And even then success is problematic. She cites the gubernatorial campaigns of Ann Richards in Texas and Dianne Feinstein in California as examples of women waging the tough and nasty campaigns usually associated with male candidates. Richards won. Feinstein lost.

After discussing a variety of reforms of the political system that would be helpful to women's candidacies, Mandel stresses the critical importance of women helping women. To make a difference women must support the women who take the daunting personal risk of playing politics differently, more honestly, and humanely, with new vision and values. These pioneering women will then be the needed models, the leaders, for women to come.

Varieties of Spiritual Experience: Women and Religion from the 1960s to the 1990s

In the prologue to Chapter 5 on the role of women in organized religion, Rosemary O'Brien writes: "Women used to use religion as a way of accepting their lives; now they use their lives to change religion." Her subsequent discussion reflects the same difficulties for women of being invisible and powerless that have confronted them in the economy, in the corporation, and in politics. In religion women have had to adjust to values, rituals, and rules defined by men. Her analysis echoes the point made by Violet Franks and Hanna Fox in Chapter 7 that male-dominated psychotherapy saw the woman, not the environment, as the problem that needed to be fixed. Therapy, like religion, has been a way of teaching women to accept their lives.

The feminism of the 1960s and the succeeding decades has brought changes to organized religion: new language in the churches, new ways of dressing and behaving for clergies, discourses about traditional ethics, arguments about women's roles in the church, ordination of women as rabbis and ministers. Women have heightened our moral awareness of issues of the environment, racial and sexual parity, and the ethic of caring. But religious structures have avoided fundamental change and women still lack authority and power.

O'Brien focuses on feminist forces for change within existing religious organizations. Women have been the mainstay of organized religion. Will they continue to provide its audience and support without more change in its patriarchal nature? Her interviews with Protestant, Catholic, and Jewish women are particularly interesting, reflecting the diversity of women's views on the possibilities of a religious reconstruction that includes feminine values.

Women's Spirituality II: An Alternative to Organized Religion

Some women have sought alternatives to organized religion rather than seeking to change its attitudes and framework. In Chapter 6 Francesca Benson describes an alternative women's spirituality that has grown out of the modern feminist movement. This spirituality seeks to express women's view of the sacred, drawing on a variety of sources—nature, modern feminist thought, ancient goddess symbolism, and women's own experiences.

Benson reviews the historical context of feminist spirituality and then turns to the words of women who are its practitioners. These women explain their dissatisfaction with their childhood experiences of organized religion and its neglect of women. They outline the steps that brought them to alternatives that expressed women's experience of the sacred. Using the example of a women's spirituality group formed in her town, Benson shows how this group came together, how it developed its activities and rituals, and how its members feel about it. She discusses some of the difficulties this group faced when conflicts developed and compares the group and its activities, structure, ritual, and membership with other groups. Members describe their interaction with traditional religions and with the community. Benson concludes with a look at the future of alternative women's spirituality.

Feminist Therapy: An Update and a Glimpse into the Future

Feminist therapy was born in the 1970s as an outgrowth of the women's movement. Clinical psychologist Violet Franks and her coauthor Hanna Fox write in Chapter 7 that feminist therapists saw that psychotherapy theory had been largely developed by male theoreticians and was geared to a male model of a sexist society. The goals of traditional therapy were to teach women to adjust to their prescribed social and economic roles as wives and mothers, teachers, nurses, secretaries, and clerical workers.

Franks and Fox describe feminist therapy as representing a radical departure from conventional psychotherapy, which was substantially based on a disease model introduced by Freud. The Freudian tack saw women who deviated from society's Victorian norms as pathological and worked to help them adapt to these norms. Feminist therapy, on the other hand, sees society rather than the individual as problematic. Feminist therapists focus on ways to strengthen the individual's ability to deal with the social, political, and economic causes of her problems. They help women reduce frequently paralyzing feelings of guilt and self-blame. They help them deal with the common paradox that leads women to feel depressed because they are told that they should feel happy and not complain when they have so much of what other people value and want for them. But what other people want for them is not what they really want for themselves.

Franks and Fox use case studies to show how women were treated by traditional and prefeminist therapists and how they are treated now by feminist therapists within the changing therapy landscape. They illustrate how women today face decisions rarely met by previous generations and how these issues have changed as women's family roles have changed.

The authors conclude with predictions about feminist therapy in the 21st century. They emphasize that feminist therapy will, of necessity, change as the economic and social realities of America change. White middle-class women, traditionally the bulk of feminist therapists' clientele, will be a decreasing proportion of the population. Growing ethnic diversity coupled with the problems of poverty, homelessness, abuse, single motherhood, and old age will present feminist therapy in the 21st century with the challenge of developing new ways of reaching a diverse population with a wide range of services.

Literary Criticism and Language

Literature and language both reflect and affect women's place in society. Like feminist therapy, feminist literary criticism developed along with the early phase of modern American feminism. Laura Curtis discusses the stages of development of feminist criticism and its growing importance since the late 1960s in academia and in the critical canon. In Chapter 8 she makes clear the disagreements within the body of feminist criticism as to the nature of women's writing as well as the divisions among various groups of authors and critics, particularly the disaffection of some lesbian and black feminists. She describes the third phase of feminist criticism—gender studies analysis—which has been heavily influenced by French poststructuralism. She illustrates how these feminist critics have used the theories of deconstruction and Lacanianism in their gender analyses of literature.

Curtis then moves on to the issue of the male-centered bias in language usage. When the issue of sexist language came to the fore in the 1970s, many men and, in fact, a goodly number of women derided feminists' concern with the effect of linguistic sexism on girls and women. They also cited customary usage and claimed that "he" and "man" were not necessarily sex-specific terms but were commonly used to reference both sexes.

Curtis points out that the use of the generic masculine has been the subject of argument since the 18th century. Prior to that time "they" was used to refer to an antecedent of unspecified or mixed sex and "they" is often used today, particularly by women. She finds that referencing with the masculine makes women both silent and invisible. This parallels the invisible situation of women that Frances Hutner describes in classical and neoclassical economic theory where "economic man" was the economic actor and the "worker" was always a "he."

As for the effect of sexist usage on females, Curtis cites arguments on both sides of this question. She includes an encouraging overview of current usage reforms in various fields such as publishing, professional organizations, scholarly books, religion, and government. She provides a helpful review of guides to nonsexism in language and suggests ways in which students, faculty, readers, and authors can exert pressure for nonsexist language.

Women and Risk

Of all the facets of women's lives discussed in this book, facing risk undoubtedly is the situation where women feel the greatest vulnerability and lack of power. The pace of technological development, the problems of toxic waste disposal, the spread of sexually transmitted diseases, and the apparently increasing threats of leukemia, and lung, breast, colon, and prostate cancer are among the factors multiplying the health risks that women must judge for their families and themselves. In her analysis of women and risk in Chapter 9, Regina Kenen says that men also face increased risks and hazards in various aspects of their lives. The main difference, she finds, is that women and men may not evaluate risk in the same way, and men usually judge the risks for women. This is the root of women's powerlessness.

Some examples of the technological changes whose risks confront women every day are the microwave in the kitchen; the computer monitor in the office; the IUD, or the birth control pill, or Norplant in the bedroom; antibiotics and hormones in meat, milk, and eggs; and pesticides on food, and in the house and yard. Pregnant women must compare the risks of amniocentesis with those of bearing a child with serious birth defects. And women in childbirth may have little choice but to endure the electronic fetal monitor, a cesarean section, or intrauterine transfusions. Kenen points out that women frequently are treated as the objects of these technological developments and interventions. If they question, protest, or refuse to use or be subjected to the recommended new technology they are considered, she says, "at best an oddity, at worst mentally unstable."

But, she asserts, women must understand that their perceptions of risk may differ from those of powerful groups like doctors, scientists, business-men, and government regulators. The cost/benefit analyses of these groups do not necessarily include the costs that women fear or the benefits that they value. The scientists' standard of significant risk may not satisfy women who are aware of some of the unfortunate consequences that may occur from taking the risks. Women are less apt to see technology as a neutral tool or to find that these groups' decisions about risk are strictly objective. Women are more likely to stress the social and cultural implications of technology and risk assessment. And some take risks even though they know the costs may be high—for example, young women who smoke, or poor women whose need for income overrides their worry about health hazards on the job.

Kenen gives helpful advice to women on how to improve their evaluation of risk. She alerts her readers to the ways in which risk assessors and risk communicators affect the perception of and reaction to risk. She analyzes how people reason about risk and suggests methods for improving their methods of reasoning and for increasing the information on which it is based. She advises risk communicators on how they can improve the public's understanding of risk. And, finally, she shows women how they can effec-tively exert influence on the decisions made by the business, government, and judicial evaluators and regulators of risk.

Women's Sexuality from the Inside Out

Our concluding chapter by Gail Walker on women's sexuality sums up the common theme of the varied topics our authors have studied. She writes: "Women's realities have been explained and organized in ways that don't always make sense to women but that make sense to those doing the de-scription and analysis.... Even the parameters of female sexuality have been male-derived." She explains that all sexuality has been modeled by men, based on their knowledge of their own sexuality and their observations of female sexuality. In surveys like the Kinsey report, for example, women may fill in the data but men have phrased the questions.

One consequence of this, she finds, is that sexuality has been viewed as static, focused on relationships to others, and goal-oriented. Sex counselors often consider that achieving orgasm is the goal of human sexual response, while some religious groups may stress the goal of producing offspring. Walker urges us to see sexuality differently, as an internal "life force" with a variety of meanings to the individual. She stresses that it exists with differing strengths at all stages and conditions of an individual's life—youth and age, pregnancy and motherhood, health and illness, stress and relaxation, disability and pain. It may be expressed or experienced in different ways. And it exists as a force within an individual even when others are not present. Sexuality is more than the sex act.

Women need to define their own sexuality, she says. They need to develop a model of female sexuality based on women's insights into women's minds and bodies. But when they begin this process they should recognize the obstacles to redefinition. Women are used to being told what they should do and not do and how they should feel—by traditional psychology and medicine, by organized religion, by government, and by the media. They may find their perceived challenges to these prescriptions greeted with ridicule and a fall from grace, with harassment, and, in the worst case, with the threat of violence.

To help women define their sexuality, Walker first encourages them to acknowledge it. Then she suggests ways of thinking about its content and context. She concludes with suggestions for future research.

LOOKING FORWARD

The authors of these chapters have a vision of a 21st century whose institutions recognize women's worth, encourage women's contributions, and are concerned about women's values. Shaping such a century means striving for changes in society's institutions to accommodate the shifts in women's and men's roles and the new needs of their families. It is a problem all of us as individuals must work on but not one we can solve alone.

NOTES

1. "Montreal Massacre," *Maclean's*, December 18, 1989, pp. 14–17. According to his high school records, Marc Lépine was intelligent. After dropping out of college, he started a computer course, but dropped that. Then he took an evening chemistry course, earning 90s. He tried to enlist in the Canadian armed forces but was refused because of "antisocial" behavior. He was unemployed at the time of the shootings.

Elliot Leyton, an anthropologist at Newfoundland's Memorial University and author of a book about multiple murderers, described Lépine as "frustrated and angry. He did not get to be who he wanted to be and it was the target group's fault. He was going to get even and go out in a burst of manly glory." "The Making of a Mass Killer," *Maclean's*, December 18, 1989, p. 22.

Herbert Pascoe, a forensic psychiatrist at Alberta Hospital, said that this resentment of successful women is common. He commented that "the fact is that many, many men feel inadequate and inferior in their relations with the opposite sex. And this can show up in some very unpleasant activities." "The Making of a Mass Killer," p. 18.

2. Anna Quindlen, "Time to Tackle This," *New York Times*, January 17, 1993, p. E17.

2

Yesterday, Today, and Tomorrow: Women's Lives at Home and at Work

Frances C. Hutner

THE QUESTION

"We're gaining on it," Vermonters say when getting ahead with a tough job. Progress may be slow and hard but as long as there is a glint of improvement then patiently, cheerfully, comes the "we're gaining on it." Are women "gaining on it"? Are they making progress, albeit slow and intermittent, in taking control of their lives and in improving their well-being and that of their families? How can they enhance that progress in the future?

The question of how far women have come and where they are and should be going is a hotly debated one. It creates controversy because it is not primarily a factual question, though there is disagreement over the facts as well as over the interpretations made from them. But it is above all a political issue. Women are perceived to be challenging the power structure and the challenge is profoundly disturbing to many men and many women with vested interests in the existing setup.

This apparent challenge raises social, cultural, and economic issues. Does women's "progress" provide needed family income, giving men more freedom, children more opportunity, and women more independence as women's advocates argue? Or does it harm children, emasculate men, and destroy the family as critics claim? Are women's breakthroughs in education and work enhancing the economy's productivity by providing needed workers who are skilled, dedicated, and, on average, better educated than men? Or are women just taking jobs from men who should be the main breadwinners? Are the changes in women's work and family roles producing divorce, single-parent households, and poverty for children? Or is it the reverse, with these situations forcing women into the work force?

Two recent books demonstrate the depth of the disturbance caused by women's perceived challenge to the patriarchy. In her best-selling book, *Backlash*, Susan Faludi documents the strong reaction by many in the 1980s to the threats they felt that women's advances posed to male authority and the social order. The debate gets heated when another best-selling author, Camille Paglia, defends male domination and even violence, like that expressed in sexual harassment and date rape, as reasonable responses of the superior sex to untamed, threatening, and inferior female biology. Paglia seems to believe we asked for it, we need it, and isn't it exciting?[1]

The discomfort over women's place is not new. "If we win, what will we lose?" This was the provocative question that began a 1972 *American Scholar* forum called "Women on Women." The journal assembled a distinguished group of women to discuss "the present ferment" about "the condition of American women today."[2] All were writers, some were college professors—Lillian Hellman was the moderator, with Carolyn Heilbrun, Alice Walker, Elizabeth Janeway, Ann Birstein, Nancy Wilson Ross, Norma Rosen, and Renata Adler as participants. The question of winning and losing that they tackled with mixed success twenty years ago seems, unfortunately, just as relevant and confusing today. We hope that a look at today's American women at home and in the workplace can help us understand where women are gaining, where losing, and where future progress lies.

WOMEN'S PLACE

With few exceptions, all American women work. They work at home without pay and outside the home for wages, with a majority of them today doing the double shift of working in both places. And many of them do unpaid volunteer work, as well. Economists who estimate the value of women's unpaid housework conclude that, if paid for, it would add 25 to 40 percent to the value of the total national output of goods and services. The U.S. Agency for International Development estimates that valuing women's unpaid household work worldwide would add $4 trillion to the world's annual economic product, increasing its stated value by one-third.[3]

Even homemakers who are welfare mothers do work of value; however, anyone listening to discussions of the "welfare problem" would certainly think they were lazing around at the taxpayer's expense, even though the welfare aid provides income levels below the poverty line. In its study of mothers' ability to earn a family wage, the Institute for Women's Policy Research reports that "in no state do AFDC benefits take a family out of poverty. In most states, an AFDC family receives an income that is only 60 to 75 percent of the poverty line even when Food Stamps and other benefits are included."[4]

In a reversal of philosophy from the early days of family aid, a growing number of lawmakers and academics do not rate homemaking and child raising as appropriate full-time jobs for poor women. Instead, faced with the cost of supporting poor families headed by women and fearful of encouraging welfare dependency, governments and their advisors are increasingly pressuring poor mothers, even mothers of very young children, to work for pay as well as run their homes. At the same time, critics often blame more prosperous women who work outside the home for many of our family and social ills. These attitudes are reminiscent of the Victorian era when society frowned on "working" by wives unless they were poor immigrant or minority women whose labor was needed in factories and domestic service. Similarly muddled reasoning can lead judges handling divorce cases to diminish the unpaid contributions of wives and mothers to a marriage and can lead potential employers to downplay the skills that homemakers and volunteer workers have acquired in their work.

This schizophrenia about the work women do and its value—or lack of value—lies at the heart of women's biggest problems. Pay inequity, occupational segregation, the double and triple shift, displaced homemakers, the feminization of poverty, the glass ceiling, the glass wall, inadequate child and parental care, meager health care—all have roots in the devaluation of women and their work.

The History

How has this devaluation of women and their work come about? Thorstein Veblen, an iconoclastic, institutional economist of the late 19th and early 20th centuries known for his sharp insights into American social and economic structures, offered a scholarly, anthropological explanation of the development of what he termed "the barbarian status of women." He started with the institution of marriage. Describing primitive societies, he wrote that women were prizes taken by victorious warring chieftains to be their wives and thereby enhance their male, warrior status. Marriage developed as an institution based on coercion and ownership, one that reflected barbarian man's mastery and status.[5]

Is Veblen's analysis too extreme? Not in an England where, according to Lawrence Stone, the recently retired Dodge Professor of History at Princeton University, "under the patriarchial system of values, as expressed in the enacted law as it endured until the nineteenth century, a married woman was the nearest approximation in a free society to a slave." The reviewer of Mr. Stone's recent book on the history of divorce in England describes "the infamous wife sales—in which wives were taken to market with halters around their necks and sold by their husbands to the highest bidders." He explains that these sales "were usually prearranged as to both price and successful bidder (although one unfortunate wife was recorded as being sold for a leg of mutton)."[6]

Nor is Veblen's analysis extreme in the United States today, where aging, powerful men often acquire young "trophy" wives in second or later marriages. According to the *Wall Street Journal*, Olivia Goldsmith, the author of a recent, "hugely successful" novel, *The First Wives Club*, got her inspiration from "a 1989 cover story in *Fortune* magazine on 'The CEO's Second Wife'—the young, glitzy, 'trophy wives' of men like Henry Kravis and Robert Mosbacher." The *Journal* article describes some of the more egregious entries in a "First Wives Contest" sponsored by the book's publisher to publicize the book.[7] A recent description by an Iranian woman, Sattareh Farman Farmaian, of her life in the Islamic world shows strong similarities with Veblen's "barbarian status of women." Raised in a harem, the author, whose name means "belonging to the greatest of all commanders," was, "like 35 siblings, four wives and 1,000 servants, very much the chattel of her princely father. Her mother, the No. 3 wife married at 12 years old to a man more than 50, wasn't allowed to leave the women's quarters of the family compound for many years," even for her parents' funeral services. The father did send his daughter to an American mission school, but declined to send her abroad for further education, saying, "It would be a waste of money.... A woman will be nothing." For college in America, she had to wait until he died.[8]

Veblen continues his discussion of the origins of women's inferior status by pointing out that in primitive societies the development of better tools made workers more productive so that men's labor was no longer required for the survival of the community. This facilitated the division of work into two distinct groups, "(a) the honorific employments [male], which involve a large element of prowess, and (b) the humiliating employments [female], which call for diligence and into which the sturdier [male warrior] virtues do not enter."[9]

Barbarian men considered an "incapacity for exploit" to be an "infirmity," Veblen wrote. And to prevent catching this "infectious infirmity, it is well for the able-bodied man who is mindful of his virility to shun all undue contact and conversation with the weaker sex and to avoid all contamination with the employments that are characteristic of the sex." At times of "manly exploit"—"hunts or warlike raids"—everything about the women becomes "ceremonially unclean to the men" despite the fact that female employments support the daily life of the community. "This imputation of ceremonial uncleanness on the ground of their infirmity has lasted on in the later culture as a sense of the unworthiness or Levitical inadequacy of women; so that even now we feel the impropriety of women taking rank with men."[10]

In his seminal work, *The Theory of the Leisure Class,* Veblen added that even when man as hunter contributed essential food to the group he still did not consider himself a laborer, like women. Barbarian man had what Veblen called "a profound sense of the disparity between man's and woman's work." This "sense of the disparity between man's and woman's work" reportedly exists today in an elemental form in some Third World countries. A *New York Times* article dated May 31, 1992, about the problem of encouraging family planning in Rwanda, Africa's most densely populated country, quotes a clinic nurse as saying: "Most of the men won't accept their wives' using contraception. They want eight children. And it's a cult of egoism. They believe if their wives take pills, they will become weak and won't be able to work in the fields. And then the men would have to work."[11]

Veblen used this anthropological insight to underpin his critique of modern American culture. He commented on the turn-of-the-century's "New-Woman" movement. More than half a century before Betty Friedan described "the problem that has no name," well-to-do women who wanted to escape from the "barbarian" status of being chattels and ornaments of men in a patriarchal society precipitated a movement for "Emancipation" and "Work." They were dissatisfied with their chief function, which Veblen described as consuming vicariously for the head of household. He coined the phrases "honorific consumption" and "conspicuous leisure" to describe these socially approved ways to show and maintain status.

Veblen explained that a woman has, even more than a man, what he calls "the instinct of workmanship." She therefore wants "to live her own life in her own way and to enter the industrial process of the community at something nearer than the second remove." But less sensitive social critics of the time could not understand why these well-educated women who were "petted" by their "devoted and hard-working" husbands, and had nothing to do but consume "largely and conspicuously," were not content with their lot. Veblen quoted one critic: "The Anglo-Saxon 'new woman' is the most ridiculous production of modern times, and destined to be the most ghastly failure of the century."[12]

Whatever the anthropological origins, mainstream economists in the classical and neoclassical traditions have perpetuated the devaluation of women and their work. They have done this most often by simply ignoring women. With a few notable exceptions, like Victorians John Stuart Mill and Harriet Taylor, women have been invisible in orthodox economic theory, whether as producers, consumers, or creators of the next generation of workers. In large part, the ignoring of women's work has stemmed from economists' and society's equating of economic value with monetary worth. Inasmuch as homemaker's work is unpaid it has no monetary value and so does not fit into either the economic or social calculus of productive labor.

Historically, this neglect goes back to Adam Smith, who considered that domestic labor for consumption purposes was unproductive. "The labour of a menial servant," Smith wrote, "adds to the value of nothing."[13] He contrasted this to productive factory labor, which added calculable market value to the costs of materials used. In his view, the providers of all types of services—and he included churchmen, doctors, lawyers, men of letters, musicians, the military—were unproductive. They consumed the produce of productive workers but produced "nothing which could afterwards purchase or produce an equal quantity of labour."[14] Although Smith did consider investment in human capital to be productive, he did not recognize women's role in this investment.

And even Mill and Taylor, sympathetic as they were to the plight of the unfree female, did not consider women's reproductive work of bearing, raising, and caring for humans to be productive labor because it was "usually incurred from other motives than to obtain [an] ultimate return, and, for most purposes of political economy, need not be taken into account as expenses of production." Mill contrasted this with the labor of those who teach and learn

the arts of production . . . this labour is really, and in general solely, undergone for the sake of the greater or more valuable produce thereby attained, and in order that a remuneration . . . may be reaped by the learner, besides an adequate remuneration for the labour of the teacher, when a teacher has been employed.[15]

In her study *Feminism and Anti-Feminism in Early Economic Thought*, Michele Pujol contrasts the criterion Mill and Taylor used for judging women's reproductive work with their treatment of the "labour of invention and discovery," a type of "intellectual speculation" that Mill and Taylor admitted was often not done for material ends. But, they argued, looked at from the point of view of society it was "highly productive." Pujol condemns this as a blatant "double standard applied to men's and women's work. They expose their flawed definition of productive labour, the shortcomings of their analysis of the sexual division of labour, and their subconscious acceptance of the ideology of the day which served to deny the economic nature of women's reproductive work."[16]

Cambridge economist Alfred Marshall was a towering figure in the 19th and early 20th century development of neoclassical economics. Through his teaching and his writing, particularly with his text, *Principles of Economics*, he had a powerful influence on subsequent generations of students and practitioners. Marshall thought that women's domestic labor was essential to producing the labor force needed for successful functioning of a capitalist economy. It was so essential, in fact, that women must be kept at home to care for their children full time. Despite the importance he attached to women's "duty of building a true home and investing their efforts in the personal capital of their children's character and abilities," Marshall followed what he called "common practice," and did not recommend including this unpaid work of homemakers in national income accounting, although he would include the work of paid servants. Thus, Pujol writes, Marshall skirts the issue of whether homemaking is productive labor and "helps to institutionalize in marginalist literature, as well as in national and international standards of income accounting, the exclusion from consideration, in theory and practice, of an important share of total production."[17]

Marshall believed that the goal of women's education should be to teach them the skills needed to be proper housewives and mothers. Because he thought that higher education should not be allowed to distract women from performing their family duties, he opposed the granting of degrees to women when this proposal came up for discussion and approval at Cambridge University. Somewhat inconsistently, he married one of the university's first women students, who was also a student of his in economics, Mary Paley Marshall. She later taught economics at Oxford and Cambridge. He became coauthor of her book, *Economics of Industry*—a book described by John Maynard Keynes as "extremely good"—and considered her able enough to help him with his writings. Yet, Keynes wrote, Marshall came "increasingly to the conclusion that there was nothing useful to be made of women's intellect" although he had benefited greatly from the advice and help of his educated and talented wife "without whose understanding and devotion his work would not have fulfilled its fruitfulness."[18]

Other economists in the neoclassical stream generally followed Marshall's analysis of women's place while adding some variations of their own. For example, A. C. Pigou, a student of Marshall's and a seminal figure in the theory of welfare economics, recommended motherhood allowances to encourage mothers to stay at home. Pujol writes:

In *The Economics of Welfare*, he [Pigou] develops a blueprint for improvements in the efficiency of capitalist societies which includes an elaborate state-run welfare system.... In this system, women are assigned to non-market reproductive work, a type of activity which is not recognized as contributing to the nation's economic welfare and which is not paid. Women must therefore rely on male family members' income and/or on state welfare payments for subsistence. Employed women are not guaranteed access to a living income, as Pigou rejects the concept of a minimum wage. He advocates a national human capital investment policy but restricts its scope to the improvement of male workers' skills. For him, the focus of women's education should be their domestic "duties."[19]

Despite the emphasis on its importance, homemaking did not, and still does not, figure in neoclassical calculations of an economy's output. Pigou said that this produced a "violent" paradox, oft quoted and supposedly amusing—that "if a man marries his housekeeper or his cook, the national dividend is diminished." He explained that the paradox arises because "the services rendered by women enter into the dividend when they are rendered in exchange for wages, whether in the factory or in the home, but do not enter into it when they are rendered by mothers and wives gratuitously for their own families."[20]

The wage earners in mainstream economics texts have typically been male. And if economists mentioned women as economic actors they have often patronized and trivialized them, as, for example, Nobel Laureate Paul Samuelson did in early editions of his famous textbook, *Economics*, with his put-down of women as brainless decision-makers. In 1973, economist Marina von Neumann Whitman, then a member of the Council of Economic Advisers, testified before the Congressional Joint Economic Committee on the economic problems of women. In her testimony she quoted from a passage in Samuelson's first edition of *Economics*, published in 1948, in which he was complaining about public reaction to rationing. He wrote: "Of course, there are always a few women and soapbox orators, who are longer on intuition than brains and who blame their troubles on the mechanism of rationing itself rather than on the shortage." Dr. Whitman points out that by the seventh edition he had changed the phrase, "women and soapbox orators" to "women and cranks." Finally, in what Whitman calls the "liberated" eighth edition of 1970, Professor Samuelson drops the "rather slighting reference" to women and simply refers to "some cranky customers." She notes that the Joint Committee is "glad to observe that finally women and economics are being included in the same breath without a knowing wink by the male economist."[21]

But when Harvard professor John Kenneth Galbraith launched his attack on the basic assumptions of neoclassical economics, he cast women in a central role in the functioning of the economy. In his 1973 book, *Economics and the Public Purpose*, Galbraith describes his view of women's place. A modern economy, he points out, depends on continual growth in production of goods and services to provide employment and increasing wages for workers, rising returns for investors, and attractive pay for business management. Women are indispensable actors in this economy as "administrators of consumption." For lack of domestic servants to perform this task women are, Galbraith writes, a "crypto-servant class" performing a "menial role" that is "critical to the expansion of consumption in the modern economy." It is, he adds, "their supreme contribution to the modern economy."[22]

Galbraith argues that, by talking about the household as a sort of monolithic decision-making unit with a male head, neoclassical economists have ignored the housewife's key function of procuring and managing a constantly growing load of possessions. In this role he sees the homemaker as the unwitting agent of big, corporate businesses—the "planning system." Conned by their advertising, the household she serves strives to keep up with the consumption standards of the neighboring Joneses. This is an ever-escalating situation that, in the years since Galbraith first wrote, has been further fueled with the tempting ease offered by credit cards and the never-ending flow of new products to consume. So in the world according to

Galbraith, women's place is essential to the functioning of our economic system. As "administrators of consumption" they are indispensable. But their place in society and the economy is not that of a productive equal and is still devalued.

This is not a situation Galbraith lauds. In a tone reminiscent of Veblen he writes:

One of the singular achievements of the planning system has been in winning acceptance by women of such a crypto-servant role—in making acquiescence a major manifestation of the convenient social virtue. And in excluding such labor from economic calculation and burying the separate personality of the woman in the concept of the household, where her sacrifice of individual choice goes unnoticed, neoclassical pedagogy has contributed competently to concealing this whole tendency even from the women concerned. It is now possible for most women to study economics without discovering in what manner they serve economic society—how they are being used.[23]

Galbraith goes on to discuss the factors needed for the emancipation of women, among them the "equitable household," equal access to good jobs and good pay, flexible working hours, professional child care, and equal access to education and training.

Women's Place Today

Galbraith's analysis of women's place is twenty years old. Does it still make sense? Since he wrote, the percentage of women, sixteen years and older, who are in the labor force has risen from 43 to 57 percent, so clearly women today are significant producers of goods and services. They are the mainstay of the fast-increasing number of female-headed families. And they are essential contributors to the incomes of many male-headed households. But is their role as administrators of consumption still critical to the performance of our economy?

The constant emphasis in the media and by political candidates on consumer confidence, housing starts, retail sales, consumer incomes, money supply, and all the other factors that reflect or produce growth in consumer spending leaves no doubt that our leaders see growth in consumption as indispensable to our economy's health. In a recent *New York Times* interview, Paul Volcker, former chairman of the Federal Reserve Bank, complains about this stress on consumption. "We seem to be in a mood as a nation that consumption is the all-important thing," he said. But, he points out, "the more you consume and the less you invest, the less efficient and productive you're likely to be."[24] Keynesian economics, however, focused attention on the relationship between spending and employment. So, in the neo-Keynesian world spending has become a modern virtue and the 19th-century virtue of saving, the flip side of spending, has consequently been discouraged. A 1991 report on *America and the New Economy* explains this phenomenon and also supports Galbraith's argument about the primacy of consumption. Its author states that growth of the 20th-century's urban, industrial economy required the support of "constantly increasing consumption to justify" its heavy investment in infrastructure and to support its expanding wage labor force.[25]

The continued central role of women as "administrators of consumption" is highlighted in a recent *Barron's* article entitled "The New Ghost Towns: A Vicious Shakeout Takes Its Toll on Shopping Malls." The problem? A steady decline in mall shopping since the mid-1980s coupled with an explosion in the building of malls and shopping centers in the last decade and a half. Consumers' hours spent at malls decreased on average from twelve per month in 1980 to four per month in 1990. Not surprisingly, mall retail sales dropped as well. And sales started dropping well before the onset of the recent recession.

The causes? An important one, according to *Barron's* research, is the decrease in real income for middle-income families that "drove women into the workforce in large part to maintain former family lifestyles." The article points out that close to 75 percent of women between the ages of eighteen and fifty-five are now in the labor force. These women "no longer have the time or energy to make a day of shopping at the mall. *Even today, women account for nearly 70% of all dollars spent in malls, according to a recent Stillerman Jones survey.*"[26]

The result is a catch-22 situation. Women have to work at paid jobs so their families can keep spending enough money to keep the economy going. But when they do work for pay they have less time to "administer consumption." And so the old question, "What do women want?" is now, more aptly, "What does society want?" Would paying women for homemaking solve the dilemma by giving women both the income to shop with and the time to organize the household and its needs?

In any case, it is clear that women serve our economy in three vital roles: first, as creators of the next generation of workers, consumers, savers, and investors; second, as both paid and unpaid producers of goods and services; and third, as the organizers and directors of the consumption of goods and services the economy produces—the function emphasized by the word "economics" in its original meaning of household management. Producing and nurturing the next generation of humans is undoubtedly the most basic of women's roles. For without women there would be no human capital, no workers, no consumers for economists to worry about, and no economists to do the worrying.

Women the world over suffer from society's failure to recognize and appropriately value their contributions. Women's place does not reflect what women do. To be sure, in the last few decades many American women have made real gains in their social, economic, and political status. But many more still suffer from poverty, low pay, occupational segregation, the glass ceiling, the glass wall, overwork, lack of adequate care for children and the elderly, and inadequate provision for illness and old age. A look at some of these problems that we still face will show us what we need to do to shape a better economic future for ourselves and our families.

PAY EQUITY: "WHY CAN'T A WOMAN BE (PAID) MORE LIKE A MAN?"

"Why can't a woman be more like a man?" Professor Higgins asks irritably in *My Fair Lady*, the musical version of George Bernard Shaw's play, *Pygmalion*. Why can't she, indeed, as far as her pay is concerned? For the sad fact is that women who are working for pay typically earn significantly less than men. Does this matter?

In 1950, 33.9 percent of women aged sixteen and over—18.5 million women—were in the labor force. These numbers increased steadily by an average of nearly a million workers a year, more than tripling to a 1991 total of 56.9 million women. By 1991, 57.4 percent of women over age sixteen were working or looking for work. In contrast, the proportion of men aged sixteen and over in the labor force fell from 86.7 percent in 1950 to 76.5 percent in 1991. In fact, from 1990 to 1991, the *number* of men dropped by almost 1.5 million, in part as a result of that year's recession. As a consequence of these dramatic changes, women are close to making up half the total labor force, as their share has risen from 29 percent in 1950 to 46 percent in 1991. Clearly women's role in the economy is far more extensive and important than economic theory, policy, and practice have recognized.

The most compelling change has been the growth in the labor force participation rates of mothers. The Institute for Women's Policy Research (IWPR) points out that "in every decade since 1950, the labor force participation rates of mothers have increased more than they have for all women.... Among married women, the... rates for those *with children* increased faster than the rates for those *with no children*." By 1990, close to 75 percent of mothers with children six to seventeen were in the work force. Moreover, 59 percent of mothers with children under six and 52 percent of those with children under two were working or looking for work.[27]

Plainly, women are in the work force because they need paid work. An IWPR study based on 1984 data found that 19 percent of all women workers were women with children who were the sole wage earners in their households. These women breadwinners made up 25 percent of all the women workers who earned "below adequate wages"—wages at or below the poverty line for a family of four. Moreover, 50 percent of all black women workers and 36 percent of all Hispanic women wage earners who had below adequate wages were the sole support of their families.[28]

Furthermore, many wives have had to go to work for pay to help maintain their families' incomes as their husbands' real earnings have fallen over the past two decades. The percentage of families in which both spouses worked rose from 31.6 percent in 1960 to 70 percent in 1990.[29] Unquestionably, what women earn matters to them and to their families. Pay equity—pay that is determined by the value of the job to the employer and not by the sex of the jobholder—is a serious workplace issue. How equitable is women's pay? Does sex discrimination lower women's wages significantly?

In 1950, women working full time in the labor force earned, on average, only 53 percent as much as full-time male workers, a percentage that drops to 45 percent if domestic workers' salaries are included.[30] This pay gap hovered around the much-publicized 59 cents per male dollar in the 1960s and 1970s. It narrowed in the 1980s to 65 percent in 1986 and 71 percent in 1990. Unfortunately, a fall in men's average earnings explains a significant part of the shrinkage in the pay gap. Men have been losing high-paying jobs in heavy industry, business, and finance as some companies have downsized and some have failed. The impact of the drop in real wages and loss of jobs has been particularly severe for less-skilled men working in the goods production sector of the economy.[31]

What accounts for the female/male pay gap? It is a question that has been exhaustively studied by puzzled (and some not so puzzled) economists. Some factors are clear. As women came into the labor force in the years after World War II they had less seniority than men. They also had less experience and job training, although in the low-level, dead-end jobs where they often worked, experience and training did not have much effect on either men's or women's pay. Women have tended to work fewer hours a week, to work less overtime, and to be less likely to hold multiple jobs. All of these decrease their annual earnings. Researchers have not found, however, that women's absenteeism and turnover rates were notable factors in the pay gap. On the contrary, some observers find women to be more committed workers than men and suggest that this commitment and uncomplaining attitude may be a factor in their low pay.[32] And in separate statistical studies of combat readiness, both the Pentagon and the Navy concluded that "even with servicewomen's loss of time because of childbearing, absenteeism among men was twice as high because of alcoholism, misconduct and routine medical problems."[33] But after taking into account all the relevant causes they can think of, researchers have still found themselves left with an unexplained "residual" of pay disparity that ranges from 20 percent in some studies to 55 percent in others.[34] Many scholars attribute this unexplained disparity to sex-based wage discrimination. Economist Claudia Goldin defines "wage discrimination": It "means that one group, here females, is paid less than another group, here males, even when the characteristics of each are identical. It measures the degree to which equal characteristics are given a different value by the market." The aim of the concept is to "measure the extent to which prejudices against women in the labor market lower their earnings compared with those of men."[35]

Some economists attribute sex disparity in earnings to human capital factors such as the amount of women's investment in education and training and to their choice of occupations. And they imply that girls and women make these choices freely. These economists, for example, would explain that the difference between the pay of someone like Supreme Court Justice Clarence Thomas and his sister, whom he accused of welfare dependency when she gave up work temporarily to care for a sick aunt, was due to his getting a college education and law degree and her failure to go beyond high school. In this instance the human capital and choice of occupations explanations are superficially right. The case is particularly interesting, however, because the discrimination leading to differences in occupation and pay began early on with the grievously unequal educational and career opportunities available to the young girl and her brother.[36]

But if unequal educational attainment explains pay differences in individual cases like that of the Thomases, it does not explain the general case. For the most striking, indeed shocking, evidence of sex-based wage discrimination is the overall lack of connection between the relative educational levels of women and men workers and their pay. In a study of "the educational careers and labor market experience of women in the high school class of 1972 through the time they were 32 years old," Clifford Adelman, senior associate in the Office of Research of the U.S. Department of Education, found what he describes as an "unhappy paradox." The paradox is, he writes, "that women's educational achievements were superior to those of men, but that their rewards in the labor market were thin by comparison."[37]

He found that

women's academic performance in high school was far stronger than that of men, and those who studied more than 2 years each of math and science performed just as well as men with the same curricular backgrounds on the SAT.... Women's grade point averages in college were higher than men's no matter what field they studied. This pattern held in individual courses, particularly in mathematics, where women earned higher grades than men in both statistics and calculus.[38]

But when he compared the labor market experience of men with the women who had not had children by age thirty-two, groups whose amount of market experience would be similar, he found that

in only seven of 33 major occupations did women achieve pay equity with men. In five other occupations, four of them in business-related fields, women who took more than 8 credits in college-level mathematics achieved pay equity. *Outside of these areas and these conditions, however, the men of the Class of '72 were paid more than the women without children no matter what unit of analysis is applied.*[39]

The earnings of women with children were significantly lower than those of women without children and much lower than the men's. Adelman attributed some of this added difference in female pay to less work experience—7.5 years on average for women with children as opposed to 7.8 years for childless women and 8.0 years for men. And more of the women with children worked part-time. But he found that the "principal difference lies in occupational distribution.... a higher percentage of women with children worked in lower paying fields (e.g., nurse, health technician, teacher)" as opposed to the higher paying professional occupations like medicine, engineering, the law.[40]

In reviewing Gary Becker's human capital theory, which relates investment in knowledge to a worker's productivity and earnings, Adelman returns to the crux of the paradox: "our archive," he says, finds "not merely that women are equally qualified—they are better qualified." Yet the data show the paradox—that notwithstanding their better qualifications the majority of women receive a smaller return on their investment than men do.[41]

Does this matter? he asks, and concludes that it does. He points out that women now make up over half of those enrolled and receiving degrees at all levels of higher education except the doctoral (where the gap is disappearing) and first professional sector. Furthermore, the Women's Bureau of the Department of Labor forecasts that women will provide 64 percent of new work force entrants in the 1990s and will make up half the labor force by the year 2000.[42] But, Adelman argues, "if we take women's knowledge contributions for granted or ignore them at the same time we treat men's knowledge as proprietary and rewardable, we have a half-economy." Men, who, he says "have been slacking off in school and college for decades, in part because they believe that to learn is 'feminine,' " are not taught that real knowledge counts. Meanwhile, women's abilities are underutilized. The result is labor market exploitation of women and economic loss to them, to their families, and to our whole society.[43] And it puts our political and business leaders in the quixotic position of agonizing over the educational deficiencies of our workers, on the one hand, and failing to reward and encourage the best use of our educated women workers, on the other.

WOMEN'S WORK: SEX SEGREGATION BY OCCUPATION AND JOB

"That's women's work"—we all know the remark and the implication of somewhat demeaning, and even "humiliating" employment, to use Veblen's characterization, that it carries. Margaret Mead, in her anthropological studies, found that in cultures where men were fishers and women were weavers, fishing had a higher status than weaving. In cultures where men wove and women fished, weaving had higher status. Segregating women's work and attributing a low value to it are prime factors in the female/male pay gap. A recent United Nations study of women around the world corroborates Mead's observations, finding that "almost everywhere, the workplace is segregated by sex" and the male-dominated occupations are the honorific ones that carry more pay. And everywhere, "*Everywhere* women are paid less than men."[44] Moreover, it observed that jobs are typically segregated by sex within the occupational groups, with men concentrated in the more prestigious, better paid jobs and women in the lower paid ranks. For example, in the teaching profession, tenured college professors are most often men while elementary school teachers are more likely to be women.

In their recent intensive study of occupational sex segregation, Barbara Reskin and Patricia Roos describe a situation in the United States that mirrors the one described by the U.N. report. Intrigued by newspaper reports about 1980 Census data indicating "women's dramatic inroads" into some predominantly male occupations during the 1970s, they supervised detailed case studies of fourteen of these thirty-three occupations and also analyzed the forces affecting the sex status of all the 503 detailed census occupational categories.[45] In their discussion of these studies they first point out that from 1900 to 1970 the degree of occupational sex segregation changed little despite major changes in the structure of the economy, as manufacturing and agriculture declined in importance relative to the service sector. Most working women were concentrated in a small number of female-dominated occupations. Most men were spread across a much broader spectrum of male-dominated occupations. Throughout the period around "two-thirds of either all working women or all working men would have had to change to a detailed occupation the other sex dominated for the sexes to be identically distributed across detailed occupational categories."[46] Although, starting in the late 19th century, women did go into some mainly male occupations—like clerical workers, schoolteachers, telephone operators, and bank tellers—men left as women entered, or, conversely, women entered as men left for better paying opportunities. Women's pay levels were low compared to the alternatives available to men. These feminized occupations were female work "ghettos" with little or no opportunity for advancement to higher paying, more prestigious positions.

During the 1970s, however, occupational sex segregation lessened. But when Reskin and Roos studied the male-dominated occupations where women had made the greatest gains in employment to see what factors helped women's entry, they found no "genuine integration." They defined genuine integration as securing "occupational equity with male coworkers of equivalent experience."[47] Instead they found that "ghettoization" was the usual result—that is, women in the same occupation as men were concentrated in different job titles, or in different firms, or in different industries.

And in several cases resegregation occurred as former male specialities turned female. Inasmuch as the feminized jobs were typically lower paid and dead-end, women's apparent "dramatic inroads" did not reduce the male/female pay gap by much. Where improvement did occur, it was mostly due to a fall in men's real pay rather than to a rise in women's. Women in these jobs did, however, tend to improve their pay compared to that of other women workers, although this improvement declined during the 1970s. All in all, Reskin and Roos conclude that "the outlook for women in these desegregating occupations, then, is not particularly promising. Although women made more headway in entering male occupations during the 1970s than in any previous decade, ultimately not much genuine integration occurred."[48]

A brief review of a few of the cases studied by Resnick and Roos illustrates their conclusions. For example, the job of editor in the book publishing industry was a low-paid but prestigious "gentleman's profession" that became feminized.[49] As conglomerates took over major publishers and had profits as their main concern, the prestige of trade book editors fell. Low-paying editing jobs no longer attracted able men and the expanding industry turned to women to fill these jobs.

In the baking industry the development of technology for processing partly finished baked goods that are "baked off" in retail stores encouraged the stores to hire women for these proliferating nonunion, often part-time, low-wage jobs. Women bakers now dominate retail baking while the higher paid, unionized production bakers are still male.

Women have also made inroads into bus driving. But they are mainly school bus drivers, typically part-time, nonunionized, and lower paid than male municipal transit drivers.

As the real estate industry expanded during the 1960s and 1970s, women entered in a large way as salespersons, but were crowded into lower paying residential real estate sales rather than in the more lucrative specialities. In 1980, women's hourly earnings in real estate averaged 65 percent of men's, not much better than women were averaging in all occupations.

Growing demand for bank managers plus pressure from sex discrimination suits brought many women into bank management. But they were concentrated in low- and middle-management positions and in retail and branch banking rather than commercial banking. And the "glass ceiling" prevented them from rising to senior positions. One commentator wrote that

by 1983 ... women held just 2% of the senior jobs, despite the fact that we represented more than 70% of the banking work force.... Five years ago, women senior vice-presidents nationwide could have been counted on two hands; today [1986], the National Association of Bank Women estimated that over 200 women have reached that rank.... But with tens of thousands of male senior vice-presidents still running the show, the gender gap at the top remains.[50]

The result of the gender gap was a male/female pay gap in bank management that, at the end of the 1970s, was greater than the gap between all full-time, year-round women and men workers.[51] Despite the gender and pay gaps, however, women found the bank jobs attractive because the pay was typically higher than in other management opportunities open to them.

THE CHALLENGE

Dramatic increases in female labor force participation have occurred in the past few decades. By 1991, close to three-fifths of working-age women were in the labor force—an increase of 200 percent since 1950. In the majority of families, both spouses worked outside the home. And perhaps the most notable change, three-fifths of women with children under six and over half of mothers of children under two were in the labor force.[52]

In these decades women have made important gains. They have entered occupations formerly off limits to them and have substantially increased their numbers in some of them, like bus driving, baking, medicine, the law, business and financial management, editing, insurance adjusting and examining, systems analysis, and public relations. They benefit from better pay in these new possibilities than in the old female ghettoes. And crowding in the stereotypical female occupations like nursing, school teaching, and clerical work is lessened, which tends to improve these pay scales as well.

Yet the "glass ceiling," limiting upward movement, and the "glass wall," blocking sideways movement, still exist. "Women at the Top: Role Models or Relics?" is the title of a *New York Times* article about a meeting of eighteen women top executives of corporations like Mattel, Liz Claiborne, Dean Witter Reynolds, and Equitable Life Assurance Company. Reporter Barbara Lyne writes:

What shook not a few of the participants was the growing suspicion that the women sitting around the table might be dinosaurs.... Relics of an optimistic group of women who went to work in the early 70's when the doors opened, and who moved up the corporate ladder in good economic times, but not forerunners of an expanding column of women climbing steadily to the top.

Some of the women executives said that, added to the frequent skepticism and covert hostility of male management, "the fight to get to the top may be even tougher for women in this decade than it was 10 years ago because of the dead economy." They also perceived that the younger corporate women "want a more balanced life style early on." Declines in the number of women applying to business schools support their observations.[53]

The male/female pay gap, while reduced, also still exists. A high degree of sex segregation by occupation and by jobs within occupations still exists. And many working women and their families still live in poverty, lacking medical care, and without good child and elder care. A recent study of Census data by the Northeastern University's Center for Labor Market Studies and the Children's Defense Fund presents a disturbing picture, finding that real incomes for families with children headed by parents under thirty years old dropped 32 percent in real dollars between 1975 and 1990. The child poverty rate in these families is now 40 percent. Real income for families with parents thirty to sixty-four years old fell by 6.4 percent, while real income for childless families rose about 11 percent in these decades. The income declines were less for more highly educated young families and higher for the less educated—a 15 percent fall when young family heads had some college education, and a 46 percent decline for high school drop-out-headed families.[54] The study ascribed about half of the income fall to the increase in single-parent families. The percentage of children living with one parent tripled to about 20 percent in the past three decades for white children, and doubled to 55 percent for black children. These families are typically female-headed and at high risk of being poor. For example, the poverty rate for white female-headed families approaches 40 percent; for black and Hispanic female-headed families it nears 55 percent. The dramatic fall in men's real wages from 1973 to 1991 also accounts for part of the family income decline, as the real wages of men with a high school education fell by nearly 21 percent, those of men not completing high school fell 26.4 percent, and real wages of young black city workers fell by 50 percent. Some analysts say men's income fall explains much of the increase in female-headed families as well, because young men find themselves unable to fill the supporting husband/father role.[55]

Not only have women's gains been inadequate to maintain or raise many family incomes, they have also had costs. In fact, one economist, Victor Fuchs, concludes that American women made *no* gains in "economic well-being" relative to men in the years from 1960 to the mid-1980s. According to his findings, women's income improvements have been offset by the costs of lost leisure time and increased family financial responsibility. The only women who have gained, he maintains, are mostly single, "young, white, unmarried, well-educated women, who made large gains relative to their male counterparts."[56]

Fuchs also cites evidence of possible costs to children, such as falling scholastic test scores, increases in substance abuse, growing rates of adolescent suicide, more eating disorders, and other signs of psychological problems. He is careful to point out that there is "considerable disagreement as to whether mother's marital or employment status has any effect" on children's school achievement and psychological health.[57] And women's paid work can benefit children by lessening family poverty.

Fuchs finds that "when economic well-being is measured comprehensively, women are worse off than men and, as a group have made no gains relative to men since 1960."[58] He does not argue that women should drop their "quest for economic equality" but rather recommends the adoption of public policies that recognize "that women's weaker economic position results primarily from conflicts between career and family."[59] The policies he favors would be child-centered, available to all mothers, whatever their income or labor force status, and paid for by society with broad-based progressive taxes. He recommends a program of unconditionally granted child allowances, financed with a broad-based tax. This, he argues, would allow women to follow their own preferences as to caring for their own children or taking paid work and buying child care, with minimum social costs from market interference and disincentive effects. Children are the poorest group in our society, he points out, and helping them would "have significant positive externalities for society as a whole."[60] He concludes: "It is their children that have made women vulnerable and dependent throughout the ages, and even today the demands of motherhood continue to take a great economic toll from women. Hasn't the time come for society to recognize this reality, to provide the resources that will simultaneously help women and their children?"[61]

The results of a five-day poll taken by the *New York Times* in 1989, questioning 1,497 men and women on the effects of two decades of the women's rights movement, support Fuchs's observations. The *Times* headline reads, "Women's Gains on the Job: Not Without a Heavy Toll." While conceding progress for women on the job, both men and women said they were

unhappy about the toll on their family and personal lives.... When asked whether women have "given up too much" in exchange for gains in the workplace, almost half of all women say yes, as do a third of the men. Most women say that what they gave up is time with their children and quality of their family life.[62]

But most also say that they work out of necessity, to support themselves and their families. The economic pressures of the past two decades have propelled low- and middle-income women into the labor force in an economy that, as the *Times* article points out, "gives parents no compensation for raising children."[63]

In her best-selling book, *The Overworked American*, Harvard economist Juliet Schor corroborates the "heavy toll" with her finding that from 1969 to 1987 the average number of hours worked per year by American employees both for pay and in the household rose by 162 hours—four weeks. Women's paid hours of work increased over the period about twice as much as their household hours of work fell, while men increased their hours somewhat in both categories.[64] Pushing up the annual paid work hours were substantial increases in moonlighting (second and third jobs). The increases for women were particularly high as they sought to piece together enough income from several low-paying jobs to maintain their families.

Sociologist Arlie Hochschild investigated the effect of dual working parents on life in families with young children by following the lives of fifty families over ten years. She found that in most of the families men were doing "incrementally more" household work but that "working mothers are still doing the lion's share of what gets done." She found that both parents together were doing less work at home than similar couples did two decades ago. She concluded that "what emerges is a portrait across the social class spectrum of the marginalization of family life. The definitions of what the family needs, what a marriage needs, what the house needs, even what the child needs, have been shoved back and reduced." She added that with "the growth of the service sector and the declining earning power of men, wives have been pulled into wage labor." Women and men and the institutions of marriage and the family and the corporation are all being forced to adapt to that change. Hochschild found that women were adjusting to what she termed a "stalled revolution" faster than men and she urged more change in men's roles at home. The other part of "unstalling a stalled revolution" is, she said, "to adjust the workplace to the new kinds of workers who now inhabit it. . . . that's the challenge before us."[65]

The challenge for American women moving into the 21st century is to understand fully the nature and value of their role in our economy and our society—its contributions and its costs. If women are going to shape a better future, they must recognize why and how their place in shaping that future is vital and central. Then they can move with conviction as well as understanding to improve the economic, political, and legal policies that affect them and their families.

Dr. Heidi Hartmann, director of the Institute for Women's Policy Research, in testimony before the U.S. Senate Committee on Labor and Human Resources, pointed out the practical importance of recognizing women's roles. "Much of our public policy is anachronistic," she asserted. "It assumes both a predominantly white male workforce, living in traditional families, and stable employment patterns with socially responsible employers providing health insurance and other vital fringe benefits." It does not recognize that this "traditional family with a working father and a mother at home now represents only a quarter of all families with children." It "does not accept that women are independent citizens, often living without men, competing in the market place with men, and being equal breadwinners with men. . . . What are needed now are new public policies that deal with new realities: women's autonomy and women's economic responsibilities."[66]

Margaret C. Snyder, founding director of the United Nations Development Fund for Women, calls the assumption behind our policies the "myth of the male breadwinner," which "dictates that a man must have higher wages than a woman because he (supposedly) is the sole or major support of a family." She describes the "traditional family" as "nearly nonexistent" worldwide, with women as sole breadwinners in a third of world households and cobreadwinners with men in another third.[67]

What are the most important practical ways to meet the "new realities?" At the top of the list is implementing pay equity—that is, eliminating sex-based wage discrimination. Basing women's pay on the value of their work rather than on their sex and race is an important policy for women at all pay ranks, but it is particularly critical at low wage levels where eliminating the pay gap could lift many families out of poverty. A 1991 Institute for Women's Policy Research study showed that sex and race discrimination are significantly related to women's low wages—that "women of color are four times as likely to be low-wage workers as are white men with comparable skills and experience," and "white women are more than three times as likely as [comparable] white men to be low-wage workers."[68]

How can employers, employees, and governments ferret out sex and race discrimination in pay? In the mid-1970s the European Economic Community and the International Labor Organization began requiring member countries to implement the policy of equal pay for work of equivalent value—sometimes called equal pay for comparable worth, or pay equity policy—which the international organizations had initiated in the 1950s and early 1960s. Australia, the federal government of Canada, and some Canadian provinces are often-cited examples of success in using the policy to help reduce the pay gap. Meanwhile, in the United States, by 1989 all but five states had undertaken public-sector pay equity initiatives and twenty states had actually made pay equity adjustments. Across the country many local governmental jurisdictions have also adopted the policy. Minnesota has been an American leader in pay equity activity with laws requiring action on both the state and local government levels.[69] In the private sector, some large U.S. corporations have quietly followed suit and equal pay for comparable worth has been a frequent topic at business, academic, and union conferences.

To eliminate sex and/or race discrimination in pay, management consultants use job evaluation tools to rank jobs according to the required responsibility, education, skill, and working conditions of the work and the value of the job to the employer. Governments and business have used job evaluation systems widely since World War II to set pay scales. But the systems used have typically incorporated and validated the sex and race discrimination of the marketplace. In the last two decades some in the profession have revised their evaluation methods to remove, or at least reduce, wage discrimination. Though the nondiscriminatory techniques work, conflicts of interest between employer and employees and between various groups of employees—male/female, white/black, professional/blue and pink collar—have sometimes limited the success of the outcome. Management science is easily overtaken by politics; therefore, who controls the evaluation process has proven key to its success or failure in reducing wage discrimination.

Furthermore, the issue of income distribution is always a hotly contested one. And raising women's pay carries an especially heavy emotional load involving male status and privilege in addition to the economic worry of its cost. Moreover, the economic worry escalates as the number of women workers keeps growing. Beginning with the Reagan administration, the Republican-controlled federal government was unalterably opposed to the policy, ridiculing it as "the looniest of loony tunes" and opposing it in court cases. The business-oriented media has forecast disaster from opening the "Pandora's box" of pay equity. And conservative economists and jurists have contended "comparable worth" is meaningless. Value, they argue, is and should be determined by the market. If a woman earns less than a man would be paid for doing the same job, it is because the market says she is worth less than a man.

Paradoxically, the same federal government commissioned and plans to implement a study by Harvard economists that has figured out how to remove the Medicare pay of doctors from the market and base it on such nonmarket factors as time spent with the patient, complexity and risk of the procedure, and education and skill requirements, using criteria and techniques similar to those used in pay equity job evaluation. According to the *Wall Street Journal,*

Until now, Medicare has reimbursed doctors according to their actual charges or the prevailing fees in their area—whichever is less costly. Under the new system, the government has assigned its own values to thousands of medical services and procedures.... In a proposed rule... federal health officials put relative values on more than 4,000 medical services. They will cover 3,000 additional procedures by the time the final rule is issued.

The goal of the new system, according to Health and Human Services Secretary Louis Sullivan, is "*to help address longstanding imbalances between Medicare payments to urban and rural physicians and between primary care physicians and certain specialties, such as surgeons. We want to provide fairer payment to all physicians,* and in particular we want to improve Medicare reimbursement for... primary care." According to the *Journal,* the fee changes will undoubtedly have a wide effect by changing payment schedules of private insurance companies as well.[70]

The American Medical Association attacked the proposed new system with angry opposition. But unlike the reception accorded the policy of equal pay for comparable worth, no uproar from economists, the Business Roundtable, the Equal Employment Advisory Commission, the *Wall Street Journal*'s editors, or the assistant attorney general in charge of civil rights has greeted this radical shift away from the market in the determination of doctors' Medicare payments. Women can learn from this that the attacks on pay equity are based on politics and cost and not on pristine principles of economics.

Properly valuing women's unpaid work as homemakers—as mothers, wives, housekeepers, caretakers of parents—is as important to improving their lives at home and at work as correctly valuing their paid work. Issues like flextime, family leave, and providing benefits to part-time workers make good sense if we value homemaking as productive work. And if full-time homemakers are seen as valuable contributors to the economy's functioning, then recognizing their need for adequate child support, medical insurance, pensions, disability benefits, and displaced homemaker assistance also seems reasonable. The Congressional Women's Caucus, the U.N. Decade for Women World Conference in Nairobi, Kenya, and other women's advocates have urged that nations account for the unpaid home labor of women in their gross national product statistics.[71] This would be the first step in making the invisible woman visible and in showing the total effects of social policies on women, families, and the economy.

CONCLUSION

American women have made progress. They have more opportunities for education and work and they have used them well. But society has still not thoroughly recognized the value of women's work, at home as well as in the workplace, and consequently has not fully understood or been willing to meet their needs. Moving ahead means that women, themselves, must understand and believe in the value of what they do. It means taking control of their lives in ways that are new to many women—for example, joining unions, political organizations, and women's advocacy groups to work effectively on their needs and goals. They must risk becoming leaders in these groups. They must understand the overwhelming importance of government in affecting their lives and the lives of their families and become active players in the political process. They must work together for changes to bring the workplace into step with the needs of families. Above all, women need to see that they are not alone but rather that they share a woman's place, a place that is common to all women whatever their race, class, or country.

NOTES

1. Susan Faludi, *Backlash: The Undeclared War Against American Women* (New York: Crown Publishers, 1991); Camille Paglia, *Sexual Personae: Art and Decadence from Nefertiti to Emily Dickinson* (New Haven, CT: Yale University Press, 1990).

2. American Scholar Forum, "Women on Women," *The American Scholar* 41 (Autumn 1972): 599–627.

3. John Kenneth Galbraith, *Economics and the Public Purpose* (Boston: Houghton Mifflin, 1973), p. 33; Michele A. Pujol, *Feminism and Anti-Feminism in Early Economic Thought* (Aldershot, England: Edward Elgar Publishing, 1992), n. 28, p. 142. U.S. Agency for International Development, "Highlights," Vol. 7, no. 3 (Winter 1990), p. 3.

4. Roberta M. Spalter-Roth, Heidi I. Hartmann, Linda M. Andrews, "Mothers, Children, and Low-Wage Work: The Ability to Earn a Family Wage" (Washington, DC: Institute for Women's Policy Research, revised September 1990), p. 6.

5. Thorstein Veblen, "The Barbarian Status of Women," in *Essays in Our Changing Order* (New York: Viking Press, 1943), pp. 50–64.

6. Lawrence Stone, *Road to Divorce, England, 1530–1987* (New York: Oxford University Press, 1990). Mr. Stone is quoted by Neil McKendrick, "Breaking Up Was Hard to Do," *New York Times Book Review*, November 4, 1990, p. 12.

7. For a discussion of modern-day "trophy wives," see the *Wall Street Journal* article, "Women Done Wrong Find a Public Outlet for Their Hostilities," May 13, 1992, pp. A1, A6.

8. *Wall Street Journal*, May 15, 1992, p. A18. Sattareh Farman Farmaian's father had a total of eight wives but Muslim law allowed only four at one time.

9. Veblen, *Essays in Our Changing Order*, p. 50.

10. Ibid., pp. 51–52.

11. Thorstein Veblen, *The Theory of the Leisure Class* (New York: B. W. Huebsch, 1918); p. 5; *New York Times*, May 31, 1992, pp. A1, A12.

12. Veblen, *The Theory of the Leisure Class*, p. 358.

13. Adam Smith, *The Wealth of Nations* (New York: Modern Library, 1937), p. 314.

14. Ibid., p. 315.

15. John Stuart Mill, *Principles of Political Economy* (London: Longmans, Green, 1929), pp. 39–40.

16. Pujol, *Feminism and Anti-Feminism*, p. 32.

17. Alfred Marshall, *Principles of Economics*, 8th ed., 1920 (London: Macmillan, reprinted 1938), pp. 524, 685; Pujol, *Feminism and Anti-Feminism*, p. 134.

18. Pujol, *Feminism and Anti-Feminism*, pp. 140–141, n. 12. Pujol quotes from John Maynard Keynes, "Obituary, Mary Paley Marshall," *Economic Journal* 54 (June–September 1944): 268, 274–275.

19. Pujol, *Feminism and Anti-Feminism*, p. 163. Also see A. C. Pigou, *The Economics of Welfare*, 4th ed. (London: Macmillan, 1932). For a discussion of the views of F. Y. Edgeworth, a neoclassical economist, known for his 1922 and 1923 *Economic Journal* articles on women's work and equal pay, see Pujol, *Feminism and Anti-Feminism*, pp. 94–112.

20. Quoted by Pujol, *Feminism and Anti-Feminism*, pp. 169–170. Pujol points out that Pigou and later economists have created this paradox by definition.

21. Joint Economic Committee, *Hearings on the Economic Problems of Women*, 93rd Congress, 1st session, Part 1, July 10, 11, and 12, 1973, p. 33.

22. Galbraith, *Economics and the Public Purpose*, pp. 33–37.

23. Ibid., p. 233.

24. *New York Times*, June 8, 1992, pp. D1, D2.

25. Anthony Patrick Carnevale, *America and the New Economy* (Alexandria, VA: The American Society for Training and Development and the U.S. Department of Labor, Employment and Training Administration, 1991), p. 6.

26. Jonathan R. Laing, "The New Ghost Towns: A Vicious Shakeout Takes Its Toll on Shopping Malls," *Barron's*, March 16, 1992, pp. 8–9, 20, 22, 24. Italics added.

27. "Are Mommies Dropping Out of the Labor Force? *No!*" Research in Brief (Washington, DC: Institute for Women's Policy Research, n.d.), p. 3. Data are drawn from the IWPR article; from U.S. Department of Labor, Bureau of Labor Statistics, *Working Women: A Chartbook*, August 1991; and from Dana Priest, "Major Changes Seen in Female Labor Force," *Washington Post*, March 25, 1992, p. A21.

28. Spalter-Roth, Hartmann, and Andrews, "Mothers, Children, and Low-Wage Work," Table 2. The study used data from the 1984 panel of the Survey of Income and Program Participation, covering 64,000 persons. The study defined "below adequate wages" as wages of $6.33 an hour or less, which comes to 100 percent or less of the poverty line for a family of four, in 1989 dollars, if earned full-time, full-year. Ibid., p. 11.

29. Priest, "Major Changes," p. A21. Statistics cited in "Major Changes" are from a study: "A Changing Work Force: Demographic Issues Facing the Federal Government," GGD–92–38, General Accounting Office, March 24, 1992.

30. Sara M. Evans and Barbara J. Nelson, *Wage Justice, Comparable Worth and the Paradox of Technocratic Reform* (Chicago: University of Chicago Press, 1989), p. 26 and Chapter 2, note 35.

31. Barbara F. Reskin and Patricia A. Roos, *Job Queues, Gender Queues: Explaining Women's Inroads into Male Occupations* (Philadelphia: Temple University Press, 1990), p. 80. The authors cite a National Committee on Pay Equity study attributing one-quarter of the increase in the ratio of women's to men's earnings between 1979 and 1986 to a fall in men's wages. National Committee on Pay Equity, "Women Have Made Slow Steady Progress in the Labor Market Since 1979, but the Wage Gap Has Not Suddenly Narrowed Significantly" (Washington, DC., 1987), p. 3. See also National Committee on Pay Equity, "Changes in the Wage Gap, 1979–1989," *Newsnotes*, April 1992. Gary Burtless discusses the declining earnings position of less-skilled men in Gary Burtless, ed., *A Future of Lousy Jobs?* (Washington, DC: Brookings Institution, 1990), pp. 1–31.

32. Frances C. Hutner, *Equal Pay for Comparable Worth* (New York: Praeger Publishers, 1986), p. 6.

33. Jamie Ann Conway, "Let Women Fly in Combat," *New York Times*, June 25, 1992, p. A31. Jamie Ann Conway is an Army captain who works in the Pentagon.

34. Barbara R. Bergmann, *The Economic Emergence of Women* (New York: Basic Books, 1986), Table 4–5, p. 78. Claudia Goldin, *Understanding the Gender Gap* (New York: Oxford University Press, 1990), pp. 87–88.

- 35. Goldin, *Understanding the Gender Gap*, pp. 86–87. See also Hutner, *Equal Pay*, pp. 4–6, for a discussion of the factors involved in the pay gap.

36. Bergmann (*The Economic Emergence of Women*, pp. 81–82, 112) cites articles by Jacob Mincer, Solomon W. Polachek, and Gary Becker as illustrative of the human capital school of thought. For a discussion of the nature and importance of sex discrimination in elementary and secondary education, see Wellesley College Center for Research on Women, *How Schools Shortchange Girls: A Study of Major*

Findings on Girls and Education, commissioned by the American Association of University Women Educational Foundation and National Education Association. 1992.

37. Clifford Adelman, *Women at Thirtysomething: Paradoxes of Attainment*, U.S. Department of Education, Office of Educational Research and Improvement, June 1991, p. v. The study is based on the National Longitudinal Study of the High School Class of 1972. It includes high school records and test scores and postsecondary school or college records.

38. Ibid., p. vi.

39. Ibid. Italics added. See also p. 23 and Tables 16, 17, and 18.

40. Ibid., p. 23.

41. Ibid., pp. 20–21. See also Gary Becker, *Human Capital*, 2d ed. (Chicago: University of Chicago Press, 1975).

42. Reskin and Roos, *Job Queues, Gender Queues*, p. 315.

43. Adelman, *Women at Thirtysomething*, pp. 30–31.

44. "The World's Women: Trends and Statistics, 1970–1990" (New York: United Nations, 1991), pp. 87–88. Italics added.

45. Reskin and Roos, *Job Queues, Gender Queues*, p. x.

46. Ibid., p. 11.

47. Ibid., p. 71.

48. Ibid., pp. 87–88.

49. Ibid., p. 47.

50. Quoted by Reskin and Roos, in ibid., p. 155, from an article by Jane Sasseen, "The Great National Bank Hold-Up." *Savvy*, March 1986, pp. 34–36.

51. Reskin and Roos, *Job Queues, Gender Queues*, p. 157.

52. Priest, "Major Changes," p. A21; Christopher Farrell, *Business Week*, June 29, 1992, pp. 90–91; Spalter-Roth, Hartmann, and Andrews, "Mothers, Children and Low-Wage Work," *Fact Sheet*.

53. Barbara Lyne, "Women at the Top: Role Models or Relics?" *New York Times*, September 27, 1992, p. F27.

54. *Washington Post*, April 15, 1992, p. A20.

55. Farrell, *Business Week*, pp. 90–91.

56. Victor R. Fuchs, *Women's Quest for Economic Equality* (Cambridge, MA: Harvard University Press, 1988), p. 3.

57. Ibid., p. 114.

58. Ibid., p. 117.

59. Ibid., p. 4.

60. Ibid., p. 147.

61. Ibid., p. 150.

62. Alison Leigh Cowan, *New York Times*, August 21, 1989, pp. A1, A26.

63. E. J. Dionne, Jr., *New York Times*, August 22, 1989, p. A18.

64. Juliet B. Schor, *The Overworked American* (New York: Basic Books, 1991), p. 35, Table 2.3.

65. Charles Brumfield, Arlie Hochschild, Rhona Rapoport, Beth Salerno, and Faith Wohl, "Men and Women: At Home and in the Workplace," Ford Foundation Women's Program Forum, May 1991, pp. 6–7.

66. Heidi Hartmann, "Women's Work, Family Diversity, and Employment Instability: Public Policy Responses to New Realities," testimony before the Committee

on Labor and Human Resources, U.S. Senate, January 7, 1991, revised January 31, 1991, pp. 1–2.

67. Margaret C. Snyder, "Letter: On Poverty," *New York Times*, December 28, 1991, p. 18.

68. Roberta Spalter-Roth and Heidi Hartmann, "Women and the Workplace: Looking Toward the Future," testimony before the Subcommittee on Employment and Productivity, Committee on Labor and Human Resources, U.S. Senate, July 18, 1991, p. 4.

69. National Committee on Pay Equity, "Pay Equity Activity in the Public Sector, 1979–1989," Executive Summary (Washington, DC, October 1989).

70. Hilary Stout, "Medicare Shift May Alter Fees For All Doctors," *Wall Street Journal*, June 3, 1991, pp. B1, B8. Italics added.

71. "If G.N.P. Counted Housework, Would Women Count for More?" *New York Times*, April 5, 1992, Week in Review, p. 5.

3

Women in Management: What It Will Take to Attain Truly Equal Opportunity

Jennifer S. Macleod

It was the 1950s. Shortly before the young woman was to receive her advanced degree in a social science from an Ivy League university, she climbed the wide staircase to the university's placement office in search of a career-starting position that would utilize her considerable skills. At the landing, a sign directed students to the men's placement office on the right, and the women's placement office on the left. Just outside each office was a large bulletin board, with announcements of openings for the specified sex of applicant.

The offerings for women were sparse. In the young woman's field, the only opportunities were as a low-paid research assistant with no advancement opportunities mentioned, or as an "administrative assistant" with secretarial skills explicitly required. On the men's bulletin board, in the same field, promising professional positions were described, with attractive salaries and specified advancement opportunities—and with no requirement for clerical skills. Although the young woman was assertive in attempting to submit applications for those positions, she was not permitted to do so.

That was the usual picture for well-educated young women in the 1950s. It took that woman five years of "assistant" jobs, and great assertiveness, before she could manage to move into the kind of positions her male classmates had been given immediately. And even when she did move up, she was routinely paid less than 60 percent of the male salaries, and promotions continued to be far harder to obtain.

Since then, the situation has changed dramatically for the better.

DECADES OF CHANGE

By the end of the 1960s, as a result of growing feminist activism (and an economic need for women's greater participation in the work force), legislation eliminated the practice of separate male and female help-wanted advertising, and gave women some legal recourse if denied opportunities because of their sex. And over the decades following the 1950s, one of the most striking changes in the world of employment was the influx of women into entry-level and even middle-level management positions, and professional positions with middle management status.

It may sometimes seem that truly equal opportunity for women in management is rapidly approaching. It generally takes two incomes to support a family adequately by today's standards, and the proportion of adult women who work outside the home is rapidly approaching that of men. In 1988, according to the U.S. Department of Labor,[1] 73 percent of women in the twenty-five to fifty-four age range were in the labor force, compared with 94 percent of men. The Department's projections for the year 2000 are that while the figure for men in that age range will stay about the same, the equivalent figure for women will rise to 81 percent. Thus the vast majority of women, like men, will spend almost all of their active adult years in the work force.

Graduate schools of business have admitted female students for quite some time, and in 1990 over a third of their graduating students were women.[2] And active discrimination against women in managerial jobs is surely a tiny fraction of what it once was.

There are those who look at the progress and conclude that women are fully "on their way"; that as current female managers gain experience, they will move to the top at a rate equivalent to their male counterparts; that the continuing evolution will soon all but eliminate the remaining pockets of discrimination.

There are others who despair, pointing out that after a quarter-century of the new feminism, of equal employment legislation, and of women entering the pipeline in managerial positions, there are still only a few female middle managers, and hardly any in top management. A 1990 study of the top *Fortune* 500 companies,[3] for example, showed that women were only 2.6 percent of corporate officers (the vice-presidential level and up). To many observers, these figures suggest that greatly increased legal, legislative, economic, and social pressure will be required if the evolutionary process is to be accelerated.

Whether people are optimistic or despairing, the remedies they propose mainly address the *symptoms* and often neglect the underlying *causes* of the situation. Unfortunately, the causes of the difficulties in attaining equity are deep, have their roots long in the past, and are built into the basic underlying structure of the work world and its institutions. Focusing only on the symptoms—even though they do indeed need to be addressed—is likely to improve the situation only in slow, agonizing steps, with many plateaus and setbacks along the way, and with almost the entire burden and cost borne by the aspiring women themselves. And that improvement may even cease entirely quite soon, if it hasn't done so already.

The remainder of this chapter describes, analyzes, and discusses those root causes. It then moves on to ways those causes, not just the symptoms, can be addressed so that truly equal opportunity for women in management can be attained.

THE MEANING OF EQUAL OPPORTUNITY: BASIC PREMISES

Let us start with the premise that equal opportunity for women in management positions, at all organizational levels including the top, is a desirable goal. This does not necessarily mean, however, that the goal must be equal *numbers* of male and female managers and executives.

Some argue that women will always be less interested than men in high-level management positions. Others believe that the abilities required of a good manager are more common in the female than in the male half of the population, so that given truly equal opportunity, managerial positions will be dominated by women rather than the other way around.

We will have a better handle on those questions if and when equal opportunities and rewards are achieved. Then, the proportions of women and men in managerial positions, at all levels in organizations, will seek their own level based on individuals' abilities and preferences. This may or may not be close to 50 percent. Be that as it may, equal opportunities and rewards have *not* yet been achieved. So the history and root causes of the inequity need to be examined and addressed.

A PERSISTENT LEGACY FROM THE PAST: THE WAY ORGANIZATIONS AND WORK ARE STRUCTURED

The basic structure of corporations was shaped many years ago, at a time when the predominant societal pattern was one in which the nuclear family was the central economic unit, with husbands/fathers the long-term full-time breadwinners. Single women (at least among the white population) might work for a short time, but as soon as they married (and most married young), they quit paid employment and spent the rest of their lives caring for home and husband, and bearing and raising numerous children.

Given those societal patterns, it was entirely sensible (fairness to women was not a consideration in those days) to structure employing organizations in such a way that only men were hired for managerial positions, or for jobs that provided opportunities to progress to management. And in office environments, it made good practical sense to place women mainly in short-term clerical positions.

There were large numbers of literate young women who needed to support themselves until marriage. They sought office jobs, where working conditions were reasonably good and they could meet potential husbands. By living with their parents or other relatives, or in shared apartments, they could manage on low income and, in fact, had little choice about it (unless they could qualify for the only somewhat better pay of nurses or teachers). Thus, employers could peg their wages very low indeed—far lower than any man would have to accept—and still easily obtain the office workers they needed.

Quite reasonably, employers did not provide these female employees with significant training or development, because they rarely stayed in the work force long enough to justify the investment. And the low pay and lack of advancement opportunity, in turn, tended to hasten young women into marriage—which must have seemed about the only way to escape permanent poverty.

Thus the office workplace was almost entirely segregated by sex. Women employees were almost all young and single. There were almost no female managers, with the exception of the occasional middle-aged single woman who might become a first-line supervisor of a group of women workers. And there were almost no male clerical workers, because men could obtain much higher pay and better advancement opportunities elsewhere.

As time went by, some women stayed in the office work force longer than a couple of years, because of later marriages or because financial need kept them in the work force until they had their first babies. Some returned to the work force after their children were grown. However, the pattern of job segregation by sex persisted because it was built into the organizational structure so thoroughly—and because employers found it economically advantageous. They could afford to pay loyal male managers and future managers enough to support a family, because they could fill essential support positions with women who had little choice but to accept what continued to be barely subsistence-level pay, with almost no advancement opportunities.

As the societal trends continued, there were increasing numbers of women who remained in the work force for extended periods or even their entire active lives. There came to be, theoretically at least, time and incentive for the employer to invest in their training and development, time for advancement and possible promotions into management.

However, male employers liked having bright and capable women as their personal assistants, and could keep them there for their entire careers by modestly increasing their salaries and status (the "executive secretary" syndrome), and continuing to deny them managerial opportunities. So change was slow, in spite of growing pressure by well-educated women with higher aspirations, most of whom nevertheless lacked economic or political clout.

The Situation for Women in Office Settings Today

The insistence that underpaid women secretaries and clerks were absolutely essential for an office to work has persisted until very recently. Now, however, ways of working are in major upheaval. Computerized word processing, electronic record-keeping and data bases, special telephone services such as call-waiting and call-forwarding, remote-controlled answering machines, fax machines, "smart" copying machines, and all the other electronic marvels are revolutionizing office work. The traditional secretary who typed, took shorthand and telephone messages, coordinated the manager's calendar, and "minded the store" when he was away is no longer nearly as necessary. Many of the traditional tasks of secretaries and clerks are now partially or entirely accomplished mechanically or electronically.

This is just as well, because the capable women who used to fill those jobs now educate themselves for, and have access to, much more varied and attractive careers. Even with increased salaries, employers find themselves extremely hard-pressed to fill secretarial jobs except with women with much lower abilities and skills than was the case in the past.

The capable, well-educated women still face significant and persistent discrimination in hiring and, especially, in promotions into and within management; and the many manifestations of that discrimination still need to be addressed. But there is a much more severely limiting barrier, that is only now *beginning* to be addressed. And it will require major structural changes to keep it from persisting and severely limiting the progress of women in management for a great many years to come.

The Great Remaining Barrier to Women's Progress as Managers

One way to describe and understand this remaining barrier to women's progress in management positions is by means of an experiential exercise that this chapter's author developed and entitled "The Short-Tall Scenario." While it was designed for administration in workshops, its essence is captured in the following:

> Imagine that you live in a society very much like the United States, except that there are two categories of people, the SHORTS and the TALLS.
> Imagine that you are a member of the TALL group. You, like

all TALLS, are six feet tall or even taller. The TALLS constitute about half of the country's population.

The other half of the population are SHORTS. All of them are well *under* five feet tall.

The SHORTS have somewhat different physiological requirements from yours: They need to eat only two meals a day, and use a bathroom only twice a day, in both cases early in the morning and late in the evening.

For historical reasons, unrelated to innate abilities or talents, SHORTS are the people who currently dominate society, government, education, and business. The executive offices of corporations have therefore until recently been almost totally inhabited by SHORTS.

As a consequence, the doors to their offices are only five feet high. Ceilings are just seven feet high, and there are numerous lighting fixtures and ceiling-mounted storage units that hang down below the six-foot level. Chairs are low, with shallow seats and low backs; desks, too, are low.

There are no restrooms in the executive areas, and no eating facilities. Executives, once they arrive in the morning, are expected not to take any work breaks, nor eat, nor leave the area. To do so is considered a sign of insufficient dedication to work.

There is also a cultural standard that requires executives always to hold their heads high. It is considered highly undignified, and even disqualifying, to stoop or to lower their heads at any time.

Recently, there have been major societal and economic changes, and TALLS, such as you, have been acquiring all the needed education and business training and experience to be fully qualified to become executives.

SHORTS no longer automatically bar you from the executive ranks. The business leaders among the SHORTS have analyzed the situation and come to a major conclusion, with which some of the TALLS concur. They say that TALLS like you have two basic options in the corporate world:

1. You can adapt to the requirements of the executive positions and offices. To get through the doors and under the lighting fixtures and storage units, you can do so and still hold your head high (as required) by moving around on your knees rather than your feet. You can blend in as best you can—for example, by never calling attention to your height or to any of height's advantages (such as a high or long reach, or the better vantage point for vision). You can somehow manage your eating habits and train your digestive system so that you can get through every working day without

either eating or using a restroom. And you can, with willpower (and by tolerating or treating backaches), adapt yourself to the office furniture and equipment ill-suited to your body's dimensions.

While this may be uncomfortable and limiting to you—and may make for much more taxing conditions than SHORTS experience—it is, after all, up to you to decide whether you care enough about the substantial rewards of success to do what it takes. Or,

2. You can decide that you do not want to do that, and instead satisfy yourself with jobs well below the executive level in content, advancement opportunities, and compensation. If you make this choice, you work in other areas of the building, where the physical environment and furniture are more suited to your needs. There is enough headroom for you to move around on your feet instead of your knees. Restroom facilities and eating facilities are usually available (though often inconvenient and of poor quality); you are permitted to use them if and when you must, although of course your pay is docked for the missed work time.

While your career will be a relatively modest one, it can be generally pleasant, and you will be congenially surrounded by other TALLS like yourself. And you will have the satisfaction of knowing that you are contributing essential support services; executives often smile and tell you, "We couldn't do it without you!"

Given these realities, which of the two options would *you* choose?

Meanings and Implications

The absurdity of forcing TALLS to choose between two such undesirable options, just because of organizational patterns that no longer suit reality, is obvious to anyone reading the above scenario. Most workshop participants who have experienced the exercise cry out that it is the *system*—the *organizational structure, physical environment, and rules*—that must change, rather than the people having to twist themselves into existing confines; that even though TALLS are now permitted in executive jobs, their access and opportunities are still vastly inferior to those of the SHORTS, for whose characteristics and needs the system was structured.

The situation in the scenario would be laughable if it were not so close to actuality, with direct parallels to current real-life situations for women managers and aspiring managers.

Today's corporations still follow the basic structure of organization and work that was formed in the old sex-segregated society in which women were only peripheral and temporary workers in corporate offices. The resulting structure is no better suited to the equal participation of women in managerial and executive jobs than the above-described organization is suited to similar participation by TALLS.

Women who aspire to managerial or executive positions are expected to deny or twist in totally unnatural ways their biological functions of pregnancy, birth, and breast-feeding, just as the TALLS who become executives are expected to go all day without eating or going to a restroom. TALL executives need to avoid leaving the executive floor to get a bite to eat, lest that be interpreted as a sign of insufficient dedication to career; similarly, it is hazardous to the career of the female executive if she takes a leave to give birth or breast-feed her infant.

Just as TALLS are expected to move around on their knees and hide the potential advantages of their height, women are expected to subordinate their inborn or culturally developed strengths—often including superior human relations skills—and to limit their behavior to that which is typical of men.

TALLS who choose the less-demanding jobs where restroom and cafeteria facilities are available are still expected to keep their use of those facilities to the barest minimum, and forfeit pay, job security, and advancement opportunities when they do use them. Similarly, those women who choose less demanding jobs in order to suit their needs and characteristics better are permitted to take only brief and often inadequate leaves, and are penalized for anything more.

In summary, it is ludicrous to insist that women, just because they happen to be latecomers to corporate management, contort themselves into the patterns designed to suit men's lives (or, to be more accurate, the lives of male executives in the days when they had full-time homemaker wives taking care of the home front), or instead accept permanently inferior status, pay, and opportunities.

However, there is surprisingly little understanding of this. Felice Schwartz, in her 1989 *Harvard Business Review* article, "Management Women and the New Facts of Life,"[4] set forth and argued in favor of the viewpoint that women should face realities and choose between those same two options, and then accept the consequences. She also argued that it may well be both reasonable and desirable for corporations to come to their own conclusions as to which pattern a particular woman fits into—and then purposefully (and not necessarily with her knowledge or approval) shape her job and development opportunities accordingly.

While there was a torrent of well-articulated protest regarding what came to be called the "Mommy Track" concept,[5] Ms. Schwartz' thesis was accepted and warmly supported by many (including some women), who considered her one of the few women who were facing reality and talking practical sense. Since then, little if anything has been done to address what is surely the greatest remaining barrier to true equal opportunity for women in management.

The Current Situation: Still Stuck in Nonfunctional Patterns

The situation, as described above, is absurd. Therefore these questions loom: Whose problem is it? Is there anything that can be done about it, and if so, what, and by whom?

Most think of it as the *women's* problem. However, it is clear that it is a problem of society in general, definitely including men. While the existing system is most markedly ill-suited to women, it is also ill-suited to current *male* life-styles.

In an era in which both husband and wife typically work outside the home, men do not have the back-up household services the wife used to provide, and men are increasingly hard-pressed by the competing pressures from their employers and their family and home lives. Many men are also becoming aware of how much they—and their children—are missing because of the employment-shaped lack of time and involvement with their children, especially since "Mom" is no longer at home either. And divorce, increasingly common, exacerbates the situation for many fathers. So the problem is men's as well as women's.

The problem is also one of corporations and other employing organizations. Under the current organizational structure, companies find it increasingly difficult to attract and retain needed employees. Able, hard-working, low-paid, compliant female clerks and secretaries are difficult or impossible to find; increasing pay levels helps somewhat, but both the quantity and *quality* of the supply continues to decline. And many of the most talented men are no longer willing to sacrifice their personal and family lives for their employers.

There is another, closely related problem faced by employers. The competitiveness of the national—and global—marketplace is continually increasing, and companies need to be *enormously flexible* to be successful. The old rigid authoritarian hierarchical organizational structure, in which carefully selected young white men, formal education complete, are anointed to move up through the hierarchy, over decades in which they compete with one another but with no-one else, lacks that flexibility.

The traditional structure also lacks the ability to draw fully on the talents of its employees. When employees (other than the top executives) are expected to perform but not to think, to respond to communications and orders from above but not to contribute their own ideas or help solve problems, all the thinking and innovating and problem solving must come from a small homogeneous group of grey-haired white men at the top of the pyramid. And one of the time-consuming priorities of that small group has to be keeping control of an underutilized and frustrated work force.

Employers, society, and government—still dominated by men and male values—are nevertheless bound to resist change unless and until they see it in their individual and collective interest to do so. Most men, and most employers, will inevitably resist pressure to make change just to "be nice to the ladies"—which is not to say that pressure should not be continually exerted.

THE TRANSFORMATION THAT IS NEEDED

A totally different, much more radical approach to the situation is needed if change is to be sufficiently rapid to meet the needs of both society and business. Instead of asking, "What modifications do we need to make in the organizational structure we now have?" we should be examining the problem in a two-step fashion. We should ask, first:

If we were starting, today, entirely afresh, to design organizations to suit today's needs, today's society, what would they be like—what assumptions would they operate from, what organizational patterns would they have?

And only after that examination and design process is under way should we move onto the practicalities of answering this question:

OK. Now, given the organizational structure and patterns that we *now* have—which are far from those that we need—how can we best get from here to there?

The New Requirements for Effective Organizations

It would be foolish to think that one can sit down and instantly develop a detailed blueprint of the structure and operating patterns of an organization well-suited to today's realities. However, one can start the process by developing, examining, and analyzing the givens, the assumptions, on which the design should be based. Here are just a few examples:

• People who are educated, qualified, experienced, and eager to work—as managers as well as in all other occupational fields—come from both sexes, all ages, and every ethnic group. Recruiting, selection, training, and advancement opportunities should be provided without regard to stereotypes based on those characteristics. This means a revolution in selection criteria and methods.

• The generally accepted principles, styles, and methods of managing based on male values and the patriarchal model cannot automatically be assumed to be applicable or effective under the dramatically new conditions and demands. A totally fresh examination must be initiated, looking at many alternatives. Sally Helgesen, for example, in her book *The Female Advantage*,[6] persuasively describes the non-hierarchical but extremely effective managerial styles of four women leaders of major organizations.

- Rapidly growing numbers of women are starting and heading their own businesses,[7] and thus having the opportunity to structure them to suit their own needs and their own managerial styles. They are often handicapped by regulations and business and banking practices based on assumptions built up when almost all entrepreneurs were male. Regulations and practices need to be rethought and restructured in the light of the changed needs.

- Education and learning are lifelong, and both women and men need to have the time, energy, and resources for continuing education and training if they are to be flexible and optimally productive. Employers must accommodate those needs.

- People live in a wide variety of personal and family situations: The U.S. Census Bureau reports that in 1990, the prototypical nuclear family of husband, wife, and one or more minor children comprised only 26 percent of all U.S. households (down from 40 percent in 1970).[8] The demands of personal and family life therefore vary enormously. Work demands and schedules, benefits, housing, education for children and adults, and types and sources of assistance must take into consideration the widely varying needs of women and men, single and divorced people, parents and nonparents, working couples as well as those in which one partner stays home, people living alone, same-sex couples, and group living arrangements of various kinds.

- Pregnancy, childbirth, and breast-feeding are natural biological processes that require accommodation from employers for several or a few years in the lives of most women. Parental leave for parents of both sexes must also be a given, at the time of birth or adoption, and if and when children are ill or hurt.

- Even when children reach school age, they are typically in school only half of the days of the year—and only until mid-afternoon. Recognizing that, employers can appropriately provide or help support child care facilities for after-school time, school vacations and holidays, and when a child is too ill to go to school but not sufficiently sick to be hospitalized.

- Many adults have responsibility for aging parents or other family members who are infirm or disabled. "Sick leave" should be expanded in definition to include care for ill family members. Large employers might provide elder-care facilities, or support such facilities in the community.

- Work schedules based on outdated assumptions and fixed to suit the convenience of the employer (e.g., 9 to 5, Monday through Friday) are often highly inconvenient for some people, particularly women—or even prevent them from working at all at various times in their lives. Flexible hours, part-time and shared positions, options of working at home temporarily or permanently, full-time or part-time, can greatly increase the pool of talent from which employers can draw and the flexibility with which they can operate.

- Vacations and holidays must be sufficient, and supplementable when needed by personal time and personal leave, for working couples and single parents to meet their personal and family responsibilities adequately and without damaging stress and conflict.

How Do We Get There from Here?

Although we are only in the early stages of examining, analyzing, and understanding the structural problems, we can nevertheless begin to shape the ways in which we can move from "here" to "there." For example, there are many possible ways to increase the number of people, particularly those in positions with the power to initiate and implement change, who understand the need to restructure the way employment is organized in order to achieve the flexibility, productivity, and quality of products and services that are rapidly becoming essential to success.

Much can be done to "spread the word" through books, articles and op-ed pieces, speeches, television news and other programs, and through changes in business education, education for public administration and the law, and workshops and seminars for adults in business and government. The analysis can be presented in such a way as to show that the restructuring will benefit men as well as women and minorities; adults as well as children; corporations as well as families and society; executives and stockholders as well as employees; the rest of the world as well as the United States.

As understanding grows, it will become easier to change the corporate policies and practices, and laws and regulations, that now get in the way. And it will become easier to exert pressure for, and create and implement *new* policies and practices, and laws and regulations, to ease, encourage, and (when necessary) force the needed changes.

As the workplace becomes more flexible and laws better structured, women's strengths, talents, and abilities will be better utilized—and their different approaches to management allowed to blossom. It will become easier for women and men to take leaves for the care of their children, particularly in the crucial first several years; day care and child care facilities will become more available, more convenient, and higher quality; women will no longer be placed on the dead-end "mommy track" just because of the biological fact that they are the ones who bear the children; women will no longer be forced to deny their own values and abilities in order to fit into the traditional "male" mode that is not even appropriate for today's men, either.

People will no longer be evaluated by their sex or age in determining their fitness for a position or a promotion, since it will be recognized that the old rules of thumb no longer apply. Companies that stick to the lock-step white male graduation-to-retirement progression up the organizational pyramid will find themselves hopelessly handicapped and unable to compete for productive employees, and unable to be sufficiently flexible in the marketplace.

It will become not only possible, but considered the norm, for both women and men to move from "full-time" to "part-time" to "temporary" to "non-employed" status, and back, perhaps several times, over their working lifetimes, in order to meet the needs of their changing circumstances and priorities.

Workplaces will become vibrant, ever-changing kaleidoscopic mixtures of women and men who participate in different ways at different times of their lives, but always as *full* participants, contributing their skills, their ideas, and their problem-solving abilities wherever they are in the structure at that moment.

NOTES

1. U.S. Department of Labor, Bureau of Labor Statistics, "New Labor Force Projections, Spanning 1988 to 2000," *Monthly Labor Review*, November 1989, p. 5, Table 2.

2. Data provided by The American Assembly of Collegiate Schools of Business, St. Louis. Also cited in *Empowering Women in Business*, The Empowering Women Series, No. 1 (Washington, DC: The Feminist Majority Foundation, 1991), p. 2.

3. Mary Ann Von Glinow and Anna Krzyczkowska, "The Fortune 500: A Cast of Thousands," University of Southern California, 1988. Data updated by Von Glinow, 1990.

4. Felice N. Schwartz, "Management Women and the New Facts of Life," *Harvard Business Review*, No. 1 (January–February 1989).

5. For example, see the lead editorial, "Why Not Many Mommy Tracks?" in the March 13, 1989, issue of the *New York Times*, and some of the letters to the editor published in the *Harvard Business Review*, May–June 1989, no. 3, in a special section entitled "Management Women: Debating the Facts of Life."

6. Sally Helgesen, *The Female Advantage: Women's Ways of Leadership* (New York: Doubleday, 1990).

7. The 1987 U.S. Census reports 4.1 million women business owners, up 57 percent from 1982.

8. From Associated Press, Washington, DC, January 29, 1991; appeared in January 30, 1991, issue of the *New York Times*, under the headline "Only One U.S. Family in Four is 'Traditional.' "

4

Doing It Whose Way? Women in Leadership

Ruth B. Mandel

WOMEN'S PROGRESS AS POLITICAL LEADERS: GAINS AND LIMITS

In one generation, women have made real progress in domains once considered almost exclusively men's birthright. In some of these areas women have advanced from complete outsiders to marginal participants. As with all paradoxes, here, too, apparent contradictions share a complex truth. It is commonly acknowledged that in professional life women have cracked open doors to entry and moved quite rapidly into lower and middle range positions, while attaining negligibly few presidential, partnership, and chief executive officer (CEO) slots at the top of large, prestigious institutions. This is certainly the case in politics and governmental leadership.

Significant progress is measured in numbers, and presence does count for something. Women's presence in American politics today contrasts sharply with their virtual absence a little over twenty years ago when feminists sounded a vigorous call for political leadership by and for the female half of the population. Certainly a scattering of influential women had been active in the political parties and in government during the half-century between passage of the suffrage amendment and the feminist call for political power in the early 1970s. Little is known about their numbers at state and local levels except to say that when the first counts were taken by the Center for the American Woman and Politics (CAWP) in the mid 1970s, elected

women represented less than 5 percent of all legislative and executive officeholders in municipal, county, and state government. In the U.S. Congress,
for which figures were available covering the years since Jeannette Rankin,
the first woman, was sworn into the House of Representatives in 1917, no
session of our national legislature had ever been convened with more than
twenty (below 4 percent) female members; and that pinnacle had been
reached only once (1961–63) in the sixty years between 1917 and 1977.
At the beginning of the 103rd Congress (1993–95), 54 women—an all-time
high of 10.1 percent women—sit among 535 House and Senate members
(47 women in the House, 7 women in the Senate; in addition, one woman
serves as the delegate to the House from Washington, DC—see Table 1 for
a dramatic illustration of women's creeping rate of progress in the U.S.
Congress over a 75-year period since the first woman entered the House of
Representatives). In state legislatures female representation quintupled in a
little over one generation, with women holding 20 percent of seats in 1993.
A pattern of incremental progress both for female candidates and for women
holding office throughout the political system stands as evidence that women
have achieved access over a remarkable generation when both sexes came
to accept women as appropriate public actors (see Tables 2 and 3).

This new access and social acceptance constitute positive change. Yet
whether in the political world, in business, the media, or higher education—
wherever women can claim new access and advancing status—women's
progress has appeared inside a narrow band on the grand spectrum of power
occupied by our social, religious, political, and economic institutions. The
range of movement occurs between Nowhere-To-Be-Seen and the Margins-
of-Participation. At the margins there are few occasions to make policy, be
understood, be taken seriously; there is scant opportunity to influence the
center of control or set the future course.

Why are women not even one-quarter of elected officials in state and federal government? Why are women's numbers minuscule elsewhere in places
of power? Notwithstanding numerical variations in women's status as
elected officials internationally as well as several prominent examples of individual women achieving high office in a few nations, why is women's general powerlessness still a worldwide phenomenon?[1] As we face a new century
witnessing staggering global challenges, women remain largely irrelevant
where far-reaching decisions are taken. Without underestimating the importance of women's growing presence in places formerly closed to them in practice if not in law, we must ask why a generation of historic effort has not
resulted in gains of greater magnitude. Formidable barriers still stall simple
numerical progress in the United States, and numerical gains accrue more
slowly at higher levels of power and competitiveness. Potent barriers include
habits and prejudices ingrained in the culture; the continuing vigor of traditional gender roles; age-old stereotypes and perceptual biases; access to am-
ple resources; the availability of an appropriately trained or experienced pool

of talent; and the complex issue of whether large numbers of women possess a consuming desire to organize their lives and schedules, focus their energies, arrange their priorities, and (re)shape their identities so as to "fit in," so as to be acceptable candidates for men's positions within men's groups inside men's domains. Chalking up greater numerical gains involves more than a will to work like the devil to acquire positions coveted by men.

Political campaigns in 1990 highlighted several aspects of the situation. For one thing, 1990 looked like others in the past twenty—that is, by small increments more women than ever before ran for office. Women had inched far enough forward by 1990 to have emerged visibly as statewide contenders, with 85 women nominated for various statewide elective executive positions. While the gubernatorial tally (8 candidates) was equal to 1986 (the last major gubernatorial election year), the 1990 group included candidates in powerful states, particularly California and Texas. National coverage of these two races disclosed an unsurprising scenario—there was only one game in town, with rules made up by men who play high stakes politics. Raise millions of dollars, hire tough political consultants, take the offense, and fight hard and nasty. In October, *Texas Monthly* magazine's cover depicted Ann Richards and Clayton Williams hoofing together beside the headline "Dirty Dancing." In a TV interview, journalist Molly Ivins dubbed their electoral encounter "foul," "nasty," "out of the gutter and into the sewer." California's Dianne Feinstein devised the campaign slogan "Tough and Caring." Presumably to reassure voters of her suitability for the job, in a campaign debate Feinstein promised to be a governor who "knocks heads." In New Jersey, Christine Todd Whitman, who ran for the U.S. Senate in 1990, posed for a photograph in a hunting jacket holding a rifle. Negative campaigning, tough talk, and tough images—female candidates recognize some hard, even brutal, realities of electoral politics as practiced today.

During her 1984 national candidacy, Geraldine Ferraro was challenged to prove her masculine readiness by saying "Yes" to a reporter on national television asking if she could "push the button." Withdrawing from the 1988 presidential primary endurance trials, Congresswoman Pat Schroeder declared herself unwilling to adjust to a dehumanized process—an airport-to-airport media blitz with the presidential candidate in planes and before cameras but rarely in contact with real folks.

A female candidate who ran for Congress in 1990 as a "nonpolitician" against "politics as usual" was viewed with cynicism by a male voter: "In order to hang out with a den of wolves, you're going to become one somewhere along the line."[2] While less cynicism may be in order, the dilemma is similar for women elsewhere. Whether other arenas are populated with wolves, foxes, tigers, or even much gentler creatures, the territory will be defended instinctively; women or other newcomers will be intruders, perhaps tolerated, certainly expected to make adjustments so as to fit in. The logic goes that if you ask admission to someone's club, you abide by its rules. Margaret W.

Table 1
Women in the U.S. Congress, 1917–93

CONGRESS	DATES	WOMEN IN SENATE	WOMEN IN HOUSE	TOTAL WOMEN
65th	1917-1919	0 (0D, 0R)	1 (0D, 1R)	1 (0D, 1R)
66th	1919-1921	0 (0D, 0R)	0 (0D, 0R)	0 (0D, 0R)
67th	1921-1923	1 (1D, 0R)	3 (0D, 3R)	4 (1D, 3R)
68th	1923-1925	0 (0D, 0R)	1 (0D, 1R)	1 (0D, 1R)
69th	1925-1927	0 (0D, 0R)	3 (1D, 2R)	3 (1D, 2R)
70th	1927-1929	0 (0D, 0R)	5 (2D, 3R)	5 (2D, 3R)
71st	1929-1931	0 (0D, 0R)	9 (5D, 4R)	9 (5D, 4R)
72nd	1931-1933	1 (1D, 0R)	7 (5D, 2R)	8 (6D, 2R)
73rd	1933-1935	1 (1D, 0R)	7 (4D, 3R)	8 (5D, 3R)
74th	1935-1937	2 (2D, 0R)	6 (4D, 2R)	8 (6D, 2R)
75th	1937-1939	2 (1D, 1R)*	6 (5D, 1R)	8 (6D, 2R)
76th	1939-1941	1 (1D, 0R)	8 (4D, 4R)	9 (5D, 4R)
77th	1941-1943	1 (1D, 0R)	9 (4D, 5R)	10 (5D, 5R)
78th	1943-1945	1 (1D, 0R)	8 (2D, 6R)	9 (3D, 6R)
79th	1945-1947	0 (0D, 0R)	11 (6D, 5R)	11 (6D, 5R)
80th	1947-1949	1 (0D, 1R)	7 (3D, 4R)	8 (3D, 5R)
81st	1949-1951	1 (0D, 1R)	9 (5D, 4R)	10 (5D, 5R)
82nd	1951-1953	1 (0D, 1R)	10 (4D, 6R)	11 (4D, 7R)
83rd	1953-1955	2 (0D, 2R)	12 (5D, 7R)**	14 (5D, 9R)**
84th	1955-1957	1 (0D, 1R)	17 (10D, 7R)**	18 (10D, 8R)**
85th	1957-1959	1 (0D, 1R)	15 (9D, 6R)	16 (9D, 7R)
86th	1959-1961	2 (1D, 1R)	17 (9D, 8R)	19 (10D, 9R)
87th	1961-1963	2 (1D, 1R)	18 (11D, 7R)	20 (12D, 8R)
88th	1963-1965	2 (1D, 1R)	12 (6D, 6R)	14 (7D, 7R)
89th	1965-1967	2 (1D, 1R)	11 (7D, 4R)	13 (8D, 5R)

90th	1967-1969	1 (0D, 1R)	11 (6D, 5R)	12 (6D, 6R)
91st	1969-1971	1 (0D, 1R)	10 (6D, 4R)	11 (6D, 5R)
92nd	1971-1973	2 (1D, 1R)	13 (10D, 3R)	15 (11D, 4R)
93rd	1973-1975	0 (0D, 0R)	16 (14D, 2R)	16 (14D, 2R)
94th	1975-1977	0 (0D, 0R)	19 (14D, 5R)	19 (14D, 5R)
95th	1977-1979	2 (2D, 0R)	18 (13D, 5R)	20 (15D, 5R)
96th	1979-1981	1 (0D, 1R)	16 (11D, 5R)	17 (11D, 6R)
97th	1981-1983	2 (0D, 2R)	21 (11D, 10R)	23 (11D, 12R)
98th	1983-1985	2 (0D, 2R)	22 (13D, 9R)	24 (13D, 11R)
99th	1985-1987	2 (0D, 2R)	23 (12D, 11R)	25 (12D, 13R)
100th	1987-1989	2 (1D, 1R)	23 (12D, 11R)	25 (13D, 12R)
101st	1989-1991	2 (1D, 1R)	29 (16D, 13R)	31 (17D, 14R)
102nd	1991-1993	4 (3D, 1R)+	29 (20D, 9R)***	33 (23D, 10R)***
103rd	1993-1995	7 (5D, 2R)++	48 (36D, 12R)***	55 (41D, 13R)***

*A total of three (2D, 1R) women served in the Senate in the 75th Congress, but no more than two served together at any one time. Part of the time two Democrats served together, and part of the time one Democrat and one Republican served together.

**Includes a Republican delegate from pre-statehood Hawaii.

***Includes a Democratic delegate from Washington, DC.

+On election day in 1992, three women served in the Senate; two were elected and one was appointed. On November 3rd, Dianne Feinstein won a special election to complete two years of a term; she was sworn in on November 10, 1992.

++Kay Bailey Hutchison (R-TX) won a special election on June 5, 1993, to serve out the remaining year and a half of a term.

Note: Table shows maximum number of women elected or appointed to serve in that Congress at one time. Some filled out unexpired terms and some were never sworn in.

© Copyright 1993. Center for the American Woman and Politics (CAWP). January 1993.

Table 2
Women Elected to Office, 1975–92

Level of Office	1975	1977	1979	1981	1983	1985	1987	1989	1991	1992
U.S. Congress	4%	4%	3%	4%	4%	5%	5%	5%	6%	6%
Statewide Elective[1]	10%	8%	11%	11%	13%	14%	15%	14%[2]	18%	18%
State Legislatures	8%	9%	10%	12%	13%	15%	16%	17%	18%	18%
County Governing Boards[3]	3%	4%	5%	6%	8%	8%(1984)	9%	9%(1988)	NA	NA
Mayors & Municipal/Township Governing Boards	4%	8%	10%	10%	NA	14%[4]	NA	NA	NA	NA

[1]These numbers do not include: officials in appointive state cabinet-level positions; officials elected to executive posts by the legislature; members of the judicial branch; or elected members of university Boards of Trustees or Boards of Education.

[2]Although there was an increase in the number of women serving between 1987 and 1989, the percentage decrease reflects a change in the base used to calculate these figures.

[3]The three states without county governing boards are CT, RI, and VT.

[4]Includes data from Washington, DC. States for which data were incomplete and therefore not included are: IL, IN, KY, MO, PA, and WI.

© Copyright 1992. Center for the American Woman and Politics (CAWP). July 1992.

Table 3
Women Running for Congress and State Legislatures, 1968–92 (major party nominees)

Year	U.S. Senate	U.S. House	State Legislatures
1968	1(1D,0R)	19(12D,7R)	NA
1970	1(0D,1R)	25(15D,10R)	NA
1972	2(0D,2R)	32(24D,8R)	NA
1974	3(2D,1R)	44(30D,14R)	1125
1976	1(1D,0R)	54(34D,20R)	1258
1978	2(1D,1R)	46(27D,19R)	1348
1980	5(2D,3R)	52(27D,25R)	1426
1982	3(1D,2R)	55(27D,28R)	1643
1984	10(6D,4R)	65(30D,35R)	1756
1986	6(3D,3R)	64(30D,34R)	1813
1988	2(0D,2R)	59(33D,26R)	1853
1990	8(2D,6R)	70(40D,30R)	2064
1992	11(10D,1R)	108(71D,37R)	2376

©Copyright 1992. Center for the American Woman and Politics (CAWP). November 1992.

Rossiter, a prominent historian of science, entitled an address to the American Association of University Professors, "Officially Encouraged, Institutionally Discouraged: Women in Academe." Muriel Siebert, who in 1967 became the first woman to acquire a seat on the New York Stock Exchange, sees Wall Street firms, "doing what they *have* to do legally. . . . But women are coming into Wall Street in large numbers—and they still are not making partner and are not getting into the positions that lead to the executive suites. There's still an old boy network. You just have to keep fighting."[3] A generation's gains have been sung to an encouraging tune of social rhetoric. All the while, institutional structures and norms stand largely unaltered, rendering the gains incremental at best, unstable at worst.

Of course, some institutional adjustments have accommodated social change. They range from the ludicrous to the pragmatic, from the installation of ladies' restrooms in legislative chambers, to the provision of child care, to flexible schedules, to creative executive contracts, to a wide variety of arrangements in workplaces that recruit new types of employees. Most of us remember nepotism rules in academia; nowadays married couples often are hired by the same schools. By and large, however, there is minimum pressure for change at the presidential/board chair/CEO levels of leadership. When corporate self-interest is served, businesses slowly adjust personnel policies to meet the needs of a changing labor force; political parties recruit female candidates when they think women can win for them. Progressive policies help employees; they also help the bottom line. In effect, liberal institutional reform—in business, politics, or higher education—supports the status quo. The status quo will produce few women in high power leadership positions, and those women will have chosen to fit into slots not fashioned by them, to adopt roles, life-styles, schedules, and priorities that of necessity will imitate men's. These few very able women will be quite comfortable doing things largely the way men have done them.

REFORMING THE POLITICAL PROCESS: WHAT IT TAKES

In electoral politics, some reforms would serve to smooth the way for greater access by greater numbers of women. Included among familiar suggestions, for example, are public funding of campaigns, expenditure limitations, and restrictions on support from political action committees. These and other measures aimed at reducing the prohibitive costs of candidacy for newcomers who have no established base of financial support would chip away at the enormous advantages experienced by incumbents, wealthy candidates, and candidates supported by affluent and powerful traditional sources of campaign money. Various people also argue that term limitations for state legislators and members of Congress would help women by wiping out the electoral power of incumbency in many campaigns and creating large numbers of open-seat races, thereby easing the way for first-time candidates and deemphasizing officeholding experience and seniority as formidable criteria for reelecting incumbents. On the other side of this debate, others argue that while term limitations would abrogate voters' rights to reelect effective, seasoned leaders, they could also benefit powerful special interests that would groom and finance their own candidates for each anticipated open seat. Women and other political outsiders would not be the likely beneficiaries of such a recruitment process.

Another suggestion for reforming the political process argues for mandated gender balance or quotas. This approach is especially appealing to activist women who are frustrated with the slow pace of progress in the United States compared with the success of women candidates in a number of countries (especially in Scandinavia) with multiparty parliamentary systems. Where party rules call for a minimum percentage of women on the party candidates list, women have taken great strides forward in increasing their numbers in elective office. In the United States, former New York Congresswoman Bella Abzug and others have been active in calling for the political parties to nominate and support women as candidates for all vacant legislative seats until there is parity in government.[4] The Democratic Party has adopted this type of approach only with regard to delegates to national nominating conventions. Under an equal division rule fought for by women and adopted in 1980, state parties must send gender-balanced delegations to nominate the Democrats' presidential candidate every four years. Gender balance is also mandated or encouraged by a number of states (for example, Iowa, Montana, Utah) and localities. Some have passed laws or resolutions or set goals to ensure that equal numbers of women and men are appointed to governmental boards and commissions, with the result that women have gained new opportunities for participation on advisory and regulatory bodies. In the case of Iowa, gender balance has been extended to include state-level judicial appointments

Realistically, in the United States the process of reforming the political system through legislation and lobbying is slow, expensive, frustrating, laced with compromise, and constantly in danger of producing unintended effects that undermine sought-for gains. The history of campaign finance reform is rife with such experiences, one of the most familiar being the explosion of independent expenditure committees in the wake of limits on campaign expenditures. Instead of fewer dollars being spent to elect candidates, large sums of money are diverted into political parties or independent expenditure committees. This diversion of funds also results in less accountability than would be the case if the candidate alone were responsible for spending campaign funds.

Given the realities of our political system, what it will take in addition to steadfast chipping away at old patterns and old powers is a series of spectacular breakthroughs by individual women who deliberately bring other women along with them, attract more women to the public arena, and by their example beckon to future generations who will be inspired to follow in their footsteps. A few contemporary political women—Shirley Chisholm, Bella Abzug, Barbara Jordan, Pat Schroeder, Sandra Day O'Connor, Geraldine Ferraro, Ann Richards, Janet Reno, Ruth Bader Ginsberg—have already accomplished much for other women. But a sparse scattering of stars signals unclear skies; some vast cloud cover or atmospheric haze obscures the full riches yet to be disclosed.

Even if grueling, the task of expanding women's numbers in traditionally male leadership slots should succeed eventually. This past generation's progress will continue, even accelerate, in a new generation with differently conditioned expectations and more varied educations. It is unlikely that acceleration will be consistently rapid; and organizational adjustments are not institutional transformations. While institutions will adjust to changing demographic and social realities, they will not voluntarily alter fundamental structures, leadership patterns, or power distributions. More likely, they will reproduce themselves, replicating their leadership norms and values. Fine for those women who fit in. But not quite the achievement of the full feminist vision of a transformed society.

WOMEN HELPING WOMEN

Little is absolutely static by nature, certainly nothing that is alive. Public policy may be made inside institutions and processes and within traditions that have evolved over time and are set in their ways, but evolution itself means change. Happily, in this recent generation of incremental progress for women in politics, some women did "do it differently.'   ˄ stories of women who found ways to infuse the standard process with something new must be collected and made available as lesson, example, and inspiration. In political office, women have influenced the public agenda, primarily in raising and giving priority to issues often undervalued or considered "soft" and less urgent than the most pressing issues. Elected women have worked for equity issues and for policies primarily affecting women, children, and families—child care, elder care, health care, domestic violence, education, social services, equal rights, pay equity, pension rights, credit equity, reproductive rights. In research about public officials (particularly state legislators), the Center for the American Woman and Politics found elected women more feminist and progressive than their male counterparts both in attitudes toward social issues and in behavior in office. Elected and appointed women also directly and indirectly bring other women into politics. While the overall impact of women in politics is still slight, the potential for advancing a progressive and feminist agenda appears linked to the numbers question. Women's distinctive perspectives should have greater influence on public policy as more women hold office.

To separate oneself by standing for something heretofore unfamiliar or undervalued takes great courage. One risks credibility and fragile acceptability by admitting one's unorthodox views. Courage is required of women in leadership positions. We must promote, protect, and honor it wherever it appears. The courage we seek also requires imagination and faith in one's own sense of how things might be done better or more humanely or more sensitively or more honestly or more clearly or more respectfully of everyone else. It will take courage and imagination to recognize new ways of doing things, and then it will take more courage to bring about change. It will take what might look like foolishness. Some of this is the courage to be women—whatever that means individually—to stand for change that feels right for women. It may be that the changes we seek are not profitable, convenient, or easy but are nonetheless important. Someone must be willing to verbalize a vision and then stand for changes that may appear impractical in the short run. Someone with credibility must take a stand—someone with a position, a public platform or a base of power. That kind of woman can help everyone.

The personal risks are great, and the courage to take them may look like foolhardiness, especially to those who thrive in the present social system. It is supremely difficult to eschew talking and behaving in the ways required for passing, approval, and earning rewards. It is stupendously difficult to bring a colleague, an office, a department, a unit, or an institution around to new standards or habits of behaving and thinking. So far, few women of high rank in politics, universities, foundations, or corporations have taken daring steps for womankind. Who can blame them? Such efforts could doom them to scorn, ineffectiveness, or professional suicide. Yet women with influence have taken smaller risks, actions that loom large in the circumstances where they were taken. It is even a risk for a woman holding a top position in a traditional institution to declare that she is a feminist. However, some elected and appointed women, some college presidents and foundation officials have done that.

How is one taken seriously if one expresses a different view or tries to reframe mainstream discussion? In the second issue of the new *Ms.* magazine,[5] editor Robin Morgan asks whether it would not be a "more accurate headline" to state that "Half of Iraq Invades Half of Kuwait," since the powers in Iraq do not consult women about political and military decisions, and the Kuwaiti women had no voice and no vote in Kuwait. Morgan wonders whether a different scenario would have developed if the other half of each society—the women—were central to the process of decision-making. Her questions catch our attention because they look at an all-too-familiar situation with a different lens. Throughout history men have arrived at an impasse, then begun to attack and kill each other as a way of resolving the impasse. In the past, those who challenged that approach to resolving conflict were viewed as foolish or crazy. Could such thinking change if the places where decisions are made continue to be filled with many men and very few women? Could such thinking change if women have come to think like men by the time they earn the credentials and occupy the places where men have made the decisions?

In the 21st century many more women will occupy mainstream positions in politics, universities, and elsewhere. How do we support these women leaders to think in new ways, to think like women? One large burden rests on educators who will teach young women to think about leadership for themselves. How can we help future generations of young women to retain their early sense of self and to bring new approaches to an old world? The old question was pragmatic—how to get women inside. The enduring questions address vision and values—how to remake the inside, transform it into a better place for everyone. Some women have talked about the need to "change the terms of the debate"; but perhaps it is still not even clear what "the debate" is about or whether there is a debate at all. There are usually two sides in debates, not one side with outsiders trying to get over there and join that team too. The debate structure itself is geared to a winner and a loser, to an assumption that complex issues can be understood sufficiently in a structure of only two opposing views and only one winner. A different world might structure many-sided discussions and many partial "winners." We must question deeply why and how we want to join in. We must know *what* it is we want to become members of. And what are *our* terms for the future?

In the musical *Annie Get Your Gun* a familiar song is entitled "Anything You Can Do I Can Do Better." A woman and man compete verbally to prove who does it better—shoot a sparrow with a bow and arrow, drink liquor, sing a higher note. This riposte is beside the point. Our question should not be whether *either* woman *or* man can do everything better, but rather what can *each* contribute that is distinctive beyond what both can do? And what can both do that neither one can do as well alone? Do we as women have another way to offer? How do we go about finding out?

The sticking point is the relationship between the so-called rate of progress issue and the impact or reframing issue. Incremental gains will not guarantee reframing, but they might suggest it if we acknowledge that the modest impact women leaders have made so far does signal progressive change. Congresswoman Martha Griffiths fought to add the word "sex" to Title VII of the 1964 Civil Rights Act, forever changing gender discussions in this country. Congresswoman Shirley Chisholm fought for a minimum wage for domestic workers. Congresswoman Bella Abzug won the appropriation to support the first and only national conference that forged an agenda for U.S. women. In 1990, Secretary of Labor Elizabeth Dole announced a "glass ceiling initiative" to pressure corporations to promote women and members of minority groups to top management positions. Because Congresswoman Patricia Schroeder and others challenged entrenched practices at the National Institutes of Health (NIH), a new NIH office has been established to conduct major research on women's health. Women legislators in the last decade have promoted increases in marriage license fees to raise funds for shelters to house victims of domestic violence. Elected women have pressed the states to pass laws mandating health insurance coverage for mammogram screening. These few examples of how a small number of political women have made a difference remind us that meaningful change can occur within traditional institutions; and it is better to be present than absent.

The sine qua non for advancing women in leadership positions at greater rates and more speedily is women supporting women. As Muriel Siebert believes about Wall Street,

equality will come...only when the women who gain power on the Street begin to use it on behalf of other women.... "It will take the decided effort on the part of major firms to make sure that women are advanced according to their abilities. And it will be up to the women who rise to the top to see that they make that effort."[6]

It is essential for women to recognize that their full empowerment will not occur unless it is sparked and fueled by women themselves, and those in positions to act must do so on the basis of that recognition. In electoral politics this means running for party or public office oneself or finding other women to run. It means aiding women candidates by donating money, volunteering time, sharing mailing lists, and contributing other precious campaign resources. It means encouraging women leaders by expressing interest in their work and calling attention to it, inviting them to meet or address audiences who may not know them, finding ways to recognize and honor them for their valued efforts.

Women's networks play key roles both in stimulating and nurturing leadership. Many female elected officials credit professional groups and women's community organizations with starting them on the road to leadership as well as providing a continuing base of support and encouragement. At the national level, without an active women's political community that has boosted candidates for elective office, even the incremental gains achieved in the 1970s and 1980s would be much smaller. By 1992, a few women's political action committees (PACs) and donor networks had grown large and influential enough to be considered major players in electoral politics.[7] The size and clout of women's political organizations still pale next to the combined strength of various special interests and the vast resources of the business world. Nonetheless, women who wish to participate in the political process today can find a helping hand and are likely to feel less isolated than the frontrunners of a few short years ago.

In politics and government, as elsewhere, the force of tradition and pattern remains enormously influential in qualifying trials, in recruitment, screening, appointing, winning positions. Egregiously different women are unlikely to pass muster and pass by the customary gatekeepers. Slightly different women can slip through the gates. We must then bolster their efforts, and also remind, cajole, and even badger them to hang on to their courage and do the right thing *as* women *for* women, because it will also be the better thing for everyone. Who can doubt that a society led by a partnership of strong women and men working together with mutual respect for each other's differences and rich diversity of experiences will be a society in which the common good is far better served.

NOTES

An earlier version of this chapter was prepared for a conference of women presidents of colleges and universities convened by the American Council on Education (ACE) in Washington, DC, December 1990. It is reprinted here with permission from ACE.

1. Figures for women's representation in governments around the globe may be found in Ruth Leger Sivard, *Women . . . A World Survey* (Washington, DC: World Priorities, 1985) and in *The World's Women, 1970–1990* (New York: United Nations, 1991). However, numbers must be read with caution, since they do not necessarily tell the story of power. In some instances, for example the former Soviet Union, gender parity in a legislative body (Supreme Soviet) meant much less than the absence of women in the powerful Politburo where decision-making took place.

2. Quoted in a newspaper story by reporter Dan Zegart, "Zimmer seen as a Maverick," *Trenton Times*, October 2, 1990.

3. Quoted by Diana B. Henriques, "Ms. Siebert, Still on the Barricades," *New York Times*, July 5, 1992.

4. In 1992 former Congresswoman Abzug launched the National Parity Campaign as a project of Women U.S.A. Fund, an organization she directs.

5. *Ms.*, 1, no. 2 (September–October 1990).

6. Henriques, "Ms. Siebert."

7. For example, EMILY's List (Early Money is Like Yeast—It makes the dough rise), a donor network for Democratic women that has grown into one of the top campaign funding sources in the country, expected to raise $5 million for U.S. Senate and House candidates in 1992. The Hollywood Women's Political Committee is another well-financed PAC for Democrats (female and male) seeking major elective offices. The WISH List (Women in the Senate and House) was established in 1992 to raise money for Republican women. Among national bipartisan feminist groups, both the Women's Campaign Fund and the National Women's Political Caucus have provided campaign dollars and/or expert advice to female candidates since the 1970s. The National Organization for Women and the Fund for the Feminist Majority have also been actively involved in supporting political women, as have a dozen or so state-based political action committees.

5

Varieties of Spiritual Experience: Women and Religion from the 1960s to the 1990s

Rosemary O'Brien

Women used to use religion as a way of accepting their lives; now they use their lives to change religion. It has been a long step from being disdained to being ordained. Clearly no one imagines that the Protestant heirarchy willingly decided to give the pulpit to females, or the Vatican to let nuns out of their cells into a world of temptations. Nor that Rome encouraged women to ignore their bishops on matters of sex; that many of them do so has a celibate male heirarchy wondering what will happen next. Not even revisions in the superfluous use of "he" and "him" in liturgical language were voluntary.

Women have attempted to redefine their roles since the industrial revolution, but the 1960s emphasis on liberation renewed the impulse for reforms on all fronts. To the extent that changes in religion have occurred it can be argued that the credit is largely due to feminists who began calling for equal rights. Yet, even granting Protestantism's historic openness to the currents of change (a condition the Church of Rome is proud to deny) it was not until women nailed their questions to the church door, so to speak, that they got a response. Why, they asked, should they accept an imagined theological inferiority, why male-dictated moral values, why an absence from ritual?

The gains, however real, may be seen as a counterpoint to the evidence uncovered in this chapter, which says that fundamental transformations in religious structures have not yet arrived, that women still face exclusion from authority. There is as yet no institutional means for allowing women to share in decision-making while keeping intact the values that govern their own moral lives. Contemporary psychological research, cited herein, tells us that women's lives condition them toward an ethic of care and responsibility rather than one of abstract morality and dominance. For religion this could mean a theology of empathy based on women's interest not so much in an engulfing male God but Jesus as a model for social action. It remains unclear whether women truly can bring their unique spiritual dimension into the churches.

The conclusions in this chapter come from listening to a cross-section of women talk about their religious experiences, as well as from reading the current literature and studying a variety of religious surveys. One thing that has emerged very clearly is how important religion continues to be to women in a pervasively secular climate. Oddly, no pollster has reported questioning women about how feminism, which rejects the institution of male dominance (the patriarchy), has affected their religious attitudes. At the same time, poll after poll report women's dissatisfaction with the way they are defined religiously. In 1989, for example, a plurality of Catholics, who are the largest denomination in the country (around 52 million members), reported in a Gallup survey their skepticism about "Vatican teachings on sexual ethics and the role of women in the public realm."[1]

The women who speak in this chapter belong to the great religious triumvirate in American life—Protestant, Catholic, and Jewish. It is remarkable how closely their views tally with what we are hearing on a larger scale. Looking ahead, it is possible for women to hope that they can act as religious reconstructionists, in transition to a stage where religion will incorporate feminine values, that it will be final proof of the decline of dogmas that rest exclusively on the traditional male God. As one woman theologian observed, "there's a very therapeutic aspect to religions today in preaching, an emphasis on healing and experience, and that's coming from women, even in the Catholic Church where women don't have any power."[2]

THE UNFINISHED WOMAN

Before "Body and Soul" was a popular blues song it was a battleground in religious theology, a metaphor for the conflict in the early Christian world between men and sexual desire, an engagement that ultimately resolved into war between the superior male and the inferior female. For thousands of years after the Fall, Eve carried a message about spiritual and political power in a patriarchal world. A prominent scholar writes that "sexuality to early Christians was an outcrop of the alien, 'animal' world into which the serpent had first led Adam and Eve."[3] The myth of the first parents thus came to signify the slavery of the human race to the sexual impulse, thanks to a disobedient female.

The sex that conjured up such negative connotations in the Hellenic world was regarded as incomplete in her essential nature, secondary to the male. According to the revered Greek physician Galen (A.D. 130–c. 200) males were those fetuses who "had realized their full potential." Anticipating Freud by seventeen centuries, he considered women to be "failed males."[4] Religious literature equated women with defilement, alleging that menstrual and postpartum blood were the proof. Plutarch, that famous first-century observer of famous men, had warned a young male friend that women "left to themselves would conceive many untoward ideas, low designs and emotions."[5] Ergo, it was up to men to keep them in check. Marriage was modeled on the idea of the state; the husband was ruler of his house.

Biblical images revolving around Mary and Martha, observes a modern woman theologian, support a dichotomy that places woman either in the position of household servant or, if she takes the higher road to virginity, a servant of God.[6] Swayed by guilt, Augustine had declared that sexuality must be firmly suppressed by the will; marriage was actually a corrupt state, celibacy the highest moral good. Shackled by male feelings about woman as threat and as perpetrator of the first sin, women came to suffer a fate worse than blame: invisibility.

Women formally were put on notice of their future religious nonexistence through various promulgations issued by misogynous churchmen from the third century on. In the fourth century the Christian Apostolic Constitution declared females eligible "only to pray and listen to those who teach."[7] The lesson for women (to paraphrase a recent comment) seems to have been that God became flesh to reinforce male superiority.[8] Women were discounted merely as reproductive systems, which were sometimes compared to sewers. There were not even words to describe organs such as the vagina until the eighteenth century. Laws and commands, these were the means by which women were defined as valuable only for their procreative abilities.

Women were left with the dilemma of how either to conform to this unwelcome oppression, or to confront it. Passivity was called their virtue. Ironically, using earlier studies of the infant-mother bond, contemporary women psychologists like Carol Gilligan and Nancy Chodorow have argued that women's avoidance of confrontation may seem to imply passivity. Females operate in a matrix of relationships based on nurturance, responsibility, and care. The key here is the attachment of daughter to mother, which sets the stage for the realization mature women achieve: that "self and other are interdependent."[9] The take-charge, rule-dominated idioms of male culture, in this construction, result from the separation of the young male from the maternal bond into a world of absolutes and control of others.

Gilligan's conclusions affront professional opinions, which hold Gilligan guilty of stereotyping, and believe gender is but one element contributing to a sense of individuality.[10] However she puts it, Gilligan has opened up questions about the normativeness of an essentially male vision of morality that places abstract notions above human realities.

Arguably, resignation as a virtue has outlived its time. Recently, Judith Plaskow, a Jewish theologian, has disclosed in her book, *Standing Again at Sinai*, how the ancient habit of textual editing managed to insure that "women are downplayed and obscured."[11] In the 1990s, on the occasion of the yearly Seder, a gathering of Jewish women celebrates an egalitarian Haggadah, the story of the Exodus that takes place during Passover. In it they attempt to rescue women from biblical silence. "We are fueled by a longing for Judaism, for religious ritual, as much as by a longing for feminism" one of them is quoted as saying.[12] They proclaim the deeds of neglected women like Miriam, a sister of Moses; her quick action saved her small brother from being slain by edict to kill first-born Jewish males in Egypt.

"Our problems between the sexes are actually outcomes of the kind of theological concepts that we have been taught, that women are inferior," declares the Reverend Hazel Staats-Westover, of the United Church of Christ, who counsels women students at Princeton University.[13] A relaxed person with an almost maternal air, she has seen the woman's movement in its various phases and has been part of the struggle to change religion. "Women must work out their own spirituality, presenting it in dialogue with the patriarchal theological concept. There can be no change unless we do that."

As a young music student at the University of Southern California, she never imagined that her religious leanings would one day translate into theological studies at Harvard Divinity School and, later, ordination as a minister. The late 1960s was a period of personal ferment for her; she was an instructor at Chicago Theological Seminary. "The woman's movement had begun, and women students came to me trying to find out how to use what they were learning at meetings of the National Organization for Women in their preparation as ministers." She decided to organize a course on Human Liberation. It became obvious right away that "the men tended to intimidate the women in their attempts to say what they felt." Out of that experience, she says, came a new realization that was to alter her life. "I began to see how women experienced theology, and how religious and theological concepts worked in their lives. It wasn't theory, it was reality. They were trying to figure out how to repattern their lives." In her own spiritual journey, Hazel Staats-Westover admits a debt to the radical theologian Mary Daly. "It was she who stretched my head. What she's talking about is that we have to take a step beyond what we know to test our faith, to move on."

Moving on can mean entering disputed territory, especially where myths are concerned. A recent example is the Goddess theory, popularized in Riane Eisler's 1987 book, *The Chalice and the Blade*. The foundations of Goddess theology were laid by Marija Gimbutas, an archeologist at UCLA. Gimbutas argued from findings in southeastern Europe that during the Stone Age, roughly from 7000 to 4000 B.C., there were in existence neolithic agricultural societies worshipping the Goddess as a benign symbol of fertility and justice. Around the fifth century B.C. the use of metals technology fell into the hands of invading Hebrew and Indo-European tribes bent on destruction. Their social forms were male-dominated and authoritarian. Thereafter, culture was used to validate dominator values.[14] The importance of the argument for its defenders is that it underlines the existence of a prehistoric matriarchal mode. Accordingly, the few traces of that idyllic universe that have survived constitute the building blocks for a future that can substitute new behaviors for the old politics of male domination. Women will direct their "intuitiveness" to good ends, replacing the "rationality" that motivates men, a paradigm that has given rise to a number of 'isms,' such as the ecofeminist claim that women will not in the future tamper with Mother Nature, as men have done. Thus, Goddess theory ties into Carol Gilligan's work, creating a possible framework for a feminist vision.

GODDESSISM AND SEX TALK

The Gimbutas thesis attracts dissent as honey draws flies and not all of it is attributable to male anxiety; the late religious philosopher Joseph Campbell endorsed it. Adherents give seminars explaining its importance. A chorus of critics laughs at it or describes it as just another version of "paradise lost" in which good women oppose evil men. Coupling it with Gilligan's ideas, a woman writer concludes that it deprives women of a way "critically to evaluate their own ideas."[15] Dr. Mary Ford-Grabowski says "it's silly. We've tried to get rid of the notion of a male god with a long beard up in the sky; why replace him with a chubby woman?"[16]

Dr. Ford-Grabowski has a decisive mind that is concealed by a wide smile. Not only a writer but editor of the journal *Fellowship in Prayer*, she holds a doctoral degree in theology. She notes that the "motherhood of God" was always present in religion, but has gotten buried in the culture. "Transcendence is what we think of as the masculine quality, distant, remote, the God who is involved in the whole cosmos; and when we think of immanence we think of the more feminine traits."

Interviewer: "You are saying God can be defined by gender?"

Ford-Grabowski: "I'm saying you could apply both masculine and feminine traits to God; it helps you to understand. But that anthropomorphizes God and the truth is, as Job discovered, God is way up above the abilities of our brains to understand. In [the book of] Job there is great poetry, especially where he surrenders, goes down on his knees, and says 'who am I to try to understand your mystery?' And he gives up; he realizes he cannot fathom the mystery, the power, the goodness of a Creator who sustains life, and ... is going to embrace us at the end. That's what God is for me, that incredible mystery."

Interviewer: "You can't set opposite to this, then, the idea of a Goddess?"

Ford-Grabowski: "Absolutely not. That's what the patriarchy is doing, cutting God in half."

Masculine spirituality, whose God was too often the God of vengeance, hurts us all, asserts Sister Lorette Piper: "It taught the evil of the prideful ego which must be beaten into submission to God's will."[17] Sister Piper, whose friends call her Resty, is a member of the Order of the Sacred Heart of Jesus, and at present she is engaged in a ministry that offers a forum for adult spirituality. She is an effective communicator with warm, brown eyes and a sparkling humor.

Perhaps the real sinfulness of women, she suggests, was "false obedience and submission, the unquestioning docility." For example, "as a spiritual director today the hardest thing I have to face is the middle-aged Catholic woman's sense of perfectionism." Her own idea of self, she continues, was altered by two things: the reforms of Vatican 2 (1962–65) and the woman's movement. She was a late bloomer in one way: "Only in the last ten or twelve years could I claim the title of Christian feminist."

Having entered the Society of the Sacred Heart of Jesus in 1960, she "was a bit sheltered from what was going on at the time. I had the Thomas Merton trappings of the monastic life; it was very appealing, but I was very unformed intellectually and emotionally, so it took me a long time ... " Her voice trails off, but when she is asked if she misses the old routine of work and prayer she immediately replies, "Well, this new life is more difficult, but it's more real, in touch with God *and* people ... but you have to have a self before you can lay down your self in service and love of your neighbor, that's where feminism comes in." Feminism has strengthened her religious commitment, drawing her into a six-year involvement in an inner-city program in Trenton, New Jersey, which serves a poor neighborhood. Sister Piper integrates her ideals and religious vows effectively; she is not in revolt against spiritual authority but finds that "the dualism of work and prayer is confining. What's religious and not religious is limiting. Before Vatican 2—this is very stylized—the point was to be good and sit in the pews and not make waves." This requirement has also been referred to by the irreverent as "pay, pray, and stay."

Sister Piper is grateful that her order allows her to make waves, what she calls "creative tension." "If the religious organization is too conforming [it] offers nothing distinctive to the Church." But there's the ever-present paradox: "We have a high degree of autonomy, at least in our order, [but] we are affected by the historical patriarchy of the Church." Still, "we have opportunities for identity and leadership that are pretty advanced, pretty remarkable compared to lay women." Sister Piper is one of those women who are in the vanguard of change.

THE UNFINISHED TASK

If their predecessors felt embattled in the terrain of the 1960s and 1970s, so do younger women today, who encounter barriers no less daunting. Seminary studies begin and end with questions about how to get from being the "groundforce" to the positions of power where change can be made. From the present perspective, oppression still lives.

"I see Jesus, his humanity, as an incredible role model" says a senior at Princeton Theological Seminary and a candidate for the clerical life.[18] "I'm saying he was a human being, not a *man*. I'm not calling him God. He advocated for the marginalized and the oppressed. This world is unjust, inhumane, we should not rest with it the way it is. It's still a patriarchal world, until the voice of woman is heard equally the whole world suffers." It is not strange that she has a vocation. It's a family tradition, from a long line of missionaries and with a grandmother who was a physician. She is strong minded and dedicated to her calling; her parents, she says, always encouraged her to follow whatever career she wanted. "I'm going to become an ordained minister, but that's not all. I feel a call to be with people who are marginalized, women's studies has helped me to find my own voice and I want to strengthen that voice. I'm not being who I am unless I do certain things." She pauses for a moment and then resumes: "I have a problem with the institutional church; we aren't meeting peoples' needs."

Interviewer: "You don't think just saving souls is enough?"

Interviewee: "Obviously that's important; it's not where we stop, it may be where we start. Ministry is not just a thing in the church, it's a way to be. I consider myself to be a radical feminist. I try to embody what I am and just by setting an example will offer people other models."

To illustrate this she cites her experience of a year in a Native American church in Oklahoma, where she found their spirituality very beautiful. "I tried in subtle ways to help them revive some of that." But it was too isolating, she found, because she lacked the support of others. "In order to minister, I need to be ministered to," she concludes. The idea of incarnational theology is appealing to her: "the modeling kind of thing; instead of telling people 'you should, you should,' it's just to be. They see your behavior."

At our meeting she wondered how long it would take for her to get a "second call," at which point her ministry will be affirmed.

"No matter where I go I carry the burden of representing all women; if I fail all fail, and then they are not going to ask another woman. Also, you feel set apart in the ministry, traditionally it's setting oneself above and apart. I don't know how to handle that." Underlying these concerns is her feeling that if you are a woman seeking a career in the church, you have to be better than the average male, "you have to be an above-average female."

Rabbi Susan Schnur was ordained in 1980 at age thirty in a non-Orthodox synagogue. She talked about her career with the interviewer one morning at her house in a small New Jersey town near Princeton. She is the mother of two children whose toys were neatly stored in the living room.

She begins bluntly: "Developmentally a lot of us are at a place right now where to be in, to lead a big conventional congregation, a big phallic congregation, presents tremendous obstacles."[19]

Interviewer: "In short, you don't feel the structure has changed very much?"

Schnur: "That's an issue for the 21st century."

What is it that leads a woman to the rabbinate? In her case, possibly, chagrin; chagrin, she writes, on learning as a child that women are dangerous (i.e., powerful). Her rabbi bandaged his hand to avoid touching females. In her words:

Sometimes I worry that I have become a rabbi not as an act of love, but of revenge. To redeem myself, not from the religious mentors of my childhood, but from that happy moron: me . . . I know I was just a child, steeped in that essence of childhood that Dylan Thomas called "once below a time." I was also in that state of pre-conscious, before-the-apple naivete with which feminists are wincingly familiar. And I was the product of a classical Jewish education, that is, a process that is blind to introspection, wherein one spends all of one's time puzzling out what others think—specifically, "the rabbi"—and no time at all appraising what one thinks one's self.[20]

As a rabbi and also a woman, she tries the personal approach. There is, of course, the fact that "people give you a margin if you're a female in a traditional male role; it's very exciting, a kind of pioneering exploration." The obverse is that you get out of sync, "mostly when you pray to a male God. Theologically you get to be in a different place. Part of it is the Hebrew language: 'Blessed art thou, Lord our God, King of the universe.' " Actually, she says, she belongs in the Orthodox or Conservative tradition; "it's because of gender issues that you end up being thrown into a tradition that's more liberal than you really should be." What's especially important at the moment is to figure out how rituals can be individualized, freed from the institutional rules. "We need to develop a vocabulary for the stuff that really works, what basic reverence means" she comments, pointing to a tiny menorah for her children's cat that she has placed on a Chanukah table nearby. "For me the questions you have to ask are domestic. Lots of people are thinking radically about ordinary life." Her goal is to inject domestic concerns into the pulpit. "Why do you think I have my office in the kitchen?" she asks with a laugh. This is not a suggestion that women become Betty Crockers again; it means she, along with others, have made the loop back to the place where they feel comfortable, where the androcentric bias that men's work is the measure of all work has lost its overarching power. Rosemary Radford Ruether, the feminist theologian, has written in similar terms, calling for an ethical process that permits sharing between the sexes in child nurturing and homemaking as well as decision-making.[21]

"I would like to get rid of the whole competition thing" declares Pam Saturnia, a seminary student who is the first member of her family to attend college.[22]

From the political point of view, to have instead of a vertical line a horizontal line, to bring to our communities everything we have, to share that with others and have them share with us.... I know it's ideology but I like to look at it that way. I like to avoid labels, but I embrace "feminist" not because of reaction to a system, but I see a better way of looking at church, coming closer to what a church should be.

She is a person of firm ideals and clear ideas. During an internship in a fishing village near Belfast she had plenty of time to consider the moral aspect of political issues. Her analysis of political and social problems rests on the idea that "people haven't learned what Jesus had to teach."

Interviewer: "Wasn't there once a consensus in American life about public behavior and public morality?"

Saturnia: "Right, and that's when blacks had to sit in the back of the bus and use different bathrooms and Native Americans were on reservations and Nisei in camps."

Interviewer: "How should clergy respond to injustice?"

Saturnia: "The church has to be aware of what's going on in people's lives. To be relevant it must include all people and life-styles, that is our mission; make church accessible to the handicapped. Some may not like it but they will learn."

Interviewer: "What role will women play in this transformation?"

Saturnia: "It is predicted that women will become predominant in church administration in fifty years. Tables will turn, it happened in teaching, nursing. People my age haven't turned their backs on the church, the church has turned against them. The church needs to be aware of what's going on in people's lives."

An example of the need to overcome clerical deafness is given by the Reverend Staats-Westover. Recently she acted as a consultant to the New Jersey Division of Women. Her mission was to sensitize male clergy to the problems of domestic abuse. "In 1989 . . . we had 52,000 calls for help from women, and 49 deaths. We didn't know the problem was so enormous. It means that clergy have a difficult time hearing their women when they say what is happening."

Interviewer: "How did clergy traditionally react to such complaints? Did they feel the women were at fault?"

Staats-Westover: "They [the clergy] would feel the women were exaggerating . . . it is in the hierarchal structure that man is the head of the household, he has the right to control women, and this includes physical punishment, at least in some fundamentalist religions. Clergy needs to preach about this kind of thing." [Also, colleges need to become more sensitive to the continual harassment of women. It often takes radical steps to change such behavior.] "Women need to be alone to do some of this work . . . but liberation doesn't take place while we're out there on a tangent . . . it must be acquired alone but shared . . . we need community for our spiritual lives."

SOMETHING OUTSIDE OF OURSELVES

A young woman studying theology at a university in Pennsylvania has made no career decisions yet but is looking to religion for answers to "the big questions."[23] She wonders what Christianity has to say about raising children, for example. Conscious that we live in a world of individualism, she treasures the feeling of community that comes from religious participation. Although her family is not active in church, she has always had the sense that there are important things "outside ourselves" and she wants to know more about them.

Her experience is that it is difficult to interest women in religious issues at this stage; they are out for fun and intent on finding spouses, not answers. She, too, will marry, she says, but she always discusses with her male friends the idea of a two-career, sharing relationship.

She combines her religious interests with wide reading in feminist literature, which has led her to develop a strong set of values. She takes her feminism for granted, though it is not based on personally experienced oppression; she stresses her belief that "the bottom line is that women should be equal." She mentions particularly Virginia Woolf, a writer who made her see the one-sidedness of marriage and of social attitudes toward women, and, as "maybe a blind optimist," she expects these things will change "perhaps in 200 years."

Meanwhile, she feels a duty to make others aware of the need for change and, possibly, after thinking it over, she will go on to graduate studies in religion. She has become involved in theater work on her campus with the object of presenting plays that offer challenges to the status quo. Her particular combination of religion and feminism is bound to lead her to an interesting future career.

A Jewish woman in her seventh decade spent an afternoon going back in her memory over her childhood religious education in a small Texas town. She, too, defined religion in terms of the "big questions."[24] For her, religious experience is replaced by a quest for answers to the inquiries "Why am I here?" "Why should I not be cruel?" "Why should I not be greedy?" and "Why should I care about others?" Although not an observing Jew, she traces the development of her sense of identity to a biography given to her on her confirmation in a Reform synagogue. The book described how an Englishwoman overcame anti-Semitism during her school days by considering her ancient heritage as a gift to be used for social betterment.

"That was just what I needed to hear." The message, she says, lifting her head high, was: "O.K. It's not just bearable to be Jewish, it's good to be Jewish, it's great to be Jewish." And in Judaism she found a morality that she described as "an aesthetic," which involves the sharing of wealth; "the person who shares with the needy person is doing the right thing."

Interviewer: "This moral aesthetic is also practical, based on a tradition of knowing how to survive, isn't it?"

Answer: "Exactly. That's what makes Jews generally hated. There are two parts to that; one is pragmatism, the other is the concept of the elite. Even poor Jews feel themselves to be set aside. It worked for me, I now see, even when I was fat and wore glasses. I can't tell how much came from the Jewish context and how much came from my mother. She encouraged me not to conform...gave me what she was denied as a young woman. What she wanted was professionalism, a career, an exciting life."

THE RETURN OF THE PROPHETESS

Religion exists today in an environment of contradictions. We live in what looks to many like a godless society, yet (or perhaps, therefore) rarely has a desire for the sacred been so urgently felt by Americans. Literally, it would seem, Christianity may be starting all over again, with clusters of wayfarers trying somehow to turn obscurity into understanding. Women are actively involved in this quest.

There is in Princeton, New Jersey, a group that meets regularly to hear a woman preacher from Philadelphia. The hostess says that she started the group in response to the drift in her church to a "too political position." One of the guests echoed this with the remark that "they don't spend any time telling you how to save your soul." As a matter of fact, she continued, "they go out of their way to avoid discussing such matters." Another, when asked her opinion of the women's movement, said with disgust, "Don't even mention it to me."[25]

There is an emotional cost in being deprived of certitude. The moral seriousness of these women extends to listening to tapes marketed by the speaker's company. One, called "Storms of Adversity," Acts 27, is a meditation on St. Paul's journey to Rome to answer charges of illegally preaching to nonbelievers in Jerusalem. Having requested judgment by a Roman court, Paul is put on board a prison ship. Off Crete the ship founders in violent storms lasting for fourteen days. When it finally runs aground, passengers pick their way over the slippery rocks to safety. The entire chapter is a sustained and beautifully written narrative of anxiety and the loss of hope, which leaves room at the end for reassurance. Moreover, it speaks to the issue of personal witness of one's beliefs, furnishing an excellent choice for inspirational speaking.[26]

The audience on that particular winter morning listened intently to the speaker's description of the great success in Asia of a recent tour by a well-known American evangelist, and of the great awakening of Christian faith that it demonstrates.

A different sort of spiritual pattern emerges in the work of a California woman whose smattering of catchy ideas parallels the pluralistic tendencies of the 1990s. A description of one homily is said to have included not only a

wide-ranging analysis of Christian symbolism, but...encompassed Jewish history and legend, Buddhist and other Eastern traditions, the hole in the ozone and air pollution, hunger and homelessness, nuclear Armageddon, the war in the Gulf, Greek tragedy, the politics of the television industry, white collar crime and the S & L crisis, the theory of evolution, brain research, Jung's theory of synchronicity, Buckminster Fuller, Snow White, Cinderella and Sleeping Beauty, and assorted manifestations of pop culture.[27]

This, concluded a reporter, is the argot of the contemporary generation. To some it might suggest a high-brow cultural bazaar, a parody of home-town religious theme parks or churches with sports facilities, barber shops, and restaurants attached.

ROADS THAT LEAD AWAY FROM ROME

The Church of Rome defines its cosmic role as the direct transmission of the teaching Jesus handed down to his disciples. It has consistently ruled that tradition, if not theology, is enough to keep women out of the priesthood. Traditions vary in weight; it is one thing (so the argument goes) to abolish the old ban on eating meat on Friday. That's tradition with a small "t." There are traditions of another sort. "The prohibition against the ordination of women belongs to the tradition with a capital 'T.' "[28] Fewer Catholics than before are accepting the distinction. Support for women's ordination has risen steadily since Vatican Two in the 1960s, in part because the faithful believed that the Council ratified a breaking away from traditional gender models.[29] Today it is not unusual to hear Catholic women, not all of whom call themselves feminists, arguing that it is their church, too, and they want to see a little more fairness toward their sex. Many call on the Church to revive the diaconate; if women could be deaconesses in biblical times, why not now? The question deserves to be considered.

Vatican Two did affirm the right of all members to participate in the church's mission, although various documents since then have wavered on the question of what it means for women to "participate" at all.

In 1985 a synod of bishops was held in Rome to consider how Vatican Two had been implemented in various parts of the world. "Although they state that the talents of women should be more effectively used in the apostolate," writes the Jesuit theologian Avery Dulles, "the Synod documents do not tackle the questions whether or not women should be installed in official, non-ordained ministries (such as lector or acolyte) or whether they might be ordained, at least to the diaconate." The writer goes on to say that although some critics were disappointed that these matters were not "openly discussed in the final report, it may be argued that the drafters showed good judgement in not trying to solve everything at once."[30] One ecclesiastical observer at the synod seems to have expressed the majority view that striving for openness had led the church, after the Vatican Two Council, into a contaminated world where "much of the faith has been called into question. Many priests and religious abandoned their vocations, and few young people felt called to the service of the church."[31]

Beyond the issue of women in the diaconate lies the more thorny question of women as priests. Whereas women did perform as deacons in the early Christian period even before the creation of the priesthood, they were never allowed to become priests. Priesthood is a role, one writer comments, and it is likely that women could perform that role. "Does the representation of Jesus become important primarily because of his maleness?" asks John Garvey in an article in the magazine *Commonweal*.[32] In any case, he concludes, it remains for the church to make a better defense than it has in the past for its teaching that men alone can become priests. The question arises: How deeply will the institution allow itself to be crippled by a shortage of priests before it starts to rethink its teaching? Laypeople already head hundreds of churches in the United States, according to a study presented at the Women's Ordination Conference in 1990.[33]

Yet when the National Conference of Bishops met to vote on the fourth draft of a pastoral letter on Women's Concerns in late 1992, it was no surprise that the text indicated a firm retreat from the more open attitudes found in early drafts. Rejecting calls by women and married couples for gender equality and more humane teachings on sex, it jeopardizes the gains from the liberalizing trend of Vatican Two.

But it is doubtful the Church has ever had to face the sort of organized resistance that now opposes it. A group called People Active in the Ministry issued a manifesto in March 1991 in advance of a Vatican meeting of bishops from all over the world. Saying they could not remain silent, the members listed among their desiderata for the Church that "women enjoy full equality and fully participate in decision-making. In this, there is still the most scandalous discrimination. Theology provides no reason to exclude women from the ministry. There can be no future church without the recognition of the equality of women."[34]

This position was endorsed by other organizations, such as the Association for the Rights of Catholics in the Church (ARCC). ARCC's president, Mary Louise Hartman, a Princeton, New Jersey, librarian, says that her specific reason for joining ARCC stemmed from her "concern about injustice," not from feminism.[35] Other organizations may be mentioned, among them the Women's Alliance for Theology, Ethics, and Ritual (WATER); the National Coalition of Catholic Nuns, and Call to Action. Perhaps the most concise statement of disaffection with Rome can be found in the Cologne Declaration of January 1989, compiled and signed by numerous European theologians, listing three areas of concern to them: biased episcopal appointments, intrusion into teaching and research, and "an attempt, theologically highly questionable, to enforce and overstep in an inadmissible way the Pope's competence in the field of doctrinal teaching."[36]

Thus, an institution formed on medieval lines with a supreme ruler and a clerical elite that enforces its decrees faces new challenges from within as well as without, and seeks to reinforce its crumbling authority. To Americans, Vatican Two's liberalism echoed democratic political ideals: the dictates of private conscience and the notion of equal participation in church affairs. The "ghetto church" is a thing of the past. Sister Piper observes: "We should worship God, not the church."

THE POSTPATRIARCHAL, POSTFEMINIST WORLD

Male domination as a mark of divine purpose has lasted long enough. But have women, in the words of the feminist historian Flora Davis, succeeded in "Moving the Mountain," as we approach A.D. 2000? Or are they at an impasse, unable to scale the "system," unable to change it?

This work tells us, first, that although local women are linked by common concerns to women everywhere, they do not speak with one voice. Change is therefore problematic. Gender alone does not magically unite women. The case of Clarence Thomas in October 1991 showed that an accusation of sexual harassment did not disqualify Thomas for the Supreme Court in the opinion of numerous women. Race and class perspectives, it is clear, must be taken into account as well. Looked at from the religious viewpoint, the women quoted in this chapter support or reject tradition, seek the Goddess or discover the already present feminine nature of the divine, preach the social Gospel or consider it politics.

Next, recent history shows us that political convergence in the 1980s between the religious right and economic conservatives has slowed women's ascent. Antifeminists hurl epithets at the woman's movement, uncovering conspiracies to destroy men as well as Christian values (which, in fact, they equate).[37] Films and television frequently show independent women as miserable and unfulfilled, not to mention dangerous, rather than as hard-working people trying to balance professional and personal lives. The message is, if women are driven back where they used to be, order would be restored. In these circumstances, coupled with rising violence against women, rights of privacy found for them by the courts in the 1970s will not survive this century. Will other accomplishments hold? The answer is complex, but there is much in this chapter to suggest that younger women take for granted what the elders wrought, and will, at least, keep alive women's hopes for change.

Interestingly, the 1981 publication of Betty Friedan's *The Second Stage* marked a turning point in which a leading feminist set aside the quest for women's rights in favor of a family orientation, advising women to "forge alliances with men."[38] In doing so, she alienated leaders of the movement she helped create. At the same time, she responded to the yearning of many women for a less "radical," profamily posture. This could be the trend of the years ahead.

Realism would indicate that while women should continue to challenge the patriarchy, justice cannot be achieved by women alone. Finally, sharing together in a human enterprise of celebrating the sacred, of restoring the environment and securing better housing, health, and child care, offers a way out of an Orwellian future. If this is the only paradise we may ever know, it will require the best insights of all of us to preserve it.

NOTES

All quotations from interviews, unless otherwise specified, are drawn from the first-cited reference.

I would like to thank the women whose interviews provided the basis for this chapter: Elizabeth Ann Davidson, Mary Ford-Grabowski, Mary Louise Hartman, Sister Lorette Piper, Pam Saturnia, Rabbi Susan Schnur, the Reverend Hazel Staats-Westover, and others who requested anonymity.

1. George Gallup, Jr. and Sarah Jones, *100 Questions And Answers: Religion in America* (Princeton, NJ: Princeton Religious Research Center, 1989), p. xiv.

2. Dr. Mary Ford-Grabowski, interview held in Princeton, New Jersey, March 1991.

3. Peter Brown, *The Body and Society: Men, Women, and Sexual Renunciation in Early Christianity* (New York: Columbia University Press, 1988), p. 9.

4. Ibid. p. 95.

5. Ibid. p. 13.

6. Elizabeth Schussler-Fiorenza, *In Memory of Her: A Feminist Theological Reconstruction of Christian Origins* (New York: Crossroads, 1985), p. 140. See also Uta Ranke-Heinemann, *Eunuchs for the Kingdom of Heaven* (New York: Penguin, 1990), for a discussion of hostility to women as reflected in pronouncements of the Roman Catholic Church over the centuries.

7. Schussler-Fiorenza, *In Memory of Her*, p. 304.

8. Mary Jo Weaver, *New Catholic Women: A Contemporary Challenge to Traditional Religious Authority* (San Francisco: Harper & Row, 1985), p. 58.

9. Carol Gilligan, *In a Different Voice: Psychological Theory and Women's Development* (Cambridge, MA: Harvard University Press, 1982), p. 75.

10. Sydney Callahan, "Person and Gender, Quelle Difference?" *Church Magazine* 6, no. 2 (Summer, 1990): 5.

11. Judith Plaskow, *Standing Again at Sinai: Judaism from a Feminist Perspective* (San Francisco: Harper & Row, 1990), p. 38.

12. Nadine Broznan, "Telling The Seder's Story in the Voice of a Woman," *New York Times*, April 9, 1990, p. B4. A Jewish Population Survey released in November 1990 reported a total of 5.5 million Jews in the United States according to Ari Goldman in "Religious Notes," *New York Times*, December 1, 1990, p. 14. The article indicated a trend toward return to traditional practices abandoned by the Reform movement as part of its search for new forms of spirituality.

13. Hazel Staats-Westover, interview held in Princeton, New Jersey, February 14, 1991.

14. Riane Eisler, *The Chalice and the Blade: Our History, Our Future* (San Francisco: Harper & Row, 1987), Introduction, passim.

15. Janet McCrickard, "Born Again Moon: Fundamentalism in Christianity and the Feminist Spirituality Movement," *Feminist Review*, No. 37 (Spring 1991): 65.

16. Mary Ford-Grabowski interview.

17. Sister Lorette Piper, RCSJ, interview held in Princeton, New Jersey, February 6, 1991.

18. Seminary student interview held in Princeton, New Jersey, March 10, 1991.

19. Rabbi Susan Schnur, interview held in Hopewell, New Jersey, December 18, 1990.

20. Susan Schnur, "HERS" *New York Times*, July 18, 1985, p. C2.

21. Rosemary Radford Ruether, *Sexism and God-talk: Toward a Feminist Theology* (Boston: Beacon Press, 1983), p. 233.

22. Pam Saturnia, interview held in Princeton, New Jersey, February 1991.

23. Anonymous, interview held in Princeton, New Jersey, in February 1991.

24. Anonymous, interview held in Princeton, New Jersey, in December 1990.

25. Anonymous, conversations held in Princeton, New Jersey, March 1991. See Susan Faludi's *Backlash: The Undeclared War Against American Women* (New York: Crown Publishers, 1991) for a review of critical media portrayals of feminists in the 1980s.

26. "Acts," *The Jerusalem Bible* (New York: Doubleday and Company, 1968).

27. Leslie Bennetts, "Marianne's Faithful," *Vanity Fair* 54, no. 6 (June 1991): 130.

28. Linda Richardson, "Catholic Women Seek to Open a Long-closed Subject: Ordination," *Washington Post*, November 11, 1990, p. A3.

29. Andrew Greeley, *American Catholics Since the Council: An Unauthorized Report* (Chicago: Thomas More Press, 1985), p. 190. Using as a definition of feminism approval of ordination, approval of women working, and a rejection of a narrow role for women at home, the author shows that over a period of fifteen years there has been a steady rise of support for these positions among Catholics.

30. Avery Dulles, S. J., *The Reshaping of Catholicism: Current Challenges in the Theology of the Church* (San Francisco: Harper & Row, 1988), p. 188.

31. Ibid., p. 191.

32. John Garvey, "Women's Ordination: Another Go at the Old Arguments," *Commonweal* 57, no. 2 (January 26, 1990).

33. Richardson, "Catholic Women Seek."

34. People Active in the Ministry, "Luzern Statement" reprinted in *ARCC LIGHT, Newsletter of the Association for the Rights of Catholics in the Church* 13, no. 2 (March/April 1991).

35. Mary Louise Hartman, conversation held in Princeton, New Jersey, May 1991.

36. "The Cologne Declaration," *The Tablet* February 4, 1989, p. 140.

37. Christina Sommers, "Hard-line Feminists Guilty of Ms-Representation," *Wall Street Journal*, November 2, 1991, p. A14.

38. Betty Friedan, *The Second Stage* (New York: Summit Books, 1981).

6

Women's Spirituality II: An Alternative to Organized Religion

Francesca Benson

While some women strive to create change within organized religion, others have moved away from established religious traditions to create spiritual alternatives for themselves. These women assert the right to express their own spiritual truth and to celebrate in their own manner, without the intervention of clergy or hierarchical structure. Their spiritual practice draws inspiration from such sources as ancient goddess symbolism, nature, modern feminist thought, and, perhaps most important, their own experience. They often gather in small, informal groups. They see themselves offering new responses to old questions and creating new rituals for often-neglected aspects of women's lives. They are among a growing number of women— and men—who are approaching spiritual issues in new ways.

In writing a chapter about women's spirituality as an alternative to organized religion, it seems fitting to let the women involved speak for themselves, rather than to have their beliefs interpreted for the reader. Thus the heart of this chapter is the words of women who are practitioners of women's spirituality. These women will be quoted in regard to various aspects of their spiritual practice throughout the chapter.[1]

HISTORICAL CONTEXT

Women's spirituality in its modern form blossomed in the early years of the feminist movement. Women had begun to question the linking of authority with maleness, and to note and comment on the prevalence of men in positions of leadership in politics, business, the media, religion. They had begun to search for reasons why females seemed to be historically relegated to second-class status. Some women saw prevailing religious belief systems as underlying factors in their subordination. Male priests and ministers preached the word of a God who was referred to as He, Lord, Father. Religious leaders quoted biblical passages and traditional texts that focused on the subservience and uncleanness of women and pictured them as tools of the devil. More and more women began to see the traditional religious view of females as detrimental to themselves. Although some thought it possible to reform existing religious perspectives, others embarked on an alternative path. One of these women, M., speaks of her religious background:

As a woman I felt ignored, overlooked and even negated by the traditional faith in which I was raised. It had no place for me and my experiences as a woman. Its language was exclusive, its ceremonies and stories were exclusive. . . . It had nothing to offer me, so for a very long time I rejected it all: soul, spirituality, ritual. . . . Then I learned about women's spirituality, which recognizes and makes meaningful the experience of being a female human in this world. I look to the women's spirituality movement to bring the balance back to humanity and our relationship with the sacred.

The budding interest in an alternative women's spirituality was sparked and nourished by the writings of a number of women researchers and authors. An early, influential voice was that of feminist theorist and scholar Mary Daly. In *Beyond God the Father*, Daly suggested that the women's movement is a spiritual revolution, concerned with the search for ultimate meaning and reality.[2] She argued that women cannot achieve liberation unless they free themselves from patriarchal religion, confront their own being, and find their own spiritual expression. According to Daly, this requires both individuation and participation in community. A sample of Daly's writing is included in *Womanspirit Rising*, a 1979 collection that serves as an excellent introduction to writings in feminist spirituality.[3]

Meanwhile, Marija Gimbutas, professor of archaeology at UCLA, was unearthing evidence of Old European cultures in which worship of the Goddess was preeminent.[4] In her writings, Gimbutas presented symbols representing a multifaceted Goddess that had been revered for thousands of years. The Goddess was portrayed in many aspects: vigorous, massively fat, youthful, pregnant, sexual, maternal, and in the forms of birds, snakes, and other animals. Modern women who were eager for positive female images of the sacred responded to Gimbutas's work and began to incorporate Goddess symbolism into their spiritual practice. One woman, N., comments on the concept of Goddess:

I don't believe in a "Goddess" who takes the place of a "God." However, for me "Goddess" is a fine symbol to substitute for the image of "God" that we grew up with, the old white bearded man who runs things. When people imagine "God" as male, it follows that men will claim leadership, but the resultant patriarchy has done a lot of damage to humanity and to the earth. Women need to see themselves as co-leaders with men in making a better world.

The image of a strong, creative Goddess can help women to affirm themselves as positive and powerful instead of sinful and weak. It can help women see their bodies as sacred and beautiful rather than unclean or overweight. Goddess legends from around the world describe the sacred as female, young, old, black, brown, yellow, red, white. To me, that's a welcome change! These legends emphasize creativity and cooperation, too, and we need this emphasis in our world.

Goddess tales do seem to highlight the multicultural aspect of women's spirituality. The wealth of Goddess stories from African, Asian, Latin American, Middle Eastern, Native American, and Oceanian traditions, as exemplified in Merlin Stone's *Ancient Mirrors of Womanhood* and other writings,[5] presents impressive evidence of the universality of the Goddess presence in human consciousness. Several of the women interviewed spoke of their childhood experience of Goddess stories as influential in their spiritual quest. L. reminisces:

When I was in sixth grade, I was fascinated by mythology. Greek, Roman, Norse myths—I read everything I could get my hands on. The goddesses in the myths were important spiritual models because they were active, they could do things. As a Catholic I was offered a few female saints as role models, but I wasn't interested in having myself martyred. I wanted to know a way to live in this world. Getting involved in women's spirituality was a way of finding the strength in those stories again.

DEVELOPING ALTERNATIVES

Women who sought alternatives began to explore and develop a spirituality that would express their own, uniquely female, view of the sacred. Noting the absence of women-centered and women-enhancing rituals, they began to design their own ceremonies and to celebrate their spirituality together. L. remarks:

There are things that are important, things that women go through in their lives, which are never celebrated. When I first got my period, there was no celebration, no sense that I had reached a new stage of my life. Marriage is celebrated in relation to a man, not in terms of a step that a woman takes. Friendship, our connection with the seasons, menopause. . . . The group gives me a place to express and celebrate my womanhood. Exploring women's spirituality has healed me in terms of my attitude towards being a woman.

How could a woman formulate her own spirituality? The question was a heady one. As time went on, women who were accustomed to accepting certain beliefs as revealed by God, as well as women who had shunned spiritual questions altogether, began the slow process of uncovering and expressing their own spiritual views, and creating rituals that marked and honored these views. As they did so, they recognized the importance of speaking from their own, female experience. They began to locate the sacred within themselves and in all things, rather than outside or above the world. They began to honor their connection with the natural world and its cycles of birth, growth, death, and rebirth. They developed an emphasis on the healing power of community. Q., one of a group of women who have been meeting together for more than ten years, describes what the group means to her:

Each month I put aside my busy life for one evening and meet in a small room with eleven other women. We enter quietly and smile at each other without speaking. The room is lit by candles; there may be flowers or evergreen branches on a low table. We sit in a circle. Two leaders, who rotate each month, begin our ceremony. The celebrations have different themes, but all of them reflect women's experiences. We mark the passages of our lives. We share our hopes, our fears, our dreams for the future. We contemplate the beauty of the earth, her changes, and our connectedness to her. We include deep breathing and silence. We sing, we dance, we laugh, we eat together.

I think our ceremonies help us to forge strong bonds of community. They help us to feel empowered so that we can go back into the everyday world renewed and better able to work for a more humane existence. No matter how tired I am, I never miss my women's spirituality group. It has become a central experience in my life.

One Example of a Women's Spirituality Group

The group to which Q. belongs has been meeting on a monthly basis in an East Coast college town for more than ten years. It had twelve members at the time of this writing, ranging in age from early twenties to mid-sixties. This group is open to women of any age, race, or sexual preference, and its membership reflects this openness. Group members have a diversity of occupations in education, business, the arts. About half are married; five have children, and at the time of this writing one was expecting her first child. The group has been "mother" to at least two other women's spirituality groups, and several other groups have been formed in the area as well.

The group meets in the home of one of its members, using a room that was formerly a children's playroom. Now that the children are grown, the room is set aside for the women's meetings so that privacy is assured. It contains a comfortable couch and folding chairs; its walls are covered with posters of women's events and happenings: a Goddess poster from the Judy

Chicago Birth Project; a painting showing women of different races dancing together; a poster of Maggie Kuhn, which proclaims "The best age is the age you are." There are drawings from Meinrad Craighead's *The Mother's Songs*[6] and a picture of the Ribbon Peace quilt. In one corner a web of yarn made by the group hangs in a prominent place; a group fingerpainting hangs near a window. A. comments:

I love having our own safe space in which to celebrate. I love the fact that it is truly a space for women. In fact, I feel that it has become sacred space, with all the rituals and celebrations that we've shared over the years. Women need space in which to be themselves. It's so rare; I feel blessed that we are able to meet together each month in that place.

The Group's Beginnings

The group was begun by two women who were active in the local chapter of the National Organization for Women. One of the women, Y., had completed studies for the ministry of the United Church of Christ, but she had begun to envision a "womanchurch" to minister to women:

My dream of what I thought we were going to do is very different from what has happened, because I was closer to the theological model then. I believe it is important for women to analyze from their own life experience what theology and spirituality are, for themselves, in their own lives. Of course women have written about spirituality—the bookstores are full of their writing. It's different though, most of it, from the way men have expressed their religious doctrine.

What has happened in our group—women sharing and celebrating what happens in our lives, and the way we really apply what we understand as the ethical, just position of the way society should be organized—has become much more important to me personally and politically than something put down in a formal, structured doctrine.

The other woman, B., was a former Roman Catholic who had long dreamed of the possibility of women designing their own rituals and celebrating their spirituality together:

I admire the women who stay in the traditional religions and work for change. However, those religions don't make sense to me, nor do they satisfy me. Women's spirituality offers me a meaningful way of expressing myself spiritually. I can celebrate my connection to the sacred in an atmosphere that in turn celebrates the sacred in me as I am, in the company of those who encourage me to be true to myself and who celebrate with me, through the music, dance and art which we make together.

The two women decided to run an ad in their local paper. At one newspaper office, the woman who took the ad looked skeptical and queried, "What is this? It sounds strange"; but at another news office, a woman responded, "This sounds terrific! I'd like to come!" The ad read:

A group of women is being formed locally to explore and share women's personal experiences of spirituality. The group is open to any woman who wishes to examine a variety of spiritual experiences, particularly from a feminist, nontraditional point of view. The group will meet on a regular basis, and will concern itself with the way in which women undertake a spiritual quest. As such, it will be process rather than product oriented. For further information . . .

The women received several phone calls from women in the area, some antagonistic, some enthusiastic. They set a date and met at Y.'s house. The first meeting was a somewhat stormy one. Nine women attended, but some felt uncomfortable with the Goddess-oriented, shared leadership model that Y. and B. had in mind. Some did not return for the second meeting. However, four women continued to meet and discuss their ideas on an irregular basis. Energy seemed to dwindle. Finally the women decided to plan an evening of woman-designed ritual. B. comments:

I remember the process of planning that ritual as clearly as if it were yesterday. A part of me was frightened. This would be a religious ceremony for me. I would be deciding for myself how I wanted to celebrate my womanhood and my participation in the sacred. All the years of my Christian training rose up before me—the words heretic, sinner. . . . Yet I knew that I would be betraying myself at the deepest level if I did not act on my belief in my right to decide how to give expression to my spirituality. And after we had lit the candles in the darkened room, and turned on the women's music, we started to dance in a circle, and I felt a moment of such ecstasy. . . . I will never forget it.

The act of creating their own rituals seemed to energize these women. Group members began to meet every month, new members joined through friendship or word of mouth, and one by one the women became more confident in developing celebrations that reflected their spiritual lives. Y. recalls:

At least one of us was willing to work at keeping the group together, calling new members, sending reminders, while another would concentrate on ritual ideas and celebrations. That combination of hard work and "spirit" is essential at the beginning. It's important not to be discouraged by slow starts; they're to be expected. It's worth it to hang in there; the work that you do together at the beginning becomes the basis for a good group relationship as time goes on.

B. agrees, and adds:

We felt strongly about sharing leadership from the start. Looking back, I think this was an important decision. Members of the group have grown because leadership is shared. I don't think a group can be an authentic women's spirituality group unless each woman has known the pleasures and responsibilities of leadership. I remember that one of our charter members didn't feel comfortable planning or leading rituals at first. We honored her wish, while continuing to offer her encouragement. Finally she decided to try leading a part of one ceremony. Little by little she felt her own power as a leader, and over the years she has led some of our most beautiful and meaningful celebrations.

Group Rituals

The group rituals took a form that has survived over the years and includes, but is not limited to, silence and meditation, visualization, chanting or singing, sharing experiences, dancing, and eating together. B. comments:

Women often ask us where we get our ideas for rituals. At the beginning, we relied on books such as Starhawk's *The Spiral Dance*,[7] but soon we began to create our own celebrations. I think this is an important step. The more the ritual belongs to the group, the more authentic it will be. Creating rituals awakens one's own creativity, too, and thus has wonderful benefits for those involved.

The group begins its celebrations by sitting or standing in a circle, a practice that is a way of creating sacred space and that seems to be common to most such groups. One of the leaders will usually walk around the circle as it is formed, acknowledging the four directions of east, south, west, and north and setting the theme for the ritual. A ritual on interconnectedness may begin, for example, as the women walk in a circle and one woman speaks:

Our circle is a woman's symbol, an earth symbol, a symbol of wholeness and of equality. As we breathe and move in this circle, we honor ourselves in our bodies, which are so often violated or oppressed. As we move, let us honor the women we are connected to, and if you want to call out a name during this time, please do so. First, let us honor all the women who came before us: women in our womanline, our mothers, our grandmothers, women who blazed a trail for us, women who spoke up for what they believed and who were often condemned for that.... Let us walk in the circle with them now. [The speaker pauses here.]

Second, let us honor women all over the world, women who struggle for their daily bread, who endure the hardships of war, who care for their families in the midst of poverty, who are afraid, abused, battered or ignored...let us walk with them now.

Third, let us honor women who are connected to us personally, women who support or encourage us, who sustain us, who love us and whom we love, who are fun to be with, who understand our pain and our joy, who share and celebrate our work...let us walk with them now.

Fourth, let us honor the women who are to come, the little girls, the female babies, those who have not yet been born, for whom we hope to make a better world, who are the next link in the womancircle...let us walk with them now.

Such an invocation connects the personal and political in women's lives. It allows women to express aspects of relationships that are meaningful and sacred to them. At the same time, it helps the women in the circle to become more aware of other women, past, present and future, with whom they are linked by virtue of their womanhood.

A silent meditation often follows the circle formation. This meditation is sometimes accompanied by a visualization that focuses on the time of year, the seasons, or the elements: air, fire, water, earth. One group member wrote the following visualization for the spring equinox:

She stirs. As light fills the sky, she awakens. Spring rains shake her with a gentle touch. Tiny flowers blossom in the branches of her hair. Small buds bloom at the edges of her fingertips. The waters of brooks and streams run freely from her breasts. Green shoots spring from her belly. Her breath grows warm. Her pulse quickens. Her blood moves as sap through the veins of trees. Her womb begins to birth its abundance. Her feet dance in the laughing wind. She is changing, growing, blossoming, creating. She is our mother; we will care for her.

Connectedness with the Earth

A connectedness with the earth as mother and female symbol is a common theme in women's spirituality celebrations. The group may be the only comfortable place for many women to express and celebrate these feelings. As A. says,

it's not an accepted thing to wax poetic about one's feelings for the earth in other places, but I can do that in the group. I can talk about how I love the out-of-doors, how the hills and woods are my sanctuary. I can speak of my absolute joy in the wind, the sight of mountain waterfalls, chickadees in the snow, bees in flowers, the full moon, and know that there are other women in the group who share my feelings.

Another woman, R., writes:

The nature of the planet is Women's Spirit. It is our Mother, it births us, feeds us, provides for us, and creates space for growth and knowledge. It is so obviously Female Power to me.

L. comments:

I was always aware of being in tune with the seasons, but I had no way to express it. I'm talking about more than just putting flowers on the table or gourds out in the fall. It seemed to me that there had to be a deeper way of expressing this, making it a part of my life.

And H. adds:

I practice women's spirituality by being in the group, and also by communing with Nature, feeling the "femaleness" of the Earth and how umbilically connected I feel to Her.

Nor does this feeling exist in a vacuum; H. goes on to say:

That results in my strong feelings of protectiveness toward the environment, and my support of organizations striving to effect political change in that area.

Her statement is echoed by other women in the group. Their celebration of the Earth seems to be linked with practical steps to preserve the environment. These women recycle, support environmental organizations, teach children about and write letters in support of environmental issues, and in general match their feelings for the Earth with specific, positive political actions. Not only does the monthly visualization reflect this connection with the Earth, but many of the songs the women sing or chant reflect this interest. They celebrate, too, the parallels between the cycles of the earth and the cycles of women's bodies. At the spring equinox, women may share stories of their first menstruation. Summer is a time for speaking of birthing and nurturing—of babies, work, or other forms of creativity. A ceremony for a woman beginning menopause might be scheduled for the fall equinox, while winter is a time to meditate on death and its mystery, and to look ahead to the sprouting of new life as the cycle of the year continues.

Empowerment

An essential feature of any women's spirituality group is the time set aside during the ceremony for sharing experiences, concerns, and convictions, often around a common theme. Many aspects of this sharing—the respectful act of listening without interrupting, the experience of being heard without judgment, the opportunity to speak and share beliefs that may be unusual or unconventional, the celebrating of women's life events—are reminiscent of earlier feminist consciousness-raising groups. The sharing often centers around a common theme, such as self-empowerment. B. comments:

To me, the crux of women's spirituality is seeing our woman selves as a part of that which is sacred or holy, and honoring that sacredness in ourselves. Many of us have been taught that the sacred is outside of us, that we are unclean, that we should be subservient or obedient to others. I believe that we partake of the sacred by being true to ourselves, by loving ourselves as women, by seeing ourselves as good and beautiful, by speaking our own truth as we understand it. We aren't often able to do that, especially in a religious context. As an example, consider the difference between the words of St. Paul, telling women to listen quietly and with submission, and the words of a song that we often sing in the group: "You can't kill the Spirit, She's like a mountain, Old and strong, She goes on and on...." The images are so different. One speaks of keeping women in their "place." The other speaks of the power of the spirit in the symbolic form of an earthy old woman. That's a nourishing symbol for me, one which helps me to visualize the sacred in myself. It's certainly different from the stereotypical modern images of older women.

A. adds:

In our circle, there is a celebration of interconnectedness with the women present and an extension of that connection to women past and future. Our ceremonies evoke earth, its seasons and our own life stages, with older sister greeting younger sister in life's passages. These celebrations help us to tap those forces which empower us, and to discard those which make us feel powerless.

How can members of a women's spirituality group practice self-empowerment? N. describes a ritual she is planning for her group:

We will be celebrating the natural beauty of each woman. We'll meditate on ways in which we embody the sacred. We'll remind ourselves about the billions of dollars spent on cosmetics and plastic surgery, and visualize ways in which that money might be better spent. We'll make a list of all the "shoulds" about women's bodies and stamp them out with our feet. We'll include a sharing in which each woman will have a chance to speak about what is beautiful about herself, her spirit, her unadorned body. We'll include time for each woman to express her own beauty through body movement to the music of the Libana chant, "Now I Walk in Beauty."[8]

G. describes a ritual that was repeated yearly in the women's spirituality group of which she was a member while in graduate school:

My favorite ritual was the one we called the fire ritual. Once a year, usually around the winter solstice, we gathered together at the house of someone who had a fireplace, and each woman brought something she wanted to burn, something she wanted to transform by fire or have fire devour or be free of or purify through fire. Each woman took her turn in front of the fire and had her choice to say or not to say what she was burning and why. Then she put whatever she brought into the fire. Some women brought objects, some paper. After each turn, we said, "What frees you, frees all of us." For me that became a very powerful ritual, which took on a life of its own. I would think at times during the year, "What do I want to burn?"

N. speaks of a similar ritual, and adds:

Whenever we do a ritual involving fire, we honor the witches, those untold numbers of women tortured and burned for "religious" reasons. Many of those condemned were poor and old. Many were midwives and healers. I'm sure that if we were living at the time of the witch craze, all of the women in our group would be burned as witches, even though none of us has studied witchcraft or claims to be a witch. To me, the common, negative view of witches shows how strong the patriarchy is. I think every woman owes it to herself to read modern historical accounts of the witch craze. One male scholar calls it the most hideous example of misogyny in European history. When we do fire rituals, I think about how I am, in a small way, affirming a woman's right to be true to her own beliefs, in spite of the attempts to keep women "in their place."

Life-Cycle Rituals

Another type of ritual seen as empowering for women is the life-cycle ritual, centering around stages in a woman's life that are usually ignored or denigrated. Q., a fifty-five-year-old woman, tells of her experience with a menopause ritual:

I wasn't close to anyone who had gone through menopause. My mother had died without speaking of it to me. I was healthy and energetic, but I felt apprehensive about aging. I mentioned that one night in the group, and the other women suggested that the group do a menopause ritual to celebrate my passage from one stage of life to the next. They urged me to spend some time in meditation before the ritual, visualizing the possibilities for this third stage of my life. They even suggested that I set new goals for myself.

The ceremony was wonderful. The other women read poems to me, sang songs in my honor, reminded me of my strengths and accomplishments, and encouraged me to approach this new stage as an explorer and adventurer. I had a chance to talk about my hopes and dreams for the future. The ceremony helped me to envision the positive possibilities of life as an older woman, rather than the negatives. It's not accidental that the past five years have been the best of my life!

Viewing older women as wise and powerful is an ancient concept that is reflected in the women's spirituality practice of honoring women at all stages of life. This concept finds expression in such writings as Barbara Walker's *The Crone*.[9]

D. makes an interesting comment about women-centered rituals such as the menopause ceremony:

Think about the more earth-centered cultures in which women and men meet separately to celebrate. There are ceremonies for girls with the women and ceremonies for boys with the men. They may also celebrate together at times. The people of those cultures must have realized in their wisdom that women need rituals with other women and that men need rituals with men. Our culture hasn't made space for that. If there is separateness, it is because males are allowed into a sacred space and women aren't. Earlier cultures had space for men and space for women that was separate and equal and important. I think women need this as a justified natural right. It feels to me as though that has been taken away. It's like "Take Back the Night"—we need to take back, to reclaim the right to celebrate separately. I think women's spirituality groups put us back in touch with how natural it is to be doing this, reclaiming our right and our need to be together.

Artistic Expression

Several of the women interviewed speak of their delight at finding a group in which they can express their spirituality in an artistic or playful form. A. says:

We did a ritual on women as weavers, weaving our stories and our daily life together, making an ongoing construction of all our continuous lives. We actually wove a web of yarn, picking colors that had symbolism for each of us. We wove the yarn together, and as we did we started to weave with our arms and then actually put our bodies through the strands of yarn. We were entangled as much as weaving, which is a kind of symbol for being the weavers and the web at the same time. We ended up laughing and having so much fun with it. It was laughter that was releasing emotion and expressing something important at the same time.

I love our celebrations at night, too. There are times when we're dancing under the light of the moon, and there's the sound of the wind chimes—there's a mystery about it, like the old mysteries.

And Q. comments:

The older I get, the more I love to dance, even though I've never been a dancer before. One of the great pleasures of the group for me is that I can express my spirituality through dancing. I can dance my fears, my hopes, my connection with what is holy to me, my spirit. Once I even designed a dance to express a transition in my life, and I danced that before the group. It felt scary but wonderful, knowing that each woman there supported me in taking that risk, knowing that I could express who I am through the dance.

Most groups end their rituals by sharing food and news. D. says:

This sharing is important to me. I like the fact that the two women who planned the evening's celebration also considered what foods would go with the theme of the evening, and especially the link with the seasons, the continuation of our appreciation of the time of year. . . . Of course the sharing of news is important, too.

L. comments:

Food is one of the most pleasurable things in my life, and the sharing together afterwards is part of the sisterhood, the sharing of where everyone is. I want to know what's going on in each woman's life. I think it helps the sharing process within the ritual, to know what is happening in the lives of the women present.

The feeling of contrast between gathering in a small group and attending a large church service is noteworthy. J. says:

In the small group, I feel that I can be much more myself and contribute in an individual way. I don't have to follow a regimen that somebody else has established. It certainly makes me think much more than in the larger setting, where everything is pretty much answered in lectures—that's how I think of sermons, as lectures. You don't have an opportunity for feedback in the larger setting, so that's frustrating. You can't say, I don't agree with that or I don't believe that. One positive thing about the large church setting is the ritual that I'm familiar with, that I'm comfortable with, that has brought me some peace in the past. . . . I think that in the large group, you're encouraged to sit back, to absorb. There's a lulling, tranquil feeling about it. In the small group, I like the parts that we do each time, the closing and opening of the circle, but it isn't exactly the same each time. Someone who opens the circle can open it in a different way, with different words. The structure is there, I like that, but there's a chance for an individual contribution.

Differences of Opinion

As in any group, there are differences of opinion. B. reflects:

I wish that we had addressed the issues of difference and conflict more directly in our early years. Conflict resolution is difficult, and there is a tendency in a women's group to avoid anything that will cause tension. However, conflict is a fact of life, and we would have been more realistic if we had expected conflict and planned ways to resolve our disagreements. It would have made sense to set up regular times to discuss where we were going and what we were doing, and to try to see differences as healthy and as issues to negotiate. We do that now, but we didn't earlier, and as a result, we had one painful meeting in which unresolved differences spilled over and resulted in unnecessary hurt for some members. At that point, the group split in two. That would probably have happened eventually in any case, since there were strong differences of opinion about the content and form of our rituals, and forming two groups allowed greater diversity. However, we didn't need to do it that way! Since then, we have worked to heal the rift, and we've even collaborated on a joint ceremony, but we could have avoided hurting each other if we had been better prepared for differences and conflicts.

Another issue that the group has faced is how to help a group member who is going through a particularly difficult life passage. Y. comments:

In our early years, one of our members was in the throes of a serious difficulty, and she needed a good deal of the group's time. Group members agreed that we would try to help her, particularly outside the rituals, but that we would also try to keep our agreement to allow equal time for each member within the framework of our ceremonies. That was a difficult balance. In recent years, we've had a similar situation, and I think we handled it better. The woman who was having such a hard time is in a much better place now, and she says we kept her going through it all. I think we all feel pleased that we were able to be a source of strength to her without neglecting our own needs within the group.

Group Membership

Groups have different approaches to integrating new members. Some groups have been hesitant to accept new women into their groups, because they feel that the bonding that takes place within the group is important to honor. Other groups make it a principle to take in any woman who wishes to join. One common solution to this problem is for a group to have several "open" ceremonies each year, and to invite new members to join at that time, which is the approach that this group takes. Another is to provide "seed" help, in the form of temporary leadership, to get a new group started.

Several women new to this group have participated in other women's spirituality groups in former years. K. contrasts her present group membership with her participation in a group in California:

For one thing, our California group—the Wheel—met once a week, so I think we got a stronger in-grouping that way.... There was more focus on what I would call raising power, although that's not the terminology that was used. We could draw on that power in our personal lives every week if we needed to, and that's very potent. The Wheel was a modified medicine wheel, drawn from Native American tradition, although only one member was Native American.... I did, and do, ritual work with ancestors, which comes out of the African tradition, my tradition. Once I realized that there was a way to recognize the ancestors, I've never not been able to feel their presence, or to feel their energy.... In both groups, the sharing is sacred. I used to think that the sacredness came from the trappings, but at some point I realized that the sacredness comes from the connection, the sharing. That's what is sacred.

G. comments on the group that she was a part of as a graduate student:

The structure was different from this one—a mailing went out once a month, before the meeting, and there was a content-related topic, such as the Shekinah, or women's bodies and their connection with spirit. We would begin to prepare for that meeting with the topic in mind. Some presentations were intellectual, with discussion; others were experiential, with spontaneous music and lots of percussion. We must have made a lot of noise! Most of the people were part of my community, too, so there were multiple connections among us. From that group came our journal, *Lady-Unique-Inclination-of-the-Night*. Some of the women saw a need to circulate some of what we were doing to more people. The journal was conceived as a way of doing that. Most of the work was done by the members of the group and all of us volunteered our time to make sure that it did get produced. The group "seeded" the journal. What's similar about the two groups is that somehow, each time, magic happens. I don't know whether to call it the sacred or the spiritual, but somehow each time I walk away having touched that. We've opened a well and it rises. I go away changed. I feel different when I wake up the next day. There is that thread that runs through our lives—like a river, a river that is so sustaining in what can be the isolation of life.

G.'s description of the *Lady-Unique* journal arising from the interaction among the members of her group reflects the manner in which women's spirituality has stimulated female creativity. An outpouring of fiction and nonfiction writing, poetry, music, art, dance, performance, and theater has been engendered by the women's spirituality movement. Goddess symbolism has proven to be a rich metaphor for the artistic expression of women's spiritual truth.

HEALING ASPECTS OF WOMEN'S SPIRITUALITY

An important aspect of women's spirituality that both feeds and is nourished by artistic expression is the recognition of each woman's individuality, of her aloneness that balances her membership in community. In *Woman Awake: A Celebration of Women's Wisdom*, Christina Feldman explores aloneness, oneness, and inner empowerment through guided meditations that can help an individual woman to companion herself.[10] Such individual companioning is essential for a woman who wishes to plumb her own depths and discover the healing power that lies within herself. F., a feminist therapist, comments on the healing aspects of women's spirituality from the point of view of her work:

The rituals themselves can be very cleansing. They celebrate renewal at every period of one's life. They help a woman to get rid of old hurts; there's a symbolic healing. The ritual is done within the context of the group; it wouldn't be as effective alone. Everyone is accepted, no one judges. I've never heard of a spirituality group that criticizes. It's a good network of support which is nonjudgmental, for which people have very little opportunity in their lives. Women will listen, but they won't give advice—I like that. It's not only a group experience, it's a grounding experience. By joining a women's spirituality group, a woman is not only not alone, but there is a group of women there, and beyond that, the whole world, because the rituals are always oriented to the seasons, the earth. A woman can see herself within a context. She can experience her place in the universe. She begins to realize that she's part of a whole female population, experiencing the stages of life—birth, regeneration, aging—without any stereotype, and experiencing not only this era, but thousands of years. She can feel the power of that heritage. For women from a religious background, it's very freeing. There are no "shoulds" to make them feel guilty or depressed. Almost 100% of the women I see come in with judgmental values, they're depressed or anxious, and these values are usually the conventional values that come from men, from religious beliefs about a woman's place. In a woman's spirituality group a woman can be away from that. It's really better than group therapy, because it's so accepting of a woman's being who she is.

SPIRITUALITY AND POLITICAL ACTION

Some feminists have been concerned that an involvement in women's spirituality diverts energy from political action. That view does not seem to be shared among the women interviewed. R. comments: "Women's spirituality and my political view are one and the same. My politics are my personal expression in thought, action, intent, relationship." N. says:

Most of the women I know who are active in women's spirituality groups are also active politically. They see political action, particularly feminist political action, as a natural outgrowth of their spiritual beliefs. They work in rape crisis centers and women's shelters. They lobby for pro-choice legislation. They're active in antinuclear and antiwar protests. I think that a woman's spiritual beliefs empower her to persevere when she meets opposition, as she surely will. I see feminist political action as an outward form of women's spirituality. Of course not all feminists would agree, but I think that to the extent that we live our beliefs, all of us practice women's spirituality.

W. gives her views:

To me, women's spirituality means a process of coming to my center, giving me a sense of myself to create the energy to do what I have to do. I'm active in feminist groups, I've done environmental work, and I'm involved in lesbian and gay issues in education. To do this work, which is so important to me, I draw on my connection with the group. I had the experience this spring of leading a workshop on how to make change in mainstream organizations. As we finished the workshop and I looked for words to bring us to closure, I said what I felt at the time, "The power is within me" (gesturing to myself), "The power is among us" (gesturing in a circle around the room), "Take the power!" I had a strong sense of power reverberating, power for being who we are, power to do what we believe and for making the changes that we believe in. I was conscious as I did that work of the importance of nourishing who we are, and of how my women's spirituality group does that for me.

Y., the ordained minister, expresses her view of the connection between women's spirituality and politics:

To me, the theological concept of inclusiveness, of equality, the concept that all human beings are valued at the same level, is essential. This is the reason for my pouring all of my energy into women's spirituality, because we have to change our concept of our relationship to the Creator. Whatever our religious concepts are affect the way we behave in community. We'll never get to the point where we can all respect each other around the globe unless we act on our vision of equality. In the women's spirituality rituals that we do, we've already experienced equality. We attempt to put aside the hierarchical structure and use one which gives equal value to each person. The way we relate to each other, we don't have any need for power structure, for dominating. We have an openness for valuing all the contributions of the women. That isn't going to happen in the community unless it happens in our spiritual practice. I think that the women's movement is a religious movement, because it has to do with valuing half the human race, who they are, and I believe that is what religious practice is, people fulfilling their created—and creative— potential. Some feminists don't accept that principle, because religion has not been a part of their background, and they see themselves arriving independently at their concepts of change, but I see it as fundamental, because I think all of the major concepts we have about women in society have come from scriptural references telling us how to behave. Inequality, reproductive rights, sexual choice.... Even people who think they are not affected by religion live in a culture that was established on the basis of certain religious principles.

WOMEN'S SPIRITUALITY AND TRADITIONAL RELIGION

Although most of the women who are members of women's spirituality groups see the groups as the focus of their spiritual practice, a number of these women are also members of traditional religious congregations. L., for example, is a long-time member of the group described above, and a Roman Catholic. She comments:

Here I am, a member of the group, and at the same time I've just joined a parish, because I made a decision that I want my child to be baptized and to be brought up Catholic. I don't feel that I have to make a choice. My understanding of what Jesus teaches has expanded to a point that I know that he was not misogynist, though people who followed him may have been. The Church is my heritage, I was raised Catholic, and I learned many good things being Catholic. In my Catholic background, how you treat *people*—not men or women—was emphasized. From the Church, I learn how to live everyday life, through the readings, the words of Jesus, illuminated by the sermons, as well as the people I meet. Women's spirituality is helpful to me in recognizing the earth, and in recognizing who I am as a woman. I think reverence is an appropriate word—in women's spirituality there's a reverence towards women, and towards being a woman, which I think is lacking in the traditional church. I'm trying to bring those two things together; somehow they fit in my mind.

S., a member of another group, remarks:

I'm a fairly observant Jew. I observe and celebrate the Jewish Sabbath and the holidays. Judaism anchors me and gives me identity. It has an important function within my family and my community. Judaism as I practice it has a great deal of latitude. Still, it is a constant struggle to get around the male dominance, imagery, terminology. Women help—my women's spirituality group, other Jewish women, and all people and institutions that are striving for more of a masculine/feminine balance.

Y. notes:

I feel that I gained a spiritual nurture from the church as a child, in spite of the negative forces. I was in a denomination that didn't ordain women. In fact, I taught the first class for women in their seminaries. I feel that it's necessary to work for change both from the outside and the inside. It will never happen from one side or the other by itself. I can still worship in my own way, in spite of anything patriarchal that's still there. I'm there in terms of reforming rather than leaving it to develop on its own. I don't think it would do that. You have to be there to help it to change, to offer different metaphors.

Y. also speculates on why some women move to an opposite religious stance, becoming members of fundamentalist groups:

I think they're afraid to separate themselves, and it *is* scary. I can remember my first visit with Mary Daly. She had written *Beyond God the Father*, and she spent the afternoon sharing that with me. I remember saying, "I can't go there with you all the way, because it's like throwing out the baby with the bath. I have to absorb this in my own understanding before I can jump with you to that degree." It was scary to me, it violated my orientation, my whole spiritual reference. My image of God since I'd been a teenager was of an old man with a white beard. It took me ten years of work to move from the Father image. Still, I would encourage *everyone* to do that. The Father image is a limiting concept—you have boxed in your thinking, you can't expand the meaning of infinity, of the spirit. . . . Most of the fundamentalist women are still living in very patriarchal family relationships. They follow the image of the hierarchical structure, they take obedience to their male leaders very seriously, and the male leaders are certainly not encouraging them to change. Nobody gives power away; power has to be taken.

B. comments:

I can sympathize with fundamentalist women. I was brought up in a very strict Catholic atmosphere. It would not have been possible for me to doubt what I was taught. That would have been a mortal sin. I remember pushing aside my doubts— I just didn't allow them to enter my mind. I believed that God, the Father, was in charge of the world, that His Son died to save us, which of course made me feel very guilty, and that Mary, the Mother of God, was obedient and good. She was the model for young Catholic girls—quiet, docile, long-suffering. It was so frightening, so wrenching for me when I started to admit my doubts to myself, when I started to allow myself to question. I remember realizing, I don't believe any of this! Actually, I do believe in one basic Christian teaching—that we as humans need to love each other. I don't believe, though, that the model of the powerful male in charge and the well-behaved woman doing what she's told is a loving model for women. It is a sexist model. It allows men to stay in power, to control politics and money. Can you imagine what would happen if women refused to go along with that? If all women—and the men who want equality, as I think many do—stopped supporting them? There would be a revolution for all of us. I dream about that. In the meantime, I work for change, and I find support, spiritual nourishment and the chance for spiritual expression within women's spirituality in general and my group in particular.

WOMEN'S SPIRITUALITY IN THE COMMUNITY

Most of the women interviewed expressed a need to celebrate their spirituality separately from men. Many also expressed support for men's rituals or for an attempt to plan some shared celebrations, in addition to separate women's rituals. S. says:

Now men's spirituality groups are beginning to form. Men need to be "liberated" from the stereotypes that are applied to them, too. Since women's spirituality has helped me to accept myself more completely, it has also helped me to accept others, including men. I think that as women's spirituality spreads, we will benefit from an increased acceptance of each other, and there will be a better balance, honoring both "feminine" and "masculine" qualities.

H. comments: "I don't see women's spirituality as separate from men's per se, despite the special bond with women. I can apply what I experience to my relationships with men." C. reflects: "My being a more empowered woman certainly seems to intimidate some men.... Men who can handle it become much closer and share in the learning process. I have several male friends who consider themselves feminists. My spiritual growth challenges them as well as myself." N. says: "We've discussed ways in which we might include men in our celebrations. We'd eventually like to hold several community celebrations a year, perhaps around the solstices, which men and other women could join. However, we feel that women still need the small group for ritual space."

Community celebrations have already appeared. In her book *States of Grace*, Charlene Spretnak describes such celebrations:

Today the solstices and equinoxes have become occasions for groups of friends and family to gather in celebration of the Earth community and to focus awareness on the particular turning of the seasons....

These rituals are communal celebrations by women, men and children around the country who give thanks for the cyclic renewal of our Earthbody and who seek to align their awareness with seasons of initiation, growth, fruition and repose.[11]

The husband of one of the women in the group gives his views on women's spirituality:

I've become aware that the intimate connection I have to my own church is largely mediated through men, and I can see that that could get annoying to someone who wasn't a man, because it's pretty annoying to me sometimes as a man. Also, from what I understand of women's spirituality, there's more of an emphasis on participation, and I think that's something that my own religion could benefit from. When I experience participation in my own religious practice, I get something out of it, and I notice that other people get something out of it. I can see where my spiritual practice could benefit from something good coming out of feminist spirituality, that it could spill over and benefit me. In the church I'm in, laypeople participate more fully when they make events happen, by bringing food, singing, distributing communion ... and I notice that women do it in a different way than men. I can see where we would benefit from more participation by women. To sum it up, I'm aware of the fact that women are left out. Even though I feel left out, I'm less left out than women. I don't want to change my religion, but I can see where we all would benefit from the insights that women have.

T., who has been a member of a women's spirituality group for several years, has facilitated several women's spirituality-type rituals open to all members of the congregation at her Unitarian church. She comments:

All of these services emphasize an egalitarian content. There is a circle leader or facilitator, but that person is not imparting wisdom or playing the part of a minister. In one ritual, we split into small groups and talked about how we thought our lives would have been different if our images of God had been female. There is always open sharing at these rituals. At a New Year's Eve service, we wrote on pieces of paper what we wanted to leave behind from the year, and threw the papers into the fire. We always have chanting and dancing. There is usually a central altar, with natural objects on it: water, the fire of candles, branches or plants. We get the entire spectrum of reactions to these services. Women, and sometimes men, come up afterwards and say, "This was great, I loved this, I've been looking for this." On the opposite end, some people—men and women—get up and leave. Men sometimes say, "I don't think of God as having a gender; I think talking about a female Goddess is just as bad as saying that God is male." Other men say that they grew up being preached at, and they appreciate being encouraged to look into themselves for spiritual answers. One thing that has surprised me is that both men and women have responded in a very positive way to the movement and dancing. There's a lot of laughing and smiling when we move and dance.

The women's spirituality group to which T. belongs grew out of the Unitarian Universalist Association's "adult seminar in feminist theology" called *Cakes for the Queen of Heaven*.[12] According to the seminar's introduction, the title comes from the book of Jeremiah in the Hebrew Bible, wherein God speaks to Jeremiah, saying: "Do you not see what they do in the cities of Judah and in the streets of Jerusalem? The children gather wood and the fathers kindle the fire, and the women knead the dough to make cakes to the Queen of Heaven and to pour out libations to other gods, in order to anger me!" This seminar, in workshop form, has been the impetus for the formation of a number of women's spirituality groups within the non-sectarian Unitarian Universalist Association. A follow-up curriculum, *Rise Up and Call Her Name: A Woman Honoring Journey into Global Earth-Based Spirituality*, is scheduled for release in late 1993/early 1994.[13] It aims to give participants (both women and men) the opportunity to encounter goddesses of Africa, Asia and the Americas, as well as to discover the feminist principles at the core of many religious traditions around the world.

THE FUTURE

Such organizational support for women's spirituality bodes well for its future as a viable spiritual movement, as do announcements of new women's studies in religion programs in universities throughout the country. At The Claremont Graduate School, for example, a new women's studies in religion program features such courses as "Visions of the Divine Feminine," "Women in Shamanism, Goddess Traditions, and Asian Religions of Inter-dependency," and "Goddesses and Women in the Mythology and Literature of the Ancient Near East." Even the *New York Times* recognizes the importance of key principles of women's spirituality, as evidenced by its 1991 Mother's Day editorial, "The Ultimate Mother":

Some of the people gathered on the Adirondack hillside called the woman a priestess, others a witch. She filled a bowl of water and pondered it for a few moments. Then she passed it to the person on her right, asking the group to concentrate on the water, putting into it prayers for their families, friends, community.

When the bowl had traveled around the circle, collecting prayers, she rose and carried it to a nearby birch tree. Pouring out the water at the base of the tree, she explained that the tree would carry it up through trunks and branches to leaves. Then the leaves would distribute the prayers on the wind.

Such is the practice of goddess worship, a new development in America's spiritual life, and one worth acknowledging on Mother's Day: it is rooted in reverence for the ultimate mother, for woman as the giver of life. Promoters of the movement cite ancient cultures that revered goddesses. In such societies, they say, life was peaceful, cooperative and egalitarian, while in societies focused on the male gods it was violent, authoritarian and stratified.

In addition, the goddess-based cultures cherished earth as nurturer of humankind. Much goddess worship today centers on the classic elements—earth, water, wind and fire—and recognizes spirits resident in animals and trees. This goddess worship resonates with modern environmentalism, and in particular with the Gaia Hypothesis—the theory, named for the earth goddess of the ancient Greeks, that the Earth and its biosphere behave like a single living organism.

The rising interest in goddess worship has also prompted ridicule. Some critics consider it so much New Age nonsense or a return to paganism. But if it appears flaky on the surface, it still warrants sympathy and respect. For it proceeds from values of nurturing, peace and harmony with nature—values as profoundly humane as motherhood itself.[14]

RESOURCES

Women who wish to begin a women's spirituality group, or to join with other women to plan such a group, would be well advised to spend some initial time distinguishing between the "outer" voice of religion and the "inner" voice of spirituality. Each woman needs to listen to herself, to be aware of what is deeply meaningful for her, to have a sense of what evokes a spiritual response in her. Nurturing the inner voice can be difficult for women, particularly those who have chosen rationality over spirituality, or those who have accepted patriarchal models of religion. Feldman's *Woman Awake* contains exercises that can be helpful for women who are doing this important work.[15]

Women who gather to create a women's spirituality group often use suggestions for rituals from Starhawk's *The Spiral Dance*,[16] now available in a revised tenth anniversary edition, and from Starhawk's later book *Truth or Dare*.[17] Starhawk's works provide a rich resource for women (and men) who are attempting to create a spiritual community. Her emphasis is on meaning rather than form; she encourages the reader to use her ideas in imaginative ways and to develop rituals that express the spirituality of the participants. Rituals that help create sacred space are described in Starhawk's books, as well as ceremonies for celebrating solstices and equinoxes and for building community. Other sources of ritual ideas include Maria Harris's *Dance of the Spirit*[18] and Barbara Walker's *Women's Rituals*.[19] The Unitarian Universalist curriculum, *Cakes for the Queen of Heaven*,[20] contains further ideas for rituals and ceremonies, and has been a source of inspiration to the many women's spirituality groups that have sprung from the use of this curriculum. The magazine *Sagewoman*[21] is another source of rituals and ceremonies from readers throughout the United States. The magazine, including back issues, is available from P.O. Box 641, Point Arena, CA 95468.

Specific sources of songs and chants for women's ceremonies are the Libana tapes *A Circle is Cast* and *Fire Within*,[22] available, along with similar tapes, through the Ladyslipper Catalogue (P.O. Box 3124, Durham, NC 27715). Other songs and chants are the subject of an appendix in Starhawk's book *Dreaming the Dark*.[23] A path to spirituality through art in the form of multimedia exercises, reflections, and meditations is offered by Adriana Diaz's *Freeing the Creative Spirit*.[24] This book honors the spirituality of each woman who uses it, an essential feature of true resources for the searching woman.

In the end, of course, women themselves will need to decide the relevance of women's spirituality to their lives. Women will need to determine whether or not the words of N. make sense to them:

Through my practice of women's spirituality, I've become an adult woman. I don't sit back any more. I take responsibility for myself. I do my own thinking. I don't do what I'm told, I do what I believe in, and I decide what this is. I'm not a good little girl anymore, I'm an adult. It's hard, it's challenging, and it's wonderful to be a free woman.

Women will need to decide whether C.'s words speak to them:

Women's spirituality is the individual empowerment of each woman as she begins to be in touch with the spirit that lives within her. The expression of that spirit is present in all that she does. Women's spirituality has just begun to influence my life. It has opened me up to imagining great power and growth for myself and the world. There is so much we have no conception of—our world view has been so limited by patriarchy. I'm beginning to see that anything is possible, beyond my wildest dreams.

NOTES

1. Many thanks to the women who contributed their inspiration, comments, suggestions, feedback, and wordprocessing expertise to this chapter: Anne, Carol L., Carol W., Cynthia, Gail, Hazel, Helaine, Judy, Marga, Margie, Maria, Maureen, Monica, Sharon, Teresa, Violet, Zantui; and many thanks also to George.

2. Mary Daly, *Beyond God the Father* (Boston: Beacon Press, 1973).

3. Carol P. Christ and Judith Plaskow, *Womanspirit Rising: A Feminist Reader in Religion* (San Francisco: Harper & Row, 1979).

4. Marija Gimbutas: *The Goddesses and Gods of Old Europe* (Berkeley: University of California Press, 1982), and *The Language of the Goddess* (San Francisco: Harper & Row, 1989).

5. Merlin Stone, *Ancient Mirrors of Womanhood* (Boston: Beacon Press, 1979).

6. Meinrad Craighead, *The Mother's Songs: Images of God the Mother* (Mahwah, NJ: Paulist Press, 1986).

7. Starhawk, *The Spiral Dance*, rev. ed. (San Francisco: Harper & Row, 1989).

8. Libana, Inc. *Fire Within* (Durham, NC: Ladyslipper, Inc., 1990).

9. Barbara G. Walker, *The Crone: Woman of Age, Wisdom and Power* (San Francisco: Harper & Row, 1985).

10. Christina Feldman, *Woman Awake: A Celebration of Women's Wisdom* (London: Arkana/Penguin, 1990).

11. Charlene Spretnak, *States of Grace* (San Francisco: Harper & Row, 1991), pp. 107, 144.

12. Shirley Ann Ranck, *Cakes for the Queen of Heaven* (Boston: Unitarian Universalist Association, 1986).

13. Elizabeth Fisher, *Rise Up and Call Her Name: A Woman Honoring Journey into Global Earth-Based Spirituality* (Boston: Unitarian Universalist Women's Federation, scheduled for publication late 1993/early 1994).

14. Editorial, "The Ultimate Mother," *New York Times*, May 12, 1991, Section E, p. 16.

15. Feldman, *Woman Awake*.

16. Starhawk, *The Spiral Dance*.

17. Starhawk, *Truth or Dare* (San Francisco: Harper & Row, 1987).

18. Maria Harris, *Dance of the Spirit: The Seven Steps of Women's Spirituality* (New York: Bantam Books, 1989).

19. Barbara G. Walker, *Women's Rituals* (San Francisco: Harper & Row, 1990).

20. Ranck, *Cakes for the Queen of Heaven*.

21. *Sagewoman: A Quarterly Magazine of Women's Spirituality* (Point Arena, CA: Arena Press).

22. Libana, Inc. *A Circle Is Cast* (Cambridge, MA: Spinning Records, 1986); *Fire Within*.

23. Starhawk, *Dreaming the Dark: Magic, Sex and Politics* (Boston: Beacon Press, 1982).

24. Adriana Diaz, *Freeing the Creative Spirit: Drawing on the Power of Art to Tap the Magic and Wisdom Within* (San Francisco: HarperSanFrancisco, 1992).

7

Feminist Therapy: An Update and a Glimpse into the Future

Violet Franks and Hanna Fox

I myself have never been able to find out precisely what feminism is: I only know that people call me a feminist whenever I express sentiments that differentiate me from a doormat, or a prostitute.

Rebecca West, 1913[1]

Feminist therapy represents a radical departure from conventional psychotherapy, which is based for the most part on a disease model initiated by Sigmund Freud. However, Freud, the father of psychoanalysis, admitted that he had a limited understanding of women. He described many of his female patients as deviant or sick, as in the classic example of Annie O., who came to him with a number of debilitating emotional symptoms. Freud diagnosed her "neurosis" as the result of unresolved infantile sexual fantasies, failing to examine the realities of Annie O. being trapped at home caring for a domineering, ill father and unable to have any life of her own. Freud saw her symptoms as feminine weaknesses rather than a desperate response to the imprisoning conditions she faced as a woman at the turn of the century in Europe.[2]

A feminist therapist would have asked Annie O. about her feelings as caretaker of her father rather than delving into her unconscious sexual feelings about him. She would have explored Annie O.'s emotional needs and tried to help her find ways to meet these needs. Annie O., realizing that she was not getting anywhere in her psychoanalysis, took matters into her own hands. She rebelled against Freud and quit her therapy. Far from being sick or nonfunctional, she subsequently assumed her real name, Berthe Pappenheim, and became a well-known turn-of-the-century European social reformer.

Freud and his contemporary followers, the therapy trailblazers, kept women in their positions, as dictated by Victorian society. They saw Annie O. and other women patients who deviated from society's norms as pathological and tried to make them fit into society. Much later, after the feminist therapy movement began, feminists adapted psychoanalysis to fit the feminist model.

In this chapter, we explain the term "feminist therapy" and its ramifications by highlighting the main trends in its development from its prefeminist era before the 1970s to its current status. We give examples of how women were treated by traditional and prefeminist therapists and how they are treated by feminist therapists within the context of an ever-changing therapy landscape. We observe how the feminist therapy perspective is affecting other disciplines, and we conclude with a glimpse into the future of feminist therapy.

THE MEANING AND BACKGROUND OF FEMINIST THERAPY

Explaining the term "feminist therapy" in the 1990s is, at best, a difficult task. The dictionary definition of "feminist" is simply "an advocate of social and political rights of women equal to those of men," but it brings mixed reactions, mainly because it is so poorly understood. The term "feminist" frequently conjures up images of bra burning and male bashing. In this final decade of the twentieth century, it is extremely important to grasp the true meaning of feminist therapy and not to placate those who are involved in backlash and in weakening the progress women have made.

Two key principles that underlie feminist therapy and have enduring qualities are viewing society rather than the individual as problematic, and focusing on methods of empowering the individual. An emphasis on cultural factors makes social activism a basic part of feminist therapy. Feminist therapists are less interested in their clients' conformity to the mainstream than in helping to identify and overcome rampant oppressive social pressures for women. Their aim is to bring about change rather than adjustment and to help clients take charge of their own lives.

Feminist therapy is an approach to therapy. It brings new ways of thinking and frees both patient and therapist from using restricting and sexist approaches. Major therapy systems may be eclectic or psychoanalytic or behavioral or Gestalt, but feminist therapists have consistently integrated feminist principles into the systems they practice. The ultimate goal of feminist therapy is the elimination of the patriarchal power structure in order to facilitate both women's and men's personal growth.

A safer title for this chapter would use the term "nonsexist therapy" instead of "feminist therapy," but this would misrepresent and weaken the main thesis. Although some therapists consider themselves nonsexist rather than feminist, the differentiation is not clear-cut. Nonsexist therapists basically believe that sexism is an issue they must deal with during the course of therapy. They may not be involved in feminist political action that focuses on radical change. At the same time, they are involved in research related to gender issues and to understanding facts that can help them combat sexism in therapy. Feminist therapists, on the other hand, believe implicitly that political action to overcome oppression for women is essential for the benefit of their clients.

There is considerable overlap in definition. Many therapists shy away from the label "feminist" but believe in feminist philosophy. Some feminist therapists identify themselves as radical feminist therapists while others see themselves as liberal feminist therapists. The main difference is that radical therapists work outside the establishment and liberal therapists work within it. For example, the liberals may have university positions and a traditional private practice. They may be less likely to take an openly radical stance because this could threaten their job situation. The radicals may work for government- and/or foundation-funded organizations, such as shelters for battered women, agencies dealing with substance abuse, and rape crisis centers. When all therapists recognize that they have reached a stage of accepting feminist theory and do not feel stigmatized by the label "feminist," real progress will be made in the treatment of women and the men involved in the lives of women.

Feminist therapy has a short history, a shaky presence, and an unknown future. If we reexamine the theories of psychotherapy of the 1950s and 1960s, many of the teachings appear blatantly sexist and ludicrous. For example, it was quite common for sophisticated therapists then to reason that women who were raped unconsciously wanted to be raped. Rape victims were seen as seductive, and therapists reinforced their patients' beliefs that they were at fault by trying to give them insights into why they wanted to be raped. Freud's viewpoint that girls had sexual fantasies about incest with their fathers was widely accepted by practicing psychoanalysts. In 1984 Jeffrey Masson challenged this viewpoint, claiming that Freud deliberately distorted the data.[3] According to Masson, Freud knew that many of his female patients actually were sexually abused, but he was afraid to make this claim in turn-of-the-century Vienna and instead attributed women's pathology to their own unreal fantasies.

Two highly publicized examples in 1991 make us wonder how far we have come from this perspective. First, Anita Hill was considered to be making up her allegations of sexual harassment by Clarence Thomas during the Senate Judiciary Committee Hearings on his appointment to the United States Supreme Court. Second, Patricia Bowman was considered to be "asking to be raped" in the State of Florida versus William Kennedy Smith case. In both instances, it seemed that not only those testifying or the defense attorneys and witnesses for the defense made these assumptions, but a large number of women and men did, as well.

When the term "feminist therapy" was coined in the 1970s, a small group of feminist therapists of all theoretical systems began to put their therapy procedures into practice. On the heels of the civil rights movement of the 1960s, these feminist therapists challenged the existing dogma of therapy, which expected women to adapt to depressing sexist conditions, and developed a new set of principles and techniques. They focused on methods of empowering women, who had very little control or real power over their lives. This new approach, practiced primarily by women therapists with white middle-class clientele, began to change the focus of therapy from an intrapsychic process to dealing with problems that clients had within their families and in society at large.

Traditionally, goals for women in therapy were sex-stereotyped and limited. As recently as the middle of this century, mainstream psychologists, along with psychiatrists and psychoanalysts, used male theories and research data, and thus questioned the intellectual capacity of women. What is more, they recommended limited education for women and encouraged them to stay home and be wives and mothers, a state considered healthier for them. Or they suggested that women prepare for the traditional female careers, such as teaching or social work. They overlooked individual talents and differences, as in the case of Susan T., who spent the greater part of the early 1960s on various psychoanalysts' couches.

Susan T. was a well-educated woman who had a strong need to express herself in the arts but was unable to break from the expectations of her family. She went to college instead of studying acting in New York. She tried a semester of graduate school in social work, dropped out, then returned and completed a Master's Degree in Education, although she didn't want to teach. Her father, who paid for her education, had said the degree was like an insurance policy. Susan T. taught for one semester and then went through a series of glorified secretarial jobs and unsatisfying affairs. Feeling she couldn't make it on her own, she married a well-established physician. Her analysts tried to help her adjust to her role of wife and mother and cautioned her to treat her acting as a hobby, even though she had leading roles in a few regional theater productions. After the birth of her daughter, she felt totally trapped and developed classic symptoms of depression—lethargy, fatigue, the inability to find any pleasure in life. The marriage deteriorated.

In the early 1970s, Susan T. and her husband went to a therapist for marriage counseling. They had joint sessions, as well as individual ones.

The therapist, using feminist therapy concepts, was ahead of his time. He helped Susan T. delineate her own needs, which seriously clashed with her husband's expectations. She continued in therapy. Her husband quit because he had gone only "to help her with her problems." It became clear that Susan's husband and her marriage were the problem. Therapy enabled her to leave her marriage, and to take herself seriously as an actress as she began building an independent life for herself and her daughter.

Feminist therapy focuses on action and change. The therapist helps the client overcome the effects of oppression. Blame and guilt are taken off the client. The therapist helps the client change her environment whenever possible. Susan T.'s therapist helped her to recognize the burden of the "shoulds" of her family, her husband, and her social milieu.

Another example is Ellen B., a so-called emancipated woman in her early thirties with a successful job as a stockbroker. In the late 1960s she started living with a domineering, prominent man twenty years older than she. When they married, she gave up her satisfying job to be his good wife. In doing so, she lost her own identity. A few years later she developed serious symptoms of panic attacks and agoraphobia. She could no longer drive or go anywhere. Her husband wanted her to be "cured" so she could resume her role of being a good wife and mother. She went into therapy in the mid-1970s. It became clear that Ellen B.'s symptoms were tied to her sense of feeling she was in a prison, one that made her helpless. After several sessions, she told the therapist her husband didn't want her to come anymore. The therapist asked her what she wanted to do. She said she wanted to continue, but that her husband was paying. The therapist pointed out that if she had not quit her job she could have paid for herself. Ellen B. admitted she felt powerless because her husband earned the money. This led to uncovering Ellen B.'s conflict between autonomy and dependence. She told her husband she was going to stay in therapy. As she acknowledged her conflicted feelings and started to assert some control over her life, her symptoms subsided. Ultimately, she achieved her own identity within the marriage. Although she did not go back to a high-powered job, she started doing things she liked to do, including civic and volunteer work in her community.

Most women tend to pattern themselves according to their early learning within their families and their communities. Frequently, they identify with other women in their lives and are likely to repeat the patterns set by their mothers, relatives, friends, and the value systems they were taught in their childhoods. Ellen B. and Susan T. were two such women. They became trapped by the very systems that shaped them. Their families became destructive and oppressive. In the cases of Annie O. and Susan T., their psychoanalyses reinforced their oppression. Susan T.'s feminist therapist had to undo the oppression reinforced by her previous traditional therapists before Susan T. could start to break destructive patterns of behavior and learn new ways of feeling and being and behaving.

DEVELOPMENT OF FEMINIST THERAPY STRATEGIES

Feminist therapists developed techniques that would help to empower their clients and enable them to change and fulfill their potentials. Instead of automatically accepting that women were depressed and angry because of unresolved issues from their childhoods and/or their "wandering wombs," they examined the real factors in their lives that were triggering these feelings, as in the case of Susan T. Her prefeminist analyst had labeled her as having a "hysterical character neurosis" and attributed her depressed feelings and angry outbursts to "injudicious acting out of oedipal and pre-oedipal conflicts," instead of recognizing her feelings of rejection because her first affair was ending. On the other hand, later when her marriage was deteriorating, her feminist therapist helped articulate her feeling of being trapped in a relationship that was destructive to who she was, and helped her face the conflict of whether to stay in a marriage that met her family's values but was detrimental to her needs. Only then could she take action and leave her marriage. Feminist therapists do not stop at the goals of insight and understanding because they believe that these two goals by themselves cannot help a client deal with her life.

The small group of pioneer feminist therapists who sought to empower their patients or clients (a term they later preferred) grew in number in the late 1970s and early 1980s. New ways of thinking about women came with this growth. Each generation challenges what was normal in the previous generation. It questions how women should act, feel, or be. We do not issue an edict on a certain date and declare that for the next decade the divorce rate will double or that 50 percent of women with preschool children will enter the work force. It happens! And when it does, therapists and their clients gradually begin to realize that women's worlds have changed and that many of them have not been prepared for these changes.

Joan R. is a classic example of the plight of some young women in the 1980s. A chic, well-educated woman in a high-powered law firm, married with three children, she "had it all." Yet she tried to commit suicide because she could not come to grips with her conflict of feeling powerless, surrounded by strong men in her firm and her strong husband at home. She felt she should continue on the fast track, but as therapy progressed she found that she really wanted to be at home with her children and use her energies by expressing herself through the arts and teaching. Joan R., like Susan T., was brought up in the 1950s by a traditional mother who projected her own fantasies—in this case, of "having it all"—onto her daughter.

Psychological expectations link women not only to what their mothers (and fathers) project, either positively or negatively; they also link them to male-dominated economic, social, and political needs of society, which often buffet women around, oblivious of individual propensities and talents. For example, during World War II, understandably, the expectation was that women would help with the war effort even if they preferred to stay home with their children. Then after the war when the soldiers returned to civilian life and needed those jobs and consumer power, women were expected to return home, even if they preferred to work in the factory. In the postwar era, if middle-class women weren't having a large number of children and taking care of their suburban households, they were seen as abnormal.

In the 1960s the women's movement initiated changes and reforms in all areas of American society, from banking to divorce laws to business practices as well as the practice of psychotherapy. Society constantly struggles with these reforms. Those in power were eager to retain the status quo. Change was threatening. Negative images were resurrected.

The early radical feminists such as Betty Friedan, Kate Millet, and Germaine Greer, who took political stances and questioned basic inequities due to gender, fueled the feminist therapy movement. These feminists helped give women a voice. Consciousness-raising (C-R) groups, an early form of feminist therapy, emerged in the 1970s to reinforce the newly found voice. Meetings were leaderless, open, and with no charge, so that women from all incomes could participate. C-R groups served as a safe harbor, where women could share their real feelings, have camaraderie, and build their confidence.

The women's movement, which started a dynamic system of change in all disciplines, challenged existing belief systems and questioned conventional values and stereotypes. Not only did many women begin to demand more from their therapists, but many therapists began to question their own clinical training. Theory and methodology of psychotherapy need updating and changing to be effective, just as good medical training is modernized as research brings in new knowledge and techniques. Until the 1970s, there was scarcely any literature dealing with psychotherapy and women's issues. Psychotherapy was predominantly a male enclave, and male clinicians developed our knowledge of the field.

In 1972, *Women and Madness*, a revolutionary book by Phyllis Chesler, advocated that women avoid all male therapists.[4] Chesler saw women's "madness" as an outcome of a male patriachal system, and she believed that male therapists were perpetuating this system. She also believed that mental hospitals were sexist and detrimental to women's mental health. Although her viewpoint may be considered radical and overstated, all revolutionary thoughts begin with an extreme viewpoint.

Feminist philosophy underlying feminist therapy called for a thorough scrutiny of environmental factors that oppress women. It questioned many basic suppositions. If women are less powerful than men and their lives are restricted and they face subtle and direct discrimination, then surely therapists have to take the condition of women into account when developing treatment strategies. The observation that the personal is political and that psychological effects result from oppression and victimization becomes obvious. For example, in certain Hispanic societies, women are more likely to accept that their men will batter them. They suffer inordinately without challenging the basic assumption of belonging to someone who has the right to abuse them. For a macho society with a built-in acceptance of physical force against women who are seen as possessions, a different approach is needed than that for white, middle-class American society, which denies this. We are just beginning to understand that we need different approaches to meet such different needs.

Early proponents of feminist therapy became politically active and asked for changes in society and for the elimination of inequitable conditions that discriminated against women. They argued that many more women than men were suffering from depression and were seeking therapy for this depression, not because women were inherently weaker and more prone to depression than men were, but because society had actually created more depressing conditions for women, as in the cases described. Studies have shown that while women were more frequently seeking therapy for depression, men often were hiding their despair and becoming workaholics and alcoholics. They were dying, and still are, on the average of seven years earlier than women.

Initially, feminist therapists expected their clients to become politically active and change society by becoming involved in issues that affected the rights of women. Subsequently, feminist therapists encouraged involvement in women's rights, both for themselves and other therapists, but they became less radical in their expectations of political involvement for their women clients. They respected a woman's individual needs, inclinations, and political differences as long as women were not being oppressed by any of these forces.

In 1980 Susan Sturdivant wrote a book, *Therapy with Women: A Feminist Philosophy of Treatment,*[5] listing specific changes for clients that feminist therapists value as desirable outcomes of therapy. Basically, she emphasized that the therapist helps the individual to actively shape her own identity. Sturdivant helped develop specific guidelines for feminist therapists. (A compiled list of guidelines for selecting a feminist therapist appears at the end of this chapter.)

A feminist therapist is committed to help her client acknowledge her identity, whether it conforms to her family's norms or not. For example, if the client's identity is lesbian, then the therapist helps her embrace lesbianism rather than allow her to suffer in her conventional role. Feminist therapy peels away old-style psychotherapy labels of "abnormal" and "pathological" when clients react with anger, or exhibit behaviors such as competitiveness and ambition.

SEX-ROLE STEREOTYPING

A now-classic study in 1970 by Broverman et al. showed that the mental health profession used a double standard in determining mental health at that time.[6] The study asked mental health workers to pick mentally healthy traits for men and then for women. For men they picked leadership, independence, and dominance as well as other masculine-type traits. For women they picked nurturance, kindness, gentleness, and other stereotyped feminine traits. Later on when they were asked to pick healthy human traits, they emphasized the masculine traits of leadership and independence. Mental health workers overvalued male traits while undervaluing female traits. Paradoxically, women who were considered well-adjusted as women were not considered to be mentally healthy adults, because they lacked the good male traits to adjust to society. After the Broverman findings, no self-respecting therapists would consciously admit to a double standard in mental health. They finally accepted the American value of rugged individualism for the female population. Feminist therapists began to show women how to discard concerns about not being feminine enough, the objective being to allow for complexity and diversity.

The term "androgyny" was introduced into the literature in the 1970s. Androgyny recognizes that well-adjusted people can have both male and female traits. Hence, the "feminine" stereotypic traits of kindness, sensitivity, and caring could combine with the "masculine" traits of independence, assertiveness, and leadership. All of these traits are desirable in both men and women. The needs to be macho, or gentle and feminine, were no longer taken for granted. If people had accepted the concept of androgyny earlier, Bella Abzug would not have been pejoratively labeled "unfeminine" when she asserted her power, and Edmund Muskie would not have been derogatorily labeled "unmasculine" when he cried in public.

The women's movement gave us all a jog. Therapists had accepted, without questioning, sexist beliefs that were detrimental to women. For example, the renowned therapist and writer, Erik Erikson, who influenced many therapists, wrote about the "empty space syndrome."[7] He felt that women who had never borne children were bound to suffer from a neurosis. This thought was not challenged until the 1970s. Another syndrome of women was labeled "the empty nest syndrome." It theorized that women were at risk when children grew up and left home. Further research challenged these assumptions. No such syndromes were discovered. There was no evidence to show that women were more neurotic and disturbed if they had never had children or after their children were grown. Women whose children had left home rated high on adjustment scales. Women whose grown children hovered around the house often suffered much more distress.

In 1983, one of the authors of this chapter, Violet Franks, coedited a book on sex-role stereotypes.[8] The introduction stated that stereotypic beliefs set limits to who we think we are and who we think we can become. It emphasized that female stereotypes can be disabling because they can imprison us, keep us down, helpless and depressed.

Interestingly, feminist thinking even affected psychiatric diagnostic categories. Before feminist therapists influenced therapeutic practice, therapists often gave a traditional diagnosis to women who were depressed and had begun menopause. This diagnosis was "menopausal depression," which was caused by menopausal changes in mid-life. Later research indicated that there was little relationship between menopause and depression. In fact, the high-risk age group for depression in women was in their twenties and not during menopause. But in the 1960s, it was not unusual to see the diagnosis of "menopausal depression" in clinical records of women who were only in their thirties and early forties. In these cases, physicians accepted their women patients' statements when they were depressed and mistakenly claimed their menopause had begun. Actually, it was their emotional condition that had contributed to their irregular menstruation and not menopause at all. Once their depression lifted, their menstruation returned to regular cycles.

In the 1980s, a strong group of feminist therapists challenged the masculine bias in establishing diagnoses. They insisted on being included in meetings of the American Psychiatric Association's panel to update diagnoses of the *Diagnostic and Statistical Manual of Mental Disorders (DSM)*, the standard reference book for professionals in mental health and related fields. These women forced the powerful traditional therapists to remove a very conventional, much-used diagnosis of masochism as a personality disorder—a diagnosis that labels a woman "sick" for behavior forced upon her—from the body of the *DSM*. The panel had to abandon its long-term concept of masochism. It finally paid attention to the women's protests, took the definition out of the manual, and put a revised version of it into the appendix.

Along with changes in therapy practice and growth of the literature was a dramatic increase of women entering professional therapy training programs. Women candidates for the doctorate in clinical psychology grew from a small number and now comprise more than half of the student population. Students of psychotherapy are demanding "sex fair" training— training that is no longer based on primarily male, prefeminist theories. Research data using male subjects and generalizing the findings to women are being challenged. In fact, as the number of women therapists increases, psychologists are worried about a new phenomenon they call "the feminization of clinical psychology." The number of women in medical school and the number of women psychiatrists have increased markedly as well.

While professional therapy circles are becoming decidedly more aware of and involved in feminist issues, the general public may have a different impression. Popular books such as Susan Faludi's *Backlash* emphasize the sexism of pop psychology and point to the proliferation of self-help books in the 1980s, which were promoted by their pop psychology authors and radio/television therapists.[9] Women were barraged with advice on how to get a man, with a nostalgia for returning to the mythical good old days when men were men and women were women. Supposedly, the advice was given to help women stave off their sense of isolation. These pop psychology talk show soothsayers and how-to book writers usually did not recognize outside factors in their analysis and treatment of women. A good example is Robin Norwood's book, *Women Who Love Too Much*, which proclaims that women are abused because they are self-destructive, without asking why there are so many abusive men.[10] The theory of codependency, which became popular in the late 1980s, used the disease model of addiction and the 12-step approach of Alcoholics Anonymous as a model for love addicts. The key to recovery for the codependent was acknowledgment of one's disease without considering the environment, a regression to prefeminist therapy concepts if ever there was one.

The impact of these messages on women in the 1970s and 1980s brought a number of new psychological problems for therapists to treat. For example, the emphasis on thinness and beauty, American advertising's prescription for career success and happiness, contributed to an increase in the number of women who developed the weight disorders of anorexia or bulimia, which can be life-threatening. These two disabilities are exacerbated by overemphasis on feelings of self-worth dependent on looks. Increasing numbers of women also underwent risky plastic surgeries to take nips and tucks, increase breast size, or eliminate lines and wrinkles. If women view themselves as commodities rather than active individuals with power, they can relinquish control over their lives and revert to self-destructive behavior. When women have a sound concept of their own value, they are unlikely to be caught up in suicidal or health-threatening behavior to meet beauty standards set by society. They set standards for themselves that are realistic and they feel good. They do not need to package themselves by using self-torture, such as starving themselves, or eating and purging in order to become valuable commodities. With a less-standardized model of beauty, women will not undergo painful and/or dangerous surgeries such as face lifts and breast implants for cosmetic purposes.

CONTEMPORARY PROBLEMS OF WOMEN IN THERAPY

In the early 1990s, feminist therapists are finding that women are bringing in new problems as well as variations of the problems they brought in the 1970s and the 1980s. For example, Barbara J., a woman in her fifties, had the benefit of the women's movement and feminist therapy to help her make changes in the past two decades. Her first marriage, when she was in her twenties, was traditional. She stayed at home and raised the children. When Barbara J.'s husband began battering her, her mother encouraged her to work out her domestic problems, and even implied that she must have done something to provoke her husband. With the help of therapy, Barbara J. broke away from her abusive husband. After her divorce, she worked her way up to becoming a high-level computer consultant in the competitive male world. She remarried and set new ground rules for the marriage.

Barbara J. recently went into therapy again because of acute anxiety. Although she has really attained power on the job, she became anxious because she failed to recognize that she is in charge. She buckled under the slightest challenge, suffering a relapse of feeling powerless, reacting to old messages from her first husband and her mother. However, within a short time in therapy, she recognized she was no longer powerless and felt comfortable taking charge of her life at work and at home. She did not have to run from her situation and is learning to acknowledge that she enjoys her power.

The rapid changes in society in the past two decades are thrusting many white middle-class American women out of their "protected nests" into a threatening jungle for which they have not been prepared or trained. Janet M., a young lawyer in her early thirties, came to a feminist therapist in 1991 because of old issues in a new guise. She is at the top of the ladder, working within the state judicial system. She finds that judges are condescending to her, and she has difficulty with the attitude of men working under her. Janet M.'s live-in boyfriend is putting pressure on her to marry. She wants to have children, but she is concerned about how that will affect her career. Her boyfriend is already implying that she should stay home to raise their children.

Women like Barbara J. and Janet M. need validation, understanding, and support to deal with a glass ceiling or other unfair practices. Often they feel isolated and alone in a male establishment. Sometimes they find themselves in the "sandwich" generation, responsible for the care of their parents, their husband's parents, and their children, all the while trying to function at a job.

Women today face decisions rarely encountered by previous generations. Their issues have changed as their roles in the family changed, and since the 1970s the family has changed rapidly. According to studies cited in Dornbusch and Strober's book *Feminism, Children and the New Families*, from 1970 to 1984 the number of single-parent families more than doubled, which meant that almost a quarter of all children under eighteen were living in single-parent families.[11] This rise can be attributed not only to the increasing divorce rate but also to a startling 500 percent increase of never-married mothers. Since most divorced persons remarry, statistics have to take into account the number of children who will be temporarily in single-parent households. Half of all American children can be expected to live in single-parent households before the age of eighteen. Reconstructed families with two sets of parents and four sets of grandparents are prevalent. Today, more than 70 percent of American women aged 20–54 are employed and 50 percent of all marriages end in divorce.

Janet M.'s contemporaries are asking themselves and their therapists if they should consider being single parents and have babies without getting married. They wonder if they should threaten career advancement by marrying and moving to another part of the country. These women have new freedoms, which bring new choices. The models and guidelines are few. Some women do extraordinarily well given these freedoms, but there are many pitfalls and hidden discriminations. The feminist perspective can contribute greatly to helping women change their feelings, attitudes, and cognitions, after which they can change their futures.

A GLIMPSE INTO THE FUTURE

The approach of feminist therapy in the 21st century will be very different than it is today because American life will be significantly different. Feminist therapy will, of necessity, change as the economic and social realities of America change. White middle-class women, traditionally the bulk of feminist therapists' clientele, will no longer be the majority population. They will either slip into poverty or not be able to afford one-on-one private therapy because their health insurance will not adequately cover it. Demographic changes in the majority population from white to nonwhite and changes in the makeup of the family, coupled with the increased use of technology, will leave their mark, requiring new approaches and techniques.

Feminist therapists of the future will treat different populations for different issues in different settings. Such factors as finding a viable income, housing, avoidance of substance abuse, medical care, child care, and education will be pressing issues of the future for a larger number of women.

The "feminization of poverty" will be a growing problem in the 1990s. Poverty brings its own mental health problems and stresses. The number of women who need and will continue to need mental health facilities undoubtedly will increase. There are the victims of domestic violence, the homeless, the chronically mentally ill. There are older women living alone on reduced incomes. Single mothers, who suffer disproportionately from poverty, will continue to be a priority group in their need for help.

Awareness has been growing for victims of incest or sexual abuse. More and more women are becoming aware of their right to speak up and to seek help. Due to the pressures of women, and particularly to actions of feminist therapists, many hospitals have developed rape crisis centers. Feminist therapists have even begun to help train police officers to understand how and when to intervene in cases of rape and family violence. Help is becoming available for battered women in the form of special shelters and special counseling. Rape treatment centers continue to grow and expand.

Yet the number of women needing services far outweighs services available. A wide array of mental health services need to be expanded to meet the needs of women. We need increased and better trained staff for services for pregnant teenagers, for pregnant addicts, for women in and out of the work force, for the poor, the powerless, and the ill. Many women are unable to avail themselves of existing services. Some do not know what facilities can be found in the community and, of those who are aware of the services, many simply do not have the strength or ability to access them. Feminist therapists can be leaders in helping these women utilize facilities and services in their communities.

Those white middle-class women who have not slipped into poverty may no longer be able to afford individual private psychotherapy because their private health insurance carriers threaten to no longer cover necessary treatment. Private insurance companies have begun to institute "managed health care," which affects the course of treatment for individuals seeking psychotherapy both on an outpatient basis and in hospitals. Managed health care determines the number of sessions an individual's insurance will cover for a client diagnosed as being acutely anxious, or an individual hospitalized for debilitating depression. When the number of sessions, or inpatient days, have been completed, the insurance company reviews the case to determine if the client or patient requires more treatment. The implications of this change in covering treatment for emotional problems are many. Not only does managed care cut down on how much insurance companies will pay for a person's treatment, but it also takes an inordinate amount of paperwork and time on the part of the therapist and the client or patient. In essence, the insurance company becomes the final decision-making body. The insurance company is substituted for the therapist in terms of professionalism.

The resulting cutback in services for individuals with private insurance, as well as the misnamed "managed health care," will lead more of these individuals to seek mental health care services from public facilities. These facilities, such as community-run mental hospitals and substance abuse clinics, became inadequate as a result of the fiscal cutbacks in the 1970s and 1980s. Although the feminist perspective has already made some inroads into social work and social welfare policy, it needs to cut deeper in order to have greater impact. To do this is a very complicated matter. The underserved population of women who are unemployed, living in poverty, trying to take care of several children and protect them from the horrors of the street, is overwhelming. Social services are lacking because staff are overworked and underpaid and suffer a high incidence of burnout. Above all, drastic budgetary cutbacks are beginning to create a situation of dramatically inadequate services available to the general public.

The feminist perspective can raise society's consciousness to new needs of a larger number of women. Since feminist therapy looks at society with fresh eyes, it can help us understand many universal principles that are often clouded by narrow and biased viewpoints. For example, it is imperative that we recognize the emerging diversity in our American population, which is moving from a mainly homogenous society to one that has a growing population of Afro-American, Hispanic, and Asian citizens.

Women in these ethnic minorities, adjusting to mainstream American society, will face problems that need special understanding. The increasing Asian population is a good example. Asian values are alien to their new culture. Asian women will need help while adjusting to our nontraditional concept of family. They may not be able to communicate in English and may feel very isolated, particularly if they remain at home with their young children. Psychotherapy will have to meet the needs of citizens of various ethnic backgrounds. Appropriate methodologies can empower all women regardless of race or national origin.

Women must stop accepting the status quo of inequality, which no longer fits in our high tech, mobile society. Women need to be concerned with one another and strive toward helping themselves and the future generations of women and men. Minority women, in particular, need their own consciousness-raising and need to come into the mainstream of the community of women.

Grass-roots mental health movements are on the rise, often with local, state, and federal government support. Examples of grass-roots services include shelters for battered women and their children and support groups for single parents, teen-age parents, and substance abusers. Many of these consumers are women.

In the future, we will see more and more minority women set up treatment programs geared to their particular problems. We will see homeless women representing themselves and helping therapists understand their needs. The recovered mentally ill women will understand the needs of other women who may not function as well as they do and need specific help to utilize facilities and therapy. Grass-roots movements can use professional, well-informed, and feminist advocates to help enhance their power, to understand their needs, and to fight for these needs within political systems in the establishment. There will be a growing need for feminist therapists, representatives of underserved groups, and for a continued grass-roots movement that helps women with special needs establish themselves.

The feminist therapy movement has always contained within its ranks differences in emphasis. We need different opinions within the movement to provide impetus to its dynamic growth. The radical feminists, by challenging the establishment, will be the pioneers and push the consciousness of society, while the liberal feminists will make changes within the institutions where they work and in the clinical therapy they teach.

Thus, feminist therapists in the future will reach a broader population than they do today, putting into practice their growing awareness of the connection between appropriate social services and political and economic reform. By the 21st century, all therapists must come out of the shelter of their one-on-one therapy in their offices and understand what is going on in their communities. Ideally, they will become advocates for all women in a concerted effort to provide human services to those needing them.

The first radical departure for feminist therapy challenged the male-dominated model of conventional psychotherapy. The present challenge is to apply the feminist therapy principles that emerged in the 1970s to all women. The next wave of the feminist therapy movement must include more services for a wider range of women, and it must create a mental health care system that merges services in the private and public sectors. The availability of human services for all is essential in a humane society that espouses ethics and democratic principles.

Women have always worn the mantle for nourishing and caring as mothers, wives, nurses, and caretakers of older family members. The new feminist therapists will help women cherish female qualities that have not been especially valued even as recently as the latter part of the 20th century. They will expect men to value caring qualities for themselves, as well. When both men and women truly value female traits and feminist teachings, the dream of "a gentler more caring society" can become a reality.

HOW TO FIND A GOOD FEMINIST THERAPIST

A good way to start your search is to ask for referrals from reputable sources, such as your state psychological association and your local universities. You have a right to shop around and to interview potential therapists. Do not be satisfied with your choice, unless you can answer "yes" to the following questions.

1. Is the therapist knowledgeable about women and their biological, psychological, and political situations?
2. Is the therapist aware of those theories and models that limit the potential of women clients and those that are useful for them?
3. Does the therapist continue to learn about issues concerning women throughout his or her career?
4. Can the therapist recognize and be aware of all forms of oppression and how these interact with sexism?
5. Does the therapist use nonsexist language and avoid sexist concepts?
6. Does the therapist ascribe no preconceived limitations on the nature or direction of potential changes in therapy for women?
7. Does the therapist refrain from engaging in sexual activity with women clients under any circumstances as well as any behavior that could be considered sexual harassment?
8. Is the therapist aware of and continually reviewing his or her own values and how they affect women clients?

9. Does the therapist support the elimination of sex bias within institutions and individuals?

10. Does the therapist practice therapy that is not constrained by sex-role stereotypes?

11. Can the therapist recognize that any violence, physical abuse, or rape is a violation against the client and illegal?

NOTES

1. Cited in Ann Blackman et al., *Time*, March 9, 1992, p. 51.

2. Josef Breuer and Sigmund Freud, *Studies in Hysteria* (New York: Avon Books, 1966).

3. Jeffrey M. Masson, *The Assault on Truth: Freud's Suppression of the Seduction Theory* (New York: Farrar, Strauss and Giroux, 1984).

4. Phyllis Chesler, *Women and Madness* (Garden City, NY: Doubleday, 1972).

5. Susan Sturdivant, *Therapy with Women: A Feminist Philosophy of Treatment* (New York: Springer, 1980).

6. I. K. Broverman, D. M. Broverman, F. E. Clarkson, P. S. Rosenkranz, and S. R. Vogel, "Sex Role Stereotypes and Clinical Judgments of Mental Health," *Journal of Consulting and Clinical Psychology* 34 (1970): 1–7.

7. Erik Erikson, *Identity, Youth and Crises* (New York: W. W. Norton, 1968), p. 278.

8. Violet Franks and Esther D. Rothblum, eds., *The Stereotyping of Women: Its Effects on Mental Health* (New York: Springer, 1983).

9. Susan Faludi, *Backlash: The Undeclared War Against American Women* (New York: Crown Publishers, 1991).

10. Robin Norwood, *Women Who Love Too Much* (New York: J. P. Tarcher, dist. by St. Martin's Press, 1985).

11. Sanford M. Dornbusch and Myra H. Strober, eds., *Feminism, Children and the New Families* (New York: The Guilford Press, 1988).

8

Literary Criticism and Language

Laura Curtis

FEMINIST LITERARY CRITICISM

The earliest phase of feminist criticism developed in the late 1960s in tandem with the earliest phase of the modern American feminist movement. Today feminist criticism has so expanded that it is strongly represented in most academic critical journals, and it has representatives in academic departments of literature all over the country. K. K. Ruthven, author of an excellent introduction to feminist literary studies, writes: "The feminist intervention strikes me as being incontestably the most important challenge faced by English studies in the twenty or more years I have been associated with it."[1]

Despite its predominance, however, feminist literary criticism is by no means a unified movement: it disagrees vigorously about many fundamental theoretical questions and it uses a wide variety of critical methods in its practice. Some of the most basic disagreements are about whether or not women's writing differs in some essential way from men's; whether, if it differs, this is due to psychological or somatic reasons; whether pragmatic studies are as valuable as criticism based on (French) theory; the role of black women and lesbians in current criticism; and so forth.

Feminist criticism is generally agreed to have passed through three stages: "In its earliest years," writes Elaine Showalter, "it concentrated on exposing the misogyny of literary practice: the stereotyped images of women in literature as angels or monsters, the literary abuse or textual harassment of women in classic and popular male literature, and the exclusion of women from literary history."[2] The outstanding book characteristic of this period was Kate Millett's 1970 *Sexual Politics*.[3] Millett examined the works of D. H. Lawrence, Henry Miller, Norman Mailer, and Jean Genet to demonstrate how the sexual power politics she described in the first part of her book was enacted in the works of these authors. Millett's approach to Miller and Mailer was in contrast to the conventional respect for the authority and intentions of the authors. She also attacked Freud and psychoanalysis for their biological essentialism or what she saw as a theory that reduces all behavior to inborn sexual characteristics. As a literary critic, Millett ignored the formal structures of the literary text and engaged in pure content analysis.

A short example of this first stage of feminist criticism can be seen in Nina Baym's article, "Melodramas of Beset Manhood."[4] Baym points out that as late as 1977, when she was contributing to a collection of essays on American literature, relying upon the going canon of major authors, she was able to find only four women writers, and none between 1865 and 1940. This was in spite of the fact that "commercially and numerically" women writers "have probably dominated American literature since the middle of the nineteenth century."[5] *Uncle Tom's Cabin* by Harriet Beecher Stowe was probably the biggest seller in American history, and Mrs. E.D.E.N. Southworth the most widely read novelist of the nineteenth century.

Although it is traditional to compare an author's work with works of predecessors to evaluate its excellence, in American literature, which aimed to be new and groundbreaking, it was regarded as unfair to compare works with works of British authorship. Instead, early critics looked for a standard of Americanness, and it began to seem as if Americanness was our standard of literary excellence.

The literary critic Lionel Trilling, whose choice of American authors is still prevalent, defined Americanness as being expressed by tension between mainstream and individual values.[6] Women were excluded from this canon by being envisioned as upholders rather than critics of consensus.

A nonrealistic, romantic narrative that neglected actual social milieux was further defined as quintessentially American by critics. The American myth depicts the confrontation of the individual with the promise of complete self-definition in a new land, free of history. The premise of the narrative is that the individual precedes society, which is secondary and artificial, thus an adversary. Nature, however, the unsettled wilderness that offers opportunity for the individual to forge his or her own destiny, is attractive.

In the canonical works of American literature, entrammeling society and the promising landscape are both presented as feminine. The necessity of the male protagonist to struggle against socializing and domesticating women, nature as feminine, virgin land, all-nurturing mother or passive bride are not themes that would attract women writers nor be comprehended by many women readers. The variations in nature depiction favored by women do not for critics fit the essential pattern as they have defined it, and hence they overlook these variations.

Finally, Baym explains how the description of the act of writing as resembling the task performed by the novel's protagonist is another idea recently much in vogue, by which women writers are excluded from the American canon. The notion that writers describe protagonists who are their own surrogates has also been used to characterize British fiction. The result, as Baym observes, is that critics have "deconstructed" Americanness and it has "vanished into the depths of what is alleged to be the universal male psyche."[7]

The second phase of feminist criticism, instead of attacking misogyny among male writers, was devoted to rediscovering lost women writers and situating them within communities of influence on other women writers. Elaine Showalter's book, *A Literature of Their Own*,[8] in which she describes a female subculture in the domestic fiction of minor nineteenth-century English women writers, is typical of this phase, the culmination of which, according to Janet Todd,[9] is *The Madwoman in the Attic* by Sandra Gilbert and Susan Gubar,[10] where the authors deal with major canonical works by women writers, discerning through close reading "some essential pattern of repetition, the suppressed female, the sense of the hidden and denied." Gilbert and Gubar sought to expose "a common, female impulse to struggle free from social and literary confinement through strategic redefinitions of self, art, and society."[11]

It was during the second phase of feminist criticism that protests from lesbians and black women began to be voiced against the movement. Bonnie Zimmerman indicts as "heterosexism" the obliteration in feminist anthologies of lesbian experience[12]—the failure to mention female companions of prominent lesbian writers, the neglect of important lesbian writers, the omission in anthologies of lesbian works by authors like Katherine Philips or Adrienne Rich. Zimmerman assails leading feminist critics like Elaine Showalter, Annette Kolodny, Ellen Moers, Patricia Meyers Spacks, Sandra Gilbert, and Susan Gubar for ignoring lesbian contributions to literature. She calls for lesbian critics to concern themselves with the integration of lesbian literature and perspectives into the mainstream of feminist texts and of traditional literature.

According to Peter Shaw, "feminist literary critics, like the male academics reluctant to express hostility to *them*, have responded to the lesbian attack with embarrassment, apologies, and tokenism. Lesbians are included but often segregated at feminist conferences and in anthologies. They have been shown acquiescence but not granted the radical reordering of literary sensibility they demand."[13] But whether a reordering were effected or not, feminist criticism would still be vulnerable to the protests of black feminist critics.

Barbara Smith, in "Toward a Black Feminist Criticism,"[14] points out that black women's books require criticism by unbiased literary commentators in order to be read, understood, and remembered. She attacks authors of well-known feminist books—Elaine Showalter, Ellen Moers, and Patricia Meyer Spacks—for failing to mention or for slighting black or Third World women writers in their works. Smith prescribes for any black feminist approach the assumption that black women writers "constitute an identifiable literary tradition" and advocates that critics help to strengthen this tradition by looking first for "precedents and insights in interpretation within the works of other black women." She ends her essay by stating that she wishes to "encourage in white women . . . a sane accountability to all the women who write and live on this soil"[15] and to assuage the sentiment of alienation among black women and black lesbians.

According to Elaine Showalter's introduction to the 1989 anthology *Speaking of Gender*, the third phase of feminist criticism, which began in the 1980s, is characterized by "the rise of gender as a category of analysis." "You can't discuss Donne or Byron," writes Showalter, "the Elizabethan stage or the modernist poem, the films of F. W. Murnau or *The Texas Chainsaw Massacre*, without talking about gender."[16]

The difference between sex and gender is that the first is given biologically, the second is socially constructed. The purpose of the distinction, writes Ruthven, "has been to free women (but inevitably men too) from sexist stereotyping based on limiting conceptions of their 'nature'; and the upshot that has been a discrediting of essentialistic theories of human behaviour which designate certain characteristics as male-specific and others as female-specific." Ruthven finds the central hypothesis of feminist literary criticism to be "that gender is a crucial determinant in the production, circulation and consumption of literary discourses."[17]

An example of gender analysis criticism can be seen in an article by Phyllis Rackin in *Speaking of Gender*. Rackin points out that the English Renaissance stage is ideal for gender studies "because women's parts were played by boys."[18] The sexual ambiguity of the boy heroine was likely to evoke a mythological tradition centering on the androgyne—the androgyne could be an example of human transcendence of sexual limits in the natural world, or of social and physical deformity. Both of these extremes are represented in the plays of Shakespeare and his contemporaries. The 16th-century ideal image of the androgyne became increasingly replaced by the deformed image as time went on.

Rackin examines a series of five plays, written between 1587 and 1609—one by Lyly, three by Shakespeare, one by Ben Jonson—illustrating a changing theatrical tradition. The plays also represent changing conceptions of gender, illustrated through their changing depictions of marriage.

Gallathea, Lyly's play, and *Epicoene*, Jonson's play, represent opposite extremes. Money is a central issue in Jonson's play, an issue that arises only in the comic subplot of Lyly's play and of no consequence in the marriage of his heroines. *Gallathea* validates both marriage and androgyny, *Epicoene* repudiates both.

According to Rackin, the three Shakespeare plays (*Twelfth Night, As You Like It*, and *The Merchant of Venice*) are "more ambivalent in their treatment of monetary considerations, the value of romantic love, and the significance of gender identity." Unlike Lyly and Jonson, Shakespeare does not "dissolve the difference between the sex of the boy actor and that of the heroine he plays; and he uses his boy heroines' sexual ambiguity not only to complicate his plots but also to resolve them." The plays end with the marriages of the boy heroines, as in Lyly, but Shakespeare's conclusions "vindicate the reality principle as well as the power of love and illusion."[19]

Although debate exists on the issue of the position of women during the Renaissance, most evidence suggests that it declined, and the five plays discussed by Rackin illustrate a pattern of decline.

Rackin goes on to discuss in detail the close relation of gender depiction to the changing notions of theatrical representation in the five plays. She claims that "gender-role transgression is intimately related . . . to the issue of theatrical representation"[20] in Elizabethan discussions of the theater, particularly in Puritan diatribes against the stage, where the complaint that poets misrepresent the world merges into Biblical injunctions against transvestism.

Both Lyly's and Jonson's plays end in the abolition of sexual ambiguity, but Shakespeare's "transvestite comedies . . . sustain that ambiguity to the end."[21] Marriage becomes more difficult in *Twelfth Night* than it was in *As You Like It*, and the former "incorporates the reality principle in its conclusion by splitting the unitary figure of the androgyne into the marvelously identical boy/girl twins who are needed to make the resolution possible."[22]

Rackin concludes by pointing out that opportunities for women available in the Renaissance were closed down by a variety of factors that we are only just beginning to understand. She claims that "changing portrayals of transvestite heroines on the Renaissance stage help to illuminate the early phase of the process, and they also give us a glimpse of a liminal moment when gender definitions were open to play."[23]

Rackin's essay is a clear example of what gender studies are, but it by no means represents a monolithic critical approach of feminist studies of gender. It is an example of the New Historicist school, a group that attempts to flesh out historical developments by following the traces they left in literature, to use literary critical techniques to elucidate history.

Peter Shaw points out that the gender studies phase of feminist criticism is distinguished more by its adoption of advanced critical theory than by its actual subject.[24] Advanced critical theory means theory influenced by

French poststructuralism, particularly deconstruction and Lacanianism. Since both these schools of theory are particularly complicated, the best way to clarify them is by describing essays that exemplify their methods.

According to Jacques Derrida, the French philosopher who is the father of deconstruction, there is no final meaning in language, which refuses to be pinned down to one stable meaning or a "transcendental signified."[25] The reasoning behind this proposition is illustrated by Toril Moi when she uses as an example the phonemes identified by Ferdinand de Saussure as the smallest signifying unit of sound in language. *B*, for example, means nothing by itself—it must be differentiated from other phonemes like *k* or *h* in order to make sense. In other words, *b* "signifies only through a process that *defers* its meaning until consideration of other differential elements in language. In a sense it is the *other* phonemes that enable us to determine the meaning of /b/,"[26] in the same way that we determine signification by comparing one signifier with the absence of others. (According to Saussure, language is a system of signs, writes Ruthven, "each of which is made up of sound-image or 'signifier' and a concept or 'signified.' ")[27] The relation of the signifier to the signified is arbitrary, as we realize when we consider the different words for the same concept—horse, for instance—in different languages. This means that language is not a representation of reality but a system of signification—words are not things but signs for things.

Derrida's meaning for his term *différence* is both "difference" and "deferred." As Moi writes,

> the interplay between presence or absence that produces meaning is posited as one of *deferral*: meaning is never truly present, but is only constructed through the potentially endless process of referring to other, absent signifiers. The "next" signifier can in a sense be said to give meaning to the "previous" one and so on *ad infinitum*. There can thus be no "transcendental signified" where the process of deferral somehow would come to an end.[28]

A "transcendental signified" would be the Christian concept of God as Alpha and Omega, origin of meaning and final end of the world. Likewise, "the traditional view of the author as the source and meaning of his or her own text casts the author in the role of transcendental signified."[29]

A practical example of deconstruction is found in Christine Froula's article, "When Eve Reads Milton: Undoing the Canonical Economy."[30] The purpose of Froula's argument is to challenge the traditional literary authority represented by the canon and to discern an alternative meaning in Milton's account of the creation of Eve, both aims in concordance with Derrida's principles.

Froula envisions canonical authority as priestly, respected by most men, challenged by most women. Many feminists have explored the politics of reading the patriarchal canon and have become resisting readers, refusing to identify with the male point of view, the position of power, against themselves. Froula quotes the author of a work on the resisting reader to make clear the political aim of questioning canonical authority: "To expose and question that complex of ideas and mythologies about men and women is to make the system of power embodied in the literature open not only to discussion but . . . to change."[31]

The first awakening of Milton's Eve is "an archetypal scene of canonical instruction."[32] In her apostrophe to Adam, Eve's own words consign her authority to Adam and to God. But next she remembers an origin innocent of patriarchal indoctrination. She remembers waking and hearing the sound of running water, going to look in the lake, and seeing reflected in it what she does not yet understand to be her own image. A voice warns her that the image is herself and that it will be better to join "hee / Whose image thou art" and to become "Mother of human race." Eve is thus described as being raised from narcissism to the purposes of Adam and God. But the actual terms of her conversion require that she abandon not only her image but herself—her self is equated by the explaining voice with her image, and Eve is not a subject at all but a shadow until she is united to Adam.

Eve recounts how she followed the voice until she saw Adam and how, though fair, he was less so than the image she had seen, so she started back to the water until Adam's voice educated her to her secondariness, her derivation from his rib, and to her role as part of Adam's whole, to whom she must cede her very self. Eve is thus converted from her own authority and experience to that of a higher authority in the same way in which readers are converted from the authority of their own experience to the authority of canonical texts.

The power moving Eve's conversion upon her first awakening is that of Milton's God, depicted as an invisible voice. The invisibility of this voice (Eve is depicted as an image, visible) is "the *secret* not only of spiritual and literary authority in Milton's poem but of cultural authority as such"[33] The authority of Christian doctrine and of church fathers is defined by its invisibility. And in Milton's text Eve is associated with visibility, Adam with invisibility: Eve's first act is to be attracted by a "maternally murmuring pool that returns an image of herself in the visible world," whereas Adam concludes that his body is not him, and looks around for a male Creator, "subordinating body and earth—all that Adam can see—to an invisible father."[34]

While it might appear that Milton is illustrating Adam's intrinsic superiority to Eve, one might also interpret Adam's attitude as "alienation from his body and the visible world, an alienation that his God and the establishment of a hierarchical relation to Eve are designed to heal." "Adam's need to possess Eve is usually understood as complemented by her need for his guidance, but Milton's text suggests a more subtle and compelling source for this need: Adam's sense of inadequacy in the face of what he sees as

Eve's perfection." Adam concentrates on the function he attributes to his rib of creating a human being, thus revealing "an archetypal womb envy as constitutive of male identity."[35]

Eve "brings the threat of woman's self-articulation into focus: it is the danger posed by her speaking from her body, from an experience that exists outside patriarchal authority, as did the untutored, self-reflective consciousness Milton represents as narcissistic. Such speech threatens the very basis of the cultural currency."[36]

It is not, then, that we no longer read the texts of a patriarchal society, but that we read them differently, "using interpretive strategies that mark a shift from a sacred to a secular interpretive model."[37] We continue to hear the other voices in *Paradise Lost* dominated by Milton, voices that, "presenting different models of literary/social authority, disrupt the canonical economy of Milton's text as the gnostic voices disrupted the economy of Christian orthodoxy."[38]

Froula's teasing of contradictory voices out of Milton's text is a particularly clear example of the way in which deconstructive criticism attempts to "decenter" or to remove the transcendental center—Eve's inferiority to Adam, as proclaimed by the voices of God and of Adam from a discourse. But Froula's article is an example of what Ruthven calls "soft deconstruction" because it undoes the given order of priorities in Milton's text but not, as in "hard deconstruction" the very system of conceptual opposition that makes that order possible. Instead, Froula decenters the traditional interpretation of Milton, the "masculine construction of reality" with "a view to centering a feminist construction of reality."[39]

The other major school of French theory characteristic of the third or gender studies phase of feminist criticism is the psychoanalytic one inspired by Jacques Lacan, the poststructuralist interpreter of Freud.[40]

One of the basic ideas of Lacan is the existence of different states of experience at different stages of an individual's life, called the Symbolic and the Imaginary Orders. The Imaginary Order exists before the Oedipal period, when the child believes itself to be part of the mother and experiences no separation between itself and the world. The Symbolic Order, which coincides with the acquisition of language, is a state in which the father has split up the unity between mother and child and forbidden the child access to the mother and the mother's body. The desire for the mother or imaginary unity with her must now be repressed, thus creating the unconscious in the child. The Symbolic Order is the realm of the Law of the Father, symbolized by the phallus, and signifies separation and loss to the child, as can be seen in his discrimination among pronouns (*I, you, he*), where he no longer claims "imaginary identity with all other possible positions."[41]

Moi writes: "To enter the Symbolic Order means to accept the phallus as the representation of the Law of the Father. All human culture and all life in society is dominated by the Symbolic Order, and thus by the phallus as the sign of lack."[42] The subject cannot remain in the Imaginary Order, for this would be equivalent to becoming psychotic. Moi suggests thinking of the Imaginary Order as Freud's pleasure principle and the Symbolic Order as his reality principle.

Sandra Gilbert's article, "Life's Empty Pack: Notes toward a Literary Daughteronomy,"[43] uses Lacan's idea of the Symbolic Order as the realm of the Law of the Father, although it does not speak about Lacan's notion of language acquisition or about his belief that the unconscious is structured like a language, another of his influential ideas. Gilbert begins by inquiring what paradigms of female sexuality have been handed down by important literary ancestresses since the 19th century. One of the fictions she analyzes for a paradigm is George Eliot's *Silas Marner*. Here she finds that Eliot, as a literary mother, speaks for the father, reminding the female child that she cannot be his inheritor. Human culture, says the literary mother, is bound by rules that "seem to constitute what Jacques Lacan calls the 'Law of the Father,' the law that means culture is by definition both patriarchal and phallocentric and must therefore transmit the empty pack of disinheritance to every daughter."[44] George Eliot as literary mother represents culture and thus inexorably tells her daughters that they cannot have a mother because they have been assigned to the Law of the Father.

Although *Silas Marner* seems to reward the daughter, actually it "becomes a female myth of origin narrated by a severe literary mother who uses the vehicle of a half-allegorical family romance to urge acquiescence in the Law of the Father."[45]

Silas Marner is depicted at the beginning as a liminal figure, alienated from society. He is integrated into the community by becoming the adoptive father of Eppie, "a child whose Christmas coming marks her as symbolically divine but whose function as divine daughter rather than sacred son is to signify, rather than to replace, the power of her newly created father."[46] The central notion of Claude Lévi-Strauss' *Elementary Structures of Kinship* is that the social order is based upon the exchange of women.[47] According to this notion, "a daughter is a treasure whose potential passage from man to man insures psychological and social well-being."[48] In this way Eppie's marriage to Aaron means that she has married Silas to the world and to herself.

Eppie's feelings about meaning all this for Silas are happy and dutiful. She claims she would have no delight if she had to go away from Silas, and she rejects her natural father and affirms Silas Marner. She is intermittently sad, however, about her lost mother, "haunted by the primal scene in the snow when she was forced to turn away from the body of the mother, the emblem of nature which can give only so much and no more, and seek the hearth of the father, the emblem of culture that must compensate for nature's inadequacies."[49] The garden finally planted by Eppie and Silas memorializes the scene—they take the furze bush against which Eppie's mother died and transplant it into "the garden of the law," where the bush will become "a symbol of nature made meaningful, controlled and confined by culture." "In the end, then," writes Gilbert, "it is Silas Marner, the meek weaver of Raveloe, who inherits the milk and honey of the earth, for he has affirmed the Law of the Father that weaves kin and kindness together."[50]

This brief survey of feminist criticism by no means exhausts all the contemporary approaches that exist. No mention, for instance, has been made of the flourishing Marxist school, nor of the well-known French theorists like Hélène Cixous and Luce Irigaray,[51] who argue that there exists a separate women's language originating from the female body.

As Ruthven points out, Anglophone investigations of women's language are much more empirical than the French, preferring to investigate evidence of its existence rather than "framing psychsomatic theories of its origin."[52] Gynocritical inquiries, initiated by the work of Robin Lakoff,[53] focus on the specificity of women's language, but the aspect of language next considered in this chapter is feminist criticism or criticism aimed at revealing androcentric bias in linguistic practices.

LANGUAGE

In 1972 *Time* magazine published an article by Stefan Kanfer attacking a phenomenon he named "Sispeak." Kanfer was objecting to the reforms of English being advocated in the 1970s by language experts and feminists, by professional and publishing organizations. He complained about *chairperson* for *chairman*, *Ms.* for *Mrs.* and *Miss*, ridiculed the basic assumption that our language reflects the sexual bias of our society, and compared "Sispeak" to George Orwell's "Newspeak," the language of the all-seeing totalitarian dictatorship of the novel *1984*. He accused the reformers of having a "touching, almost mystical trust in words"[54] in their efforts to change the dictionary, and scoffed at the notion that a society's values change in tandem with its language changes. Kanfer ended by asserting that it is our duty to resist neologisms or else we demonstrate our prejudices against reason and meaning.

Kanfer's puns and witticisms at the expense of the most extreme of suggestions for language change that he could identify should be countered by a sober examination of what sexist practices in English are, what are the remedies proposed by reformers, and what are the arguments advanced against and for change.

The psychologist Nancy M. Henley divides sexist practices in language into three categories: defining, deprecating, and ignoring women.[55] Under defining, she mentions references to women in terms of their relations to other people, such as *wife of* or *mother of*, *Miss*, or *Mrs.* (men are usually referred to by their occupations); the genderizing of professional or occupational nouns by adding suffixes or modifiers even when sex is irrelevant, as in *poetess, aviatrix,* or *lady doctor,* which has the effect of marking women as different, unusual, or inferior; and putting men before women in pairing the sexes: *men and women, his or hers, Adam and Eve,* and so forth.

Under deprecating, Henley classifies female-specific nouns that have acquired debased or obscene connotations in contrast with their male-specific nouns (*courtesan/courtier, mistress/master, governor/governess*); trivializing, negative, or stereotyped references like *little woman, weaker sex, primitive man*; treating a woman's sex as if it were her salient characteristic. Henley reports that sexual insult is used for women but hardly for men: 220 terms have been found to exist for a sexually promiscuous woman but only 22 terms for a sexually promiscuous man.[56]

When examples of the above practice are brought to their attention, most people would admit that they were sexist, but they would probably dispute the exclusiveness of practices Henley lists under ignoring women, her third category of sexism in language. The "generic masculine" or the grammatical rule requiring a masculine pronoun in reference to an antecedent of an unspecified or mixed sex ("the typical New Yorker drinks *his* coffee with cream and sugar"; "a boy or a girl must put *his* towel in *his* locker") is the chief area of conflict in the battle to make the English language less sexist than it is at present. Many claim that this practice is innocuous, but tests continue to demonstrate that *he, his, him,* and other masculine terms "do not function generically and in fact do bias interpretations."[57]

The generic masculine by which women are rendered silent and invisible has been in dispute since the 18th century and became a popular topic as early as 1884,[58] but a concerted onslaught upon it and on sexist language in general by linguists, sociolinguists, grammarians, lexicologists, psychologists, communications experts, publishers' and professional organizations, government bodies, and feminists has been a feature of the American scene only since the 1970s. Dale Spender reminds us that the generic masculine is a relatively recent practice in the history of English, unknown before the 15th century.[59] One of the first to proclaim that since males come first in the natural order, they should come first in the structure of language, was Thomas Wilson, who wrote the *Arte of Rhetorique* in 1553. Prescriptive grammarians wrote increasingly in favor of the generic masculine during a time when common usage relied upon *they* for sex-indeterminable references ("Everyone has their rights"). In 1746 John Kirkby formulated *Eighty Eight Grammatical Rules,* which included one stating that the "male gender was *more comprehensive* than the female."[60] Despite the efforts of two centuries of grammatical prescriptivists and of the educational and publishing establishments to ban its use on the grounds of grammatical incorrectness, however, *they* continued and continues to be used commonly as a singular long after Kirkby's 18th-century rules, and *he* was almost always sex specific. In fact, it required a decree of Parliament in 1850 to make it clear that *he* legally included *she* in parliamentary acts.[61]

Examples of the use by great writers of a tradition other than that of the generic *he* can be seen in the following, cited by Casey Miller and Kate Swift in their *Handbook of Nonsexist Writing*:

Each of them should...make themself ready. (William Caxton)

God send everyone their heart's desire. (William Shakespeare)

If a person is born of a gloomy temper...they cannot help it. (Lord Chesterfield)[62]

In other words, those who cite tradition as a reason for refusing to tamper with generics are presumably unaware that the history is far from monolithic.

"Over the centuries, the efforts to create a sex-neutral pronoun have concerned more language reformers and resulted in more solutions than any other question involving language and gender," writes Dennis Baron.[63] Reformers have attempted to make English pronouns simple, logical, regular, and fair to men and women. The most advocated reform has been the attempt to introduce a common gender pronoun to replace the generic masculine *he* in a sentence like "Everyone loves *his* mother." From the 18th century to the present, more than eighty epicene (common to both sexes) pronouns have been proposed, but none of them has been widely accepted in place of *he*, certainly not new pronoun coinages like *ne*, *ter*, *thon*, *heer*, *shem*, *et*, *ip*, *per*, *tey*, *co*, and not even familiar words like *she*, *one*, or *it*. *They*, as mentioned above, has been the most popular substitute for *he* in speech and in writing, and its very popularity demonstrates a widespread malaise about the use of the generic *he*.

A common argument against change is based on the assumption that the dictionary dictates the use of the generic *he* and prescribes that it include *she*, but, as we have seen, the history of this grammatical phenomenon is mixed and attempts to correct imprecision and ambiguity have been frequent. Another argument derives from the belief that the intention of the speaker or writer or the feeling of inclusion or exclusion of one particular woman determines whether a statement has generic or sex-specific impact. But here research results for many people are a more reliable indication than the reactions of specific individuals. Sixteen studies from 1971 to 1980 showing that "*he* does not function generically, that is does not reference both female and male, but rather most readily produces images and ideas of males,"[64] are cited by Henley. She explains that the tests used subjects from five years to adult, that the subjects were given written or spoken phrases, sentences, or stories and asked to identify the sex of those mentioned in their samples by generic nouns or pronouns. The tests found universally that the generic masculine was interpreted as sex-specific—it indicated predominantly males.

Henley's other descriptions of test results include the information that females have been found less likely to use the masculine generic than males, more likely to avoid it by using *he and she* or *they*.

Indications abound that gender marking other than generics influences people's behavior and attitudes. Preschool boys and girls were motivated more than they had been by hearing a story of the accomplishments of males and females, respectively; women aspired more to tasks labeled as feminine; and high school students responded preferentially to jobs cued to their own sex.

Students at Yale University and in a New York high school rated courses as less enjoyable and stimulating when they were to be taught by a *Miss* or *Mrs.* than when they were to be taught by *Ms.*, *Mr.*, or an untitled instructor. Feelings and evaluations were also affected by gender when paragraphs ascribed to professional women were rated lower if the woman had a sex designation of "lady" or "ess" than if she had one of "woman" or "female." Henley points out that the evaluation of a job candidate was $6,000 higher in terms of salary when the candidate was referred to as a *woman* instead of a *girl*. She concludes her discussion of tests about feelings and attitudes evoked by generic masculines by citing one test that showed "women exposed to the feminine generic have reported feelings of pride, importance, superiority, freedom, and power."[65]

Men who argue that *he* is generic and includes *she* often resent the same status's being claimed for *she*. For years, for instance, *she* was the preferred pronoun in educational circles for teachers, and the word *teacher* became regarded as a "covert feminine noun."[66] Men in the profession objected, claiming that this feminization of teaching was the cause of low status and low pay for teachers. By the 1960s the generic masculine became predominant, and in the 1970s protests started coming from women teachers who disliked being rendered invisible. A National Education Association publication, *Today's Education*, claimed to be a leader in the shift; but then, coming to understand the conflict, called for a common-gender pronoun.[67] Ironically, Dennis Baron observes, "although the use of the generic *she* has declined in education, the status and salaries of teachers have not improved significantly."[68]

A third serious argument against finding alternatives to the false generic *he* or *man* in addition to the ones discussed above—an incorrect notion of grammatical tradition and the belief that individual response determines whether a person feels included or excluded by the generic *he* or *man*—is that sexist language exists, as does sexist social practice, but changing the language has nothing to do with changing society. Even some feminists feel this way, as illustrated by the 1977 jingle of Nina Yablok: "If I had my choice, if I had my druthers / I'd take equal rights. Leave equal words to the others."[69] Those who advocate this argument consider that feminists have too magical a notion of the power of words.

It is true that since the 1940s the linguistic theories of Edward Sapir and Benjamin Whorf have exerted much influence among professionals and led them to regard language as perhaps more powerful than it is. The Sapir-Whorf hypothesis proposed that "the structure of one's language directly shapes one's view of the world, and that different structures impose on the consciousness a different perception of reality."[70] An example frequently used to illustrate this notion is that of Eskimos, who have many different words for varieties of snow and therefore have been credited with being able to perceive finer distinctions about it than are English speakers. From the Sapir-Whorf hypothesis succeeded the notion, accepted by many feminists, that cultural biases can be changed by changing the language in which they are expressed. But recent evidence demonstrates that it is incorrect to assume that language determines thought[71] and, as a result, the hypothesis has been reinterpreted to mean that language *influences* our world view by reflecting and thus reinforcing cultural biases. So changing biases in linguistic patterns will not automatically change social biases, but it will help to influence them. This weaker version of the Sapir-Whorf hypothesis should eliminate any tendency among feminists to attribute to words semimagical power to change society.

Arguments in favor of changing generic *he* focus upon the injustice of the status quo and its frequent ambiguity and incongruity. Francine Frank and Paula Treichler quote the lexicographer Alma Graham on the injustice:

If you have a group half of whose members are A's and half of whose members are B's and if you call the group C then A's and B's may be equal members of group C. But if you call the group A, there is no way that B's can be equal to A's within it. The A's will always be the rule and the B's will always be the exception—the subgroup, the subspecies, the outsiders.[72]

One of the many fine examples in Frank and Treichler of the incongruity of the generic *he* comes from a *New York Times* book review: "A novelist's vice usually resembles his virtues, for what he does best he also tends to do to excess."[73] The virtues and vices are further detailed, and then there follow paragraphs on Thomas Hardy and Charles Dickens. Finally we learn that the novelist under discussion is Toni Morrison!

Ambiguity of generics is illustrated in Frank and Treichler by the following:

The depressed person often becomes aware of strong feelings of self-dislike; he feels worthless and guilty about his shortcomings. He believes that nothing he can do will alleviate his condition.... Crying spells may set in, the person loses weight, finds himself unable to get to sleep.... Food no longer tastes good, sex is not arousing, and people, even his wife and children, become wholly uninteresting.[74]

The depressed person, a gender-neutral term, is the antecedent of *he*. With the appearance of *wife and children*, however, *he* must be reinterpreted as masculine. It is now ambiguous what the antecedent of *he* is meant to be: Does the passage apply to men only? Married men with children? Or depressed persons of either sex, married or single?

Most changes advocated by language reformers consist of different kinds of circumventions to eliminate gender-specific terms from usage or to substitute neutral terms. Some, however, advocate change through emphasizing feminine terms. The rationale here, according to Maija S. Blaubergs, is that the visibility of women in whatever the roles they play will contribute to the women's recognition of role models and provide a means of self-assertion; for men, awareness and appreciation of women's contributions to society will ensue.[75] Conflict is possible between the two approaches, universal or androgynous experience versus feminine experience (Does one favor *authoress* or decry it? Does one choose *chairwoman* or *chair*?) but so far it has been minimal.

Nevertheless, the different approaches typify a basic split among feminists, described by Ann Snitow as a conflict between maximizers and minimizers.[76] The former are those who want to keep the category "woman" but "want to change its meaning, to reclaim and elaborate the social being 'woman,' and to empower her";[77] the minimizers want to undermine the category "woman" and to minimize sex differences. Fluctuations between periods of minimization and maximalization or between radical feminism and essentialism, rather than a process of thesis, antithesis, and synthesis between the two positions, are the normal process of feminist history, claims Snitow.

SIGNS OF CHANGE

Most large publishing houses and professional and scholarly associations have drafted guidelines suggesting alternatives to traditional sexist usage. The form of the guidelines differ, ranging from one sentence in *PMLA*, the journal of the Modern Language Association, to short booklets. Francine Wattman Frank and Paula Treichler inform their readers that the guidebooks produced by textbook publishers often include, in addition to language usage, matters like "appropriate illustrations and balance in the content of the text."[78] The 1981 Houghton Mifflin guidelines, entitled "Eliminating Stereotypes," treat in addition to antifeminine bias, bias against the disabled, older persons, and other stigmatized groups.

Existing guidelines resemble each other in what they consider necessary to achieve nondiscriminatory language, making the following recommendations:

Use true generics or sex-neutral terms when reference includes both sexes—for example, *poet* and *nurse* for both sexes, *chair* or *chairperson* instead of *chairman*, *worker* instead of *workman*, *humanity* or *human beings* instead of *mankind*, *the average person* for the *man on the street.*

Use parallel or symmetrical expressions for both genders—for example, *men and women* or *husbands and wives* instead of *the men and their wives*; *Lytton Strachey and Virginia Woolf* instead of *Lytton Strachey and Mrs. Woolf*; *King and McEnroe* instead of *Ms. King and McEnroe.* Some guidelines also recommend attention to order in expressions such as these to ensure that men do not always precede women.

Treat women and men as individuals instead of defining them solely by their relationship to others—for example, *Jane Russo*, not *Mrs. Louis Russo*; *Mr. and Mrs. Rosen* or *Louis and Jane Rosen*, not *Mr. Rosen and his wife*; *Mary and Joseph Smith*, not *Mary Smith and her husband, Joseph.*

Use neutral references rather than biased or stereotyped terms—for example, *woman* instead of *gal* or *chick*; *drive*, not *masculine drive*; *house* or *office cleaner* or *domestic worker*, not *cleaning lady*; *feminist*, not *libber.*

Use an alternative to the "pseudogeneric" *he, his*, or *him* when referring to a person of unspecified sex. For example, omit the possessive *his* or replace it with an article where appropriate: *The good teacher respects students* instead of *The good teacher respects his students*; *The writer tells the reader* instead of *The writer tells his reader.* Other alternatives include recasting the sentence in the plural, using the second person *you*, or using both feminine and masculine forms such as *he or she.*[79]

Guidelines of professional associations and journals tend to be shorter than those of publishers. Professional guidelines are likely not to be as mandatory as the publishers' guidelines are. Newspapers usually treat sexist usage in their style manuals, while general handbooks of nonsexist usage are easily available for reference.

The effect of guidelines on usage appears to have been mixed. According to Frank and Treichler, Robert Cooper, who studied the use of androcentric generics in American magazines, newspapers, science magazines and the *Congressional Record*, found a dramatic decline from 1971 to 1979: androcentric generics fell from 12.3 per 5,000 words in 1971 to 4.3 per 5,000 words in 1979.

Effects are mixed in eliminating sexist usage in textbooks. Publishers have attempted to do it, but many older texts are still in use. In addition, efforts to restore traditional values in education may succeed in turning the clock back in some cases in the cause of nonsexist usage.

Trade books are generally not affected by guidelines; usage is left to the individual authors. In contrast, many university presses and scholarly journals have guidelines and these have been highly effective. As Frank and Treichler correctly point out, "these policies have had a notable effect on the language of scholarly writing in the past ten years."[80]

They find that usage in the mass media varies. There is a trend toward nonsexist usage, but a paper like the *New York Times* took until 1986 before adopting the title *Ms.* and giving the names of women athletes the same treatment as those of men.

Frank and Treichler conclude that, in spite of newspaper attacks against feminists by spokesmen like John Simon and William Safire, feminists should be encouraged by the victories scored in the campaign against nonsexist language.[81] If the campaign succeeds, it will be the first time since the eighteenth-century that a small but vocal group of activists have achieved a major reform in usage.

DICTIONARIES AND GUIDES

Compilers of some recently published dictionaries have taken careful note of feminist perspectives and have done their best to reduce lexicographic sexism. Morton Benson compares the 1968 edition of the *Thorndike Barnhart Beginning Dictionary* with the 1983 edition of the *Scott-Foresman Beginning Dictionary* and finds noteworthy improvements in the 1983 publication.[82] Benson and two colleagues report that the ninth edition of *Webster's Collegiate* has advanced beyond the eighth, giving as evidence the following:

The 8th defines sense 1 of *effeminate* as "having feminine qualities (as weakness or softness) inappropriate to a man...." The 9th reads: "having feminine qualities untypical of a man...." As an expression of greater objectivity, the new definition no longer equates feminine qualities with "weakness" or "softness," and, furthermore, no longer claims that the possession of "effeminate" qualities is "inappropriate," but rather "untypical for a man."[83]

Garland Cannon and Susan Roberson, studying three recent American dictionaries, Barnhart, 1973 and 1980, and Merriam-Webster, 1983, come to the "tentative conclusion that neutral-to-positive terms referring to women are now coming into the language more rapidly." They point out that negative items, those biased against women, are still well-established, so that progress has taken place "in terms of adding appropriate counter-items, never in getting rid of objectionable items."[84] Cannon and Roberson pinpoint changes in the area of pronouns—avoidance of *he* as a generic—alternatives to *man*, and alternatives to masculine or feminine items in neutral terms, such as "flight attendant" for stewardess. Their conclusion is that "the sexual, less-than-equal, less-important stereotype remains strong. Yet the lexical image of women is considerably improving and is beginning to be reflected in positive terms."[85]

Richard Bernstein, in the June 11, 1991, *New York Times*, describes the May 15, 1991, edition of a new Random House *Webster's College Dictionary* as in line with the current mood of linguistic sensitivity among the public. "The most publicized features of this dictionary," writes Bernstein, "are, first, its claim to have eliminated sexist language from its definitions and, second, the scrupulous attention it pays to the potential of words to give offense. Many guidelines to usage are appended to its definitions, warning when words are 'offensive' or 'disparaging' and sometimes offering alternatives."[86] The Random House dictionary avoids *he* for a person of an unknown sex and includes an appendix called "Avoiding Sexist Language." Some critics and scholars object to the Random House dictionary, and Bernstein asks whether it "is the politically correct dictionary of the 1990's."[87]

In addition to the changes in dictionaries taking place in response to feminist pressure, individual feminists have published dictionaries and guides that have become familiar and well-regarded. *The Handbook of Nonsexist Writing* by Casey Miller and Kate Swift is a lively and interesting discussion of major types of sexist usage.[88] There is a chapter on *man* as a false generic with suggested alternatives to "generic" *man*, a chapter on the false generic pronoun *he*, with suggestions for solving pronoun problems, discussion of salutations for letters, and much other information and advice about common problems of sexist usage.

Cheris Kramarae and Paula A. Treichler's *A Feminist Dictionary* was published in 1985.[89] It is a list of words, mostly nouns, that are of particular interest to feminists. In other words, you cannot find *Philippic* there, but you can find extensive descriptions of words like *phallus* and *phallogocentrism*. The definitions are in most cases based upon writing by women, in order that the compilers can show women as "linguistically creative speakers." Many definitions include commentary on general culture from a feminist viewpoint and are antiauthoritarian.

A handy guide is Rosalie Maggio's 1987 *Nonsexist Word Finder: A Dictionary of Gender-Free Usage.*[90] Designed to help writers avoid using sexist terminology—"language that promotes and maintains attitudes that stereotype people according to gender"—the *Nonsexist Word Finder* steers a delicate course in suggesting nonsexist synonyms that are minimally jarring to those who espouse sexist language. "The fact is," writes Maggio, "that it is possible to use inclusive language without offending or startling people and without sounding like someone with a poor command of the language." Maggio's directions are clear and succinct, and her Appendix A, which offers descriptions and lists of different categories of sexist words, is a useful overview of the most typical problems one encounters in attempting to keep one's writing gender free.

A Women's Thesaurus: An Index of Language Used to Describe and Locate Information by and about Women, edited by Mary Ellen Capek, was developed by the National Council for Research on Women, a coalition of feminist research and policy centers around the country.[91] It is not the usual thesaurus, with synonyms and antonyms of selected words, but a thesaurus of subject areas, many of them particularly pertinent to contemporary women, with lists supplied of related subjects, narrower and broader terms, so that a user may consult these lists as guides for constructing his or her own filing system, looking for additional subjects categories, and preparing indexes for books. The editor writes that the more than 5,000 thesaurus entries "are intended to encourage common usage of terms for sharing information among different types of users—standardized terms for filing information and for indexing books, reports, government documents, magazines, scholarly journals, newspapers and newsletters, as well as for the compilation of multisource indexes and reference guides."[92]

STRAWS IN THE WIND

Statistical studies of amelioration of sexism in language are not available in all areas, so we now cite examples of individual changes in order to provide an impressionistic picture of what has been happening in the United States during the last decades.

On College Campuses

• *The Chronicle of Higher Education* reported in November 1985 that the official motto of the California state university system, *vir veritas vox* (man, truth, voice) had been changed to *vita veritas vox* to avoid gender specificity. The change was proposed by W. Ann Reynolds, then the chancellor.

• The spring 1986 issue of *Women and Language* announced that M.I.T. had decided to acknowledge that one-quarter of its students were women by changing the alma mater song from "Arise Ye Sons" to "In Praise of M.I.T."

• The spring 1987 issue of *Women and Language* reported that President William E. Bowen had announced that Princeton had adopted gender-neutral lyrics to replace references to *sons* and *boys* in Princeton's alma mater song, "Old Nassau."

In Standard Reference Books

• *Women and Language* reported in spring 1982 that the latest edition of the then 130-year-old *Roget's Thesaurus* had added or reclassified 20,000 words to eliminate male bias, replacing *mankind* with *humankind*, *countryman* with *countrydweller*.

• Also in the spring 1982 issue of *Women and Language*, it was reported that the then 45-year-old *How to Win Friends and Influence People* by Dale Carnegie had had its revisions explained in a preface to the new edition. The aim was to avoid quaint, outdated phrases; some of the changes were *person* instead of *man* and *clerk* instead of *salesgirl*.

• The 13th edition of the *Chicago Manual of Style* was revised and expanded and one of its major changes was the inclusion of nonsexist language.

• Dr. Benjamin Spock revised the latest editions of his best-selling *Baby and Child Care* to eliminate sexist language.

In Governmental Agencies

• The U.S. Department of Labor in 1975 published its *Job Title Revisions to Eliminate Sex- and Age-Referent Language from the Dictionary of Occupational Titles, Third Edition.* (A new edition was published in the summer of 1991.) Some of the job-title changes, listed by Miller and Swift,[93] were:

From	*To*
Advertising layout man	advertising layout planner
airline steward, stewardess	flight attendant
cameraman, camera girl	camera operator
charwoman	charworker
draftsman	drafter
fisherman	fisher
forelady, foreman	supevisor
gateman	gate tender
hat-check girl	hat-check attendant
junior executive	executive trainee
laundress, laundryman	laundry worker
lineman	line installer, line repairer
longshoreman	stevedore
maid	house worker
office boy, girl	office helper
pressman	press operator
repairman	repairer
salesman	sales agent, sales associate
seamstress	sewer, mender
signalman	signaller
watchman	guard

• Effective December 1, 1976, San Diego county adopted guidelines for all county staff to help eliminate sex-biased language.
• The *Federal Times* of January 1979 contained a brief list and discussion of usage of nongender-specific terms, put out by the U.S. Defense Department's Office of Equal Opportunity. "Bachelor housing," for instance, becomes "unaccompanied personnel housing."

• The National Weather Service altered its practice on personifying hurricanes as female around 1979. Now every other hurricane has a man's first name.

• The *New York Times* of November 1980 reported that the U.S. Supreme Court had dropped "Mr. Justice" for "Justice" as a mode of address. It was speculated that this was an attempt to avoid "Madam Justice."

• The 1980 Census began using nonsexist forms, updating the old form, which had acknowledged only husband-headed households.

• The *Washington Post* reported in March 1983 that the Justice Department had sent guidelines to its agencies, requiring them to cite laws that might or did still discriminate on the basis of gender.

• The *Chicago Tribune* reported in June 1983 that construction signs in New York City had replaced "Men Working" with "People Working," to go along with a 1980 amendment to abolish gender terms.

• The *Minneapolis Star and Tribune* of February 1986 reported arguments in the Minnesota House over occupational titles in state laws. Eventually the House passed a bill to eliminate sexual bias from the laws of Minnesota.

In Religion

• The *Peninsula Times Tribune* of January 1980 reported that Unitarians had eliminated masculine pronouns referring to God. Instead of pronouns, the word *God* is repeated, or other phrases, such as *Source of Love*, are substituted.

• The United Presbyterian Church in the United States in 1979 issued a 48-page booklet addressing sexual bias in language, entitled *The Power of Language among the People of God and the Language about God "Opening the Door."*

• In 1987 the Catholic Bible translation changed language seen as biased against women. It does not use *man* or *men* constantly when referring to people of unknown sex. Here are two of the changes in the Gospel of Matthew:

1970: "Not on bread alone is man to live."

1987: "One does not live by bread alone."

1970: "Your light must shine before men."

1987: "Your light must shine before others."

Much of the information in this "Straws in the Wind" section comes from the journal *Women and Language*. Although it is not a quantitative survey, it can supply suggestions for individual efforts to eliminate sexism in language. If you are a college student, member of the staff, or faculty person, speak up about songs, mottoes, publications on campus. Others have plenty of scope for pressure in community or government bodies of which they are members or by which they are affected. Write to authors and publishers of books you use, how-to guide and dictionaries, as well as books you read only once. Write letters to the editors of journals and newspapers. Exercise pressure on your church or synagogue group to eliminate sexist language in publications used in religious services. Finally, check your own writing, referring, if necessary, to publishers' guidelines or to feminist handbooks and dictionaries like the ones described above. There is no lack of opportunity for reformers to exert pressure for nonsexist language.

NOTES

1. K. K. Ruthven, *Feminist Literary Studies: An Introduction* (Cambridge: Cambridge University Press, 1984), p. 7.

2. Elaine Showalter, ed., *The New Feminist Criticism: Essays on Women, Literature, and Theory* (New York: Pantheon Books, 1985), p. 5.

3. Kate Millett, *Sexual Politics* (Garden City, NY: Doubleday, 1970).

4. Nina Baym, "Melodramas of Beset Manhood: How Theories of American Fiction Exclude Women Authors," in Showalter, *The New Feminist Criticism*, pp. 63–80.

5. Ibid., p. 64.

6. Lionel Trilling, *The Liberal Imagination* (Garden City, NY: Doubleday, 1953), p. 21.

7. Baym, "Melodramas," p. 79.

8. Elaine Showalter, *A Literature of Their Own* (Princeton, NJ: Princeton University Press, 1977).

9. Janet Todd, *Feminist Literary History: A Defence* (Cambridge: Polity Press, 1988), p. 28.

10. Sandra Gilbert and Susan Gubar, *The Madwoman in the Attic* (New Haven, CT: Yale University Press, 1979).

11. Quoted in Todd, *Feminist Literary History*, p. 28.

12. Bonnie Zimmerman, "What Never Has Been: An Overview of Lesbian Feminist Literary Criticism," *Feminist Studies* 7 (1981): 451–475.

13. Peter Shaw, "Feminist Literary Criticism: A Report from the Academy," *The American Scholar*, Autumn 1988, pp. 507–508.

14. Barbara Smith, "Toward a Black Feminist Criticism," in Showalter, *The New Feminist Criticism*.

15. Ibid., pp. 174–175.

16. Elaine Showalter, ed., *Speaking of Gender* (New York: Routledge, 1989), p. 1.

17. Ruthven, *Feminist Literary Studies*, pp. 8, 9.

18. Phyllis Rackin, "Androgyny, Mimesis, and the Marriage of the Boy Heroine on the English Renaissance Stage," in Showalter, *Speaking of Gender*, p. 113.

19. Ibid., pp. 116, 117.

20. Ibid., p. 123.

21. Ibid., p. 126.

22. Ibid., p. 127.

23. Ibid.

24. Shaw, "Feminist Literary Criticism," pp. 198–199.

25. Quoted by Toril Moi, *Sexual/Textual Politics* (London: Methuen, 1985), p. 106.

26. Ibid.

27. Ruthven, *Feminist Literary Studies*, p. 37.

28. Moi, *Sexual/Textual Politics*, p. 106.

29. Ibid.

30. Christine Froula, "When Eve Reads Milton: Undoing the Canonical Economy," *Critical Inquiry* 10 (December 1983).

31. Ibid., p. 323.

32. Ibid., p. 326.

33. Ibid., p. 330.

34. Ibid., pp. 330, 331.

35. Ibid., pp. 331, 332.

36. Ibid., p. 335.

37. Ibid.

38. Ibid., p. 336.

39. Ruthven, *Feminist Literary Studies*, p. 56.

40. Moi, *Sexual/Textual Politics*, p. 99.

41. Ibid.

42. Ibid., p. 100.

43. Sandra Gilbert, "Life's Empty Pack: Notes toward a Literary Daughteronomy," *Critical Inquiry* 11 (March 1985).

44. Ibid., p. 358.

45. Ibid., p. 359.

46. Ibid., p. 360.

47. Claude Lévi-Strauss, *Elementary Structures of Kinship*, rev. ed., trans. James Harle Bell, John Richard von Sturmer, and Rodney Needham (Boston: Beacon Press, 1969).

48. Gilbert, "Life's Empty Pack," p. 361.

49. Ibid., p. 364.

50. Ibid., p. 365.

51. Hélène Cixous and Catherine Clément, *La Jeune Née* (Paris: Union Générale d'Éditions, Séries Féminin Futur, 1975), p. 235. *La Jeune Née* is available in an English edition, *The Newly Born Woman*, Betsy Wing (Minneapolis: University of Minnesota Press, 1986). Luce Irigaray, *Spéculum de L'Autre Femme* (Paris: Éditions de Minuit, 1974), p. 53. The English edition is *Speculum of the Other Woman*, trans. Gillian C. Gill (Ithaca, NY: Cornell University Press, 1985).

52. Ruthven, *Feminist Literary Studies*, p. 100.

53. Robin Lakoff, *Talking Power* (New York: Basic Books, 1990).

54. Stefan Kanfer, "Sispeak: A Misguided Attempt to Change Herstory," *Time*, October 23, 1972, p. 79.

55. Nancy M. Henley, "This New Species That Seeks a New Language: On Sexism in Language and Language Change," in *Women and Language in Transition*, ed. Joyce Penfield (Albany: State University of New York Press, 1987), pp. 3–5.

56. Ibid., p. 4.

57. Ibid., p. 5.

58. Donald McKay, "Prescriptive Grammar and the Pronoun Problem," in *Language, Gender and Society*, ed. Barrie Thorne, Cheris Kramarae, and Nancy Henley (Rowley, MA: Newbury House, 1983), p. 49. Also see Dennis Baron, *Grammar and Gender* (New Haven, CT: Yale University Press, 1986), p. 100.

59. Dale Spender, *Man Made Language* (London: Routledge and Kegan Paul, 1980), p. 148.

60. Cited in ibid., p. 148.

61. A survey of several hundred years of Canadian law reveals that, far from females being included within the definition of the generic masculine, its ambiguity "has allowed judges to include or exclude women, depending on the climate of the times and their own personal biases." Controversy about whether women are included generically in regulations referring to *he* and *man* has arisen in U.S. law as well as in Canadian. See Wendy Martyna, "Beyond the He/Man Approach: The Case for Nonsexist Language," in Thorne et al., *Language, Gender and Society*, p. 32.

62. Casey Miller and Kate Swift, *The Handbook of Nonsexist Writing* (New York: Lippincott and Crowell, 1980), p. 36.

63. Baron, *Grammar and Gender*, p. 189.

64. Henley, "This New Species," p. 6.

65. Ibid., p. 8.

66. Baron, *Grammar and Gender*, p. 175.

67. National Education Association, *Today's Education*, annual publication of the National Education Association, 1982–1986/1987.

68. Baron, *Grammar and Gender*, p. 177.

69. Quoted by Martyna in "Beyond the He/Man Approach," p. 28.

70. Frederick J. Newmeyer, *The Politics of Linguistics* (Chicago: University of Chicago Press, 1986), p. 110.

71. Michael J. Schneider and Karen A. Foss, "Thought, Sex, and Language: The Sapir-Whorf Hypothesis in the American Woman's Movement," *ORWAC Bulletin* 1 (Spring 1977): 2.

72. Francine Wattman Frank and Paula A. Treichler, *Language, Gender, and Professional Writing* (New York: The Modern Language Association of America, 1989), p. 146.

73. Ibid., p. 149.

74. Ibid., p. 153.

75. Maija S. Blaubergs, "Changing the Sexist Language: The Theory behind the Practice," *Pychology of Women Quarterly* 2 (Spring 1978): 254–255.

76. Ann Snitow, "Pages from a Gender Diary," *Dissent*, Spring 1989, p. 206.

77. Ibid., p. 206.

78. Frank and Treichler, *Language*, p. 123.

79. Ibid., pp. 123–124.

80. Ibid., p. 129.

81. Ibid., p. 133.

82. Morton Benson, "A Note on the Elimination of Sexism in Dictionaries," *Women and Language* 13 no. 1 (Fall 1990).

83. Ibid., p. 51.

84. Garland Cannon and Susan Roberson, "Sexism in Present-Day English: Is It Diminishing?" *Word* 36 (April 1985): 29, 33.

85. Ibid., p. 33.

86. Richard Bernstein, "Nonsexist Dictionary Spells Out Rudeness," *New York Times*, June 11, 1991, p. C13.

87. Ibid., p. C18.

88. Miller and Swift, *Handbook*.

89. Cheris Kramarae and Paula A. Treichler, *A Feminist Dictionary* (London: Pandora Press, 1985).

90. Rosalie Maggio, *Nonsexist Word Finder: A Dictionary of Gender-Free Usage* (Phoenix: The Oryx Press, 1987), p. 165.

91. Mary Ellen Capek, ed. *A Women's Thesaurus: An Index of Language Used to Describe and Locate Information by and about Women* (New York: Harper & Row, 1987).

92. Ibid., p. xiii.

93. Miller and Swift, *Handbook*, pp. 29–30.

9

Women and Risk

Regina H. Kenen

THE PROBLEM

Increasingly, women are faced with evaluating new risks and hazards in various aspects of their lives.[1]

St. Gabriel, Louisiana: Kay Gaudet, the village pharmacist, started keeping her list one year ago. The first name on it was Peggy, her younger sister. The next nine were friends and neighbors. All had been pregnant about the same time, but there were no babies to show for it only the private agony of miscarriage.... Was it coincidence? How many other women in St. Gabriel, population 2,100, had suffered similar fates?... Today, the names total 63. St. Gabriel lies along an 85-mile industrial corridor where about one-fifth of America's petrochemicals are produced. ... The air, ground and water along this corridor are so full of carcinogens, mutagens, and embryotoxins that an environmental health specialist defined living there as "a massive human experiment," the state attorney general called the pollution "a modern form of barbarism," and a chemical union leader now refers to it as "the national sacrifice area."[2]

These risks can range from exposure to toxics in the environment and the workplace, to the chance of contracting AIDS or a sexually transmitted disease, to the choice of accepting a given medical intervention—for example, cesarean section, hysterectomy, hormone replacement therapy. As women's life-styles become more similar to those of men, they begin to face risks that were formerly thought of as mainly male risks. For example, lung cancer overtook breast cancer as the leading cancer killer of women in the late 1980s and the trend is expected to continue.[3] The basic question in trying to deal with these risks and hazards is: How do you make a decision on a course of action in a world of uncertainty where answers are given in terms of probability, and the evidence on which the probability is based is usually incomplete?

The incorporation of a wide variety of new technologies into daily life further exacerbates the difficulty in arriving at a well-thought-out decision regarding which risks to accept and which risks to try to eliminate or reduce. Technological advances have changed women's tasks in many ways over the years. These advances have been improvements in terms of efficiency and productivity, but in terms of possible adverse effects on health, they have been mixed blessings.[4] The more indirect effects of technology pose even greater risks to both the health and integrity of women. Women, too frequently, become "the object" of technological intervention;[5] and to further complicate matters, social class can become an ingredient in unstated policies toward the use of health-related technology. Sometimes those who are most at risk get the least care and vice-versa.[6] Furthermore, the courts are increasingly inserting themselves into women's reproductive lives, particularly those women who are poor, uneducated, and on welfare. A number of court-ordered cesarean sections and intrauterine procedures have been documented.[7] These intrusions, probably constitutionally illegal, have also been based on insufficient medical knowledge.[8]

This interventionist trend by the legal system is very worrisome. More and more women are likely to become victims of such a misplaced sense of righteousness until women gain enough power to gain their rightful place in the social process that leads to negotiation of acceptable risks. They need to make critical comparisons of the various claims as to what constitutes a risk when their own lives and those of their loved ones are at stake. How are women going to accomplish this vital, but somewhat daunting, task?

1. By understanding value claims and power dimensions. As women become more self-confident about the validity of their knowledge base and begin to contest the biases of those in authority, the present power imbalance will begin to shift.

2. By learning how to evaluate risks. As women learn to understand probability, become alert to the common heuristic traps, and become comfortable about living with uncertainty, they will be better able to separate genuine high risks from those blown out of proportion by the media or vested interests.

3. By deciding what to do. As women learn how to be more effective in playing the power game and become more knowledgable in their understanding of risks and hazards, they will be able to choose the paths toward change that they feel are most appropriate to their own situations.

UNDERSTANDING VALUE CLAIMS AND POWER DIMENSIONS

Women need to understand that their own perceptions of risk, as well as those of other consumer and citizen groups, may differ from those of scientists, physicians, governmental regulatory agencies, and corporations. They must also learn that their perceptions are just as valid as those of more powerful groups. Groups vary in the amount of clout they have, not only in decision-making but in defining their perspectives as legitimate and in their ability to enforce their judgments. Women suffer from both an information gap and a power gap. This is gradually changing as women become more knowledgeable and more vocal.

For example, as recently as 1990, women were excluded from participation in most research protocols for new drugs. Pressure from women's groups, among others, persuaded researchers to begin to include women in their study designs and now the National Institute for Health is beginning to consider women's health issues as a priority item for study.

Furthermore, women tend to be seen as reproductive vessels whether they intend to procreate or not. If woman is vessel and fetus is person, it does not take a genius to determine whose rights will be subjugated. This can be seen in companies' Fetal Protection Policies—preventing fertile women from working in certain hazardous jobs. Many major corporations have such policies. The *United Auto Workers vs. Johnson Controls* case involving the effect of lead exposure on a potential fetus was the most recent *cause célèbre*. Both the lower court and the appellate court upheld the company's fetal protection policy forbidding *all women of childbearing age* (with the ludicrous upper limit of 70 years old) to work in certain jobs involving lead, despite the fact that government standards provided the same lead safeguards for men and women.[9]

No one denies that high lead levels in pregnant women's blood or tissues can harm their fetuses. But the majority of the justices on the Court of Appeals for the Seventh Circuit "ignored important studies of men with high lead exposures, showing adverse effects on their sperm as well as high rates of birth defects among their children."[10] Again, women were not given credit for being able to take care of their lives and their bodies. This case was brought to the United States Supreme Court and in March 1991 the Supreme Court ruled in favor of the women.

UAW vs. Johnson Controls is an extremely important case as both jobs in other industries and women workers' rights are at stake. These rights are based on Title VII of the Civil Rights Act of 1964, barring discrimination on the basis of sex, and the 1978 Pregnancy Discrimination Act, barring discrimination on the basis of pregnancy.

The *Johnson Controls* case is also a clash of rights on another dimension—that of defining risk. Who has the right to decide what is an acceptable occupational risk, the woman or the employer? But even in victory, some of the press and media commentators emphasize that women have now gained the opportunity to put themselves, along with men, in danger. This implies that women are not very wise in their judgments. The headline on page 1 of the March 21, 1991, edition of the *New York Times* states "COURT BACKS RIGHT OF WOMEN TO JOBS WITH HEALTH RISKS." Yet the broad coalition of health groups, women's groups, and women's rights groups that challenged the fetal protection policy of the country's largest manufacturer of automobile batteries ultimately want to obtain healthier workplaces for both women and men. By excluding fertile women not only are the majority of women employees prevented from attaining high-paying jobs, but the impression is left that the workplace is safe for all the other workers. This is not true. Risks are just denied, not reduced or eliminated.

Risk Communication

Perceptions of risk come from human experience. Obviously, Johnson Controls frames risks differently than the women who work there. Because women's place in society differs from men's, their perceptions of risk, their willingness to take certain risks and to avoid others may also differ. The concept of risk as a social process is based on the premise that "it is *people*, and not independent facts, who constrain the way concepts are framed, questions posed, and research goals set."[11] Both risk evaluation and risk communication are part of a social process within a cultural context.[12]

Because women wield so little power on both individual and societal levels, the senders of the risk messages (usually scientists, physicians, or government regulators) have neglected to include the women message receivers as an integral part of the social process. Scientists and governmental regulatory agencies do not understand women's underlying concerns and worries, or dismiss them as irrational. They operate from a scientific perspective and believe that all women need to understand in order to make "proper" risk judgments are the ideas of randomness, probability, and sample size. The scientists and officials see it as their job to teach women these basics—in other words to make an uninformed or misinformed public informed. Once they are informed, women are expected to make the decisions that the officials consider to be rational based on the regulators' own risk-benefit models. When women do not think or act according to these preconceived assumptions, the "risk assessors" tear their hair out in horror, condemning women for their irrational and hysterical behavior.

But women often have different concerns and agendas than scientists, businessmen, or governmental regulators. For example, pregnant workers frequently worry about risks of possible harm to their fetuses from hazards in the workplace. Risk-taking choices are not based only on some rational calculations of costs and benefits. Multiplying severity of the risk and probability is a necessary, but not sufficient, condition upon which to base a decision. Choices are shaped by what women see on television or read about in magazines and newspapers, what other people have experienced and women's own experiences with risk-taking.

When I took x-rays, I was afraid of the scatter radiation (during my pregnancy). We tried to work it out that the other girl would take more of the x-rays. Sometimes it worked. Sometimes it did not.

Rosie, dental assistant

During my pregnancy, I just didn't deal with the computer at all. If I had a lookup, I would get someone else to do it for me. I felt I didn't even want to be around the radiation in the area, just knowing it was inside of the machine was enough for me.

Dori, clerk

Women do not want to be the guinea pigs if insufficient testing is done before a chemical is allowed on the market, or to find out at some later date that the scientists' currently acceptable statistical criteria for exposure was erroneous. Even more important, women workers are concerned about the thousands of chemicals already available that either have not been tested at all or have been inadequately tested.

They had masks, but they didn't give them to you. Sometimes they didn't even have the masks, so you would breathe in this stuff the whole night.

Cary, production line worker

Scientists strive to maintain the integrity of their professional disciplines and require a high standard of proof. They want to be 95 or 99 percent sure that their conclusion is not due to chance alone before they will state that a given substance does or does not cause harm. (This is technically known as statistical significance.) Obtaining this high level of proof depends on the number of individuals in the study, the strength of the toxic substance, the amount of exposure to the substance, the number of other factors that might cause the harmful effect, and the length of time the people are studied. This information may take many years to obtain.

Once scientists have studied a hazard and identified its impact, the regulatory agencies have to make a policy decision: whether to ban that substance entirely or determine an acceptable risk level. Public health agencies also have to determine whether to undertake a health promotion campaign, and if so, they need to decide who is the target population and what kind of campaign will lead to behavior change. Many past efforts have increased knowledge but did not influence behavior. For example, many young women have ignored the quit-smoking campaigns. They understand the association between smoking and disease, but they also know that it takes years of smoking for serious complaints to develop. They may believe that they have plenty of time to quit or that a cure will be found by the time they are likely to develop lung cancer.

Business interests also want to "go slow" because, as in the case of cigarettes, reduction in consumption means reduction in profits. When it comes to cleaning up toxic hazards in the workplace, or toxic dumpsites in the community, corporations often argue that the high cost of the required improvements will force them to close their plants.

Business support risk-benefit analyses that claim to provide objective ways to measure expected hazards against expected benefits of technology. They argue that regulatory agencies can set politically neutral decisions based on this risk analysis data combined with data on workplace experience. Frequently, business representatives deny that there are involuntary risks. Management argues that all it has to do is explain the risks and then people can decide either to voluntarily take the risks or avoid them. They point out that many people are willing to undertake risks if they are paid enough.

This is a flawed argument. Workers who are bearing the risks are in a weaker power situation than companies imposing the risks. If women need money urgently, job loss or reduction in take-home pay may be too high a price to pay for a reduction in health hazards. Women workers are frequently reluctant to talk about health problems for fear of losing their jobs. Based on previous experience they have little faith in management's desire or efforts to minimize health hazards. Some women might be willing to accept hazard pay to improve the financial security of their families under certain circumstances, but this trade-off is a "no win" solution and if a woman is pregnant, this is certainly not a viable option.

Governmental regulatory agencies are often caught in a squeeze. They are pressured by the business and scientific communities that, for different reasons, advocate a cautious approach, and by pressures from workers and consumers who demand immediate action. Each side uses research studies in the persuasion effort. Perhaps a new way of looking at evidence of health hazards is needed during the interim period when more conclusive proof is not yet available. The scientific standard of making no recommendation unless there is at least 95 percent certainty that a given substance is harmful may be too stringent a criterion to use when possible severe health damage is at issue. The standard used in evaluating scientific research may not be appropriate when a woman is trying to protect her own well-being and that of her family.

Respecting and answering women's concerns instead of trying to dismiss them is a better approach. Women who are primarily homemakers and those who work outside the home may have different priorities and preferences, but they have the same basic concerns: protecting themselves, their pregnancies, and their loved ones from unnecessary harm. Women expect the "experts" to listen to them if they are expected to listen to the "experts."

What women want the experts to hear is the importance in the risk evaluation equation of many more facets than just mortality statistics. Listed below are some of the other characteristics influencing individuals' attitudes toward risks and hazards that are neglected in statistical summaries presented by scientists and regulatory agencies:

1. voluntariness

2. controllability

3. familiarity

4. immediacy of consequences

5. threat to future generations

6. ease of reducing risk

7. fairness in the distribution of risk

8. an indication of the probability and magnitude of extreme losses (people are worried about the worst-case scenario)

9. trust and recognition that both experts and laypeople have something important to contribute.[13]

Risk assessors and risk communicators are just beginning to realize that how people perceive risks determines how they react to them. Still too often, risk presenters seem to be experts trained to ignore feelings. Then the public gets angry, yells louder, and listens less because it is frustrated and enraged by its powerlessness. People seem to learn more and assess and process information more efficiently when they exert some real control over the ultimate decision—for example, presenting women at possible risk from exposure to a workplace hazard with a list of alternatives and a procedure for judging them.[14]

Hazard and Outrage

Though risk and hazard issues are framed as being objective and scientific, the power of vested interest groups (usually male, corporate, or scientific) and value systems (positivist-science) shapes how risk is estimated and evaluated. In addition, the power of the mass media to promote a social agenda greatly influences the public's perceptions of what is a hazard, how great the risk is, and what should be done about it. As Peter Sandman, director of the Environmental Communication Research Program at Rutgers University, so pithily puts it, there is hazard and there is outrage. Hazard is what risk assessments are designed to estimate. Outrage is everything else that goes into laypeople's risk perceptions. And they are not always the same.[15]

The public tends to dichotomize risk. Either the risk is very frightening, in which case the response is some mix of fear, anger, panic, and paralysis: or the risk is dismissed as trivial, in which case the response is apathy.

Scientists and managers who study risk for a living are consistently irritated that the public seems to worry about the "wrong" risks—which is often true if you take mortality statistics as your standard. But rather than see this as a perceptual distortion on the part of the public, it is more useful and more accurate to see it as an oversimplification on the part of the scientists and managers.[16]

Because of miscommunication between those explaining risks and those facing risks, the risk communication process itself often plays a larger role than the hazard in creating outrage.

LEARNING HOW TO EVALUATE RISKS IN AN UNCERTAIN WORLD

While we like to think in terms of certainty, the reality is that we live with uncertainty, which affects not only how we live our lives but how much control we feel we have. On a daily basis, the lives of poor, minority women are full of uncertainty as well as specific risks and hazards. Those who are more affluent and worry about the polluted environment or the "technological fix" also make decisions within a framework of uncertainty because final answers are not yet available and conflicting evidence abounds.

Those warnings to remain indoors on smoggy summer days might not always be such great advice. A fragmentary but growing body of evidence being collected by Government agencies, scientists and private industry indicates that indoor air pollution can often be as dangerous to health as polluted outdoor air—and sometimes more so.[17]

New warnings about radon in homes, which Federal officials said last month may cause 5,000 to 20,000 lung cancer deaths a year, have touched off a row among scientists over the true extent of the hazard.

Several points, however, are in dispute: What is the probable cancer risk at a given level of radon exposure? How many houses have dangerous indoor radon concentrations? Above what concentration should citizens be urged to take corrective action?[18]

Media Messages

How do people attempt to make sense out of what sometimes seems like chaos? Here the media plays an important role as most of the public obtains its information from newspapers, magazines, and television. People often assume these reports to be more accurate than they actually are, possibly because they are seeking firm answers. But the media are not always accurate. Scary headlines sell newspapers, sources of advertising revenue color interpretations, and the media frequently set their own social or political agendas.

There are certain biases in media reporting. For example, initial stories receive far more coverage than follow-up stories. Sometimes a newspaper article cites a substance as causing a specific illness or gives an exposure a clean bill of health and a later story contradicts the original. Only a few people, however, are aware of this additional report, as the follow-up is often buried in the back pages. Newspapers, magazines, and television need to attract large audiences in order to survive financially. Increasing circulation and ratings are the name of the game.

The media overreport dramatic events involving a large number of injuries and fatalities that occur at one time because these stories attract readers and viewers. The more common everyday risks and hazards causing an equivalent or even larger number of diseases, injuries, or premature deaths over a longer period of time do not get equal coverage. They may be of more concern to society, but they are not news.

Furthermore, reporters write under deadlines. Frequently, it is faster for them to obtain information from government offices or corporations that have community relations departments than to track down the individuals exposed to toxic substances and obtain their sides of the stories. Sometimes, important information contradicting the highly publicized version can only be found in the newsletters of public interest and women's groups. Mainstream newspapers and magazines appear on every newsstand. The advocacy press is harder to find.

The media also take editorial positions and feature stories dealing with those social issues and perspectives supporting their viewpoints. Both sides of issues are usually presented, but one side gets more coverage and is highlighted. Women reading about these suspected hazards can become adept at detecting less than even-handed coverage when they are sifting and evaluating what they read. If they are extremely concerned about a specific hazard, they will probably have to do further investigation. They should do this before becoming overly worried or making a hasty decision. Listed below are some questions to pursue:

What sources were used?

1. Government agencies
2. Businesses and corporations
3. Labor groups
4. Academic scientists
5. Public interest groups
6. Women's groups

Was the information cross-checked with other sources?

Was just one perspective presented?

How many and whose studies was the article based on?

Who were the studies conducted on—humans or animals?

Are you told in the article who funded the study?

Does the article describe weaknesses of the study and tell you whether more research is needed before the findings should be acted upon?

Does the article tell where you can obtain a copy of the original scientific report?[19]

The Omnipresence of Uncertainty

Living in a world of uncertainty, women have several choices. They can shove their heads in the sand and ignore risks and hazards or refuse to make any choices at all. Since everything is harmful, why bother? The better option is to try to judge risks and hazards, even though uncertainty is the normal state of affairs. This task is difficult and few can do it well because most people lack the necessary information, skills, and training. It is like trying to do a jigsaw puzzle when only a few pieces are available and there is no copy of the picture. Many women do not have the patience and give up in frustration. They pretend that nothing bad will happen. Others claim that it has already happened, so it is too late to do anything about it. Yet underneath this facade, women are worried and would like to reduce their risks.[20]

The extent of uncertainty involved in evaluating risks and hazards may make it seem like an impossible task, but research on the accuracy of public perceptions of health risks shows that people have a surprisingly good idea of the relative frequency of most causes of death, even though their knowledge about the risks may not be precise. Because of the complexities involved and the overload of things to be concerned about, people tend to use short-cuts—called heuristics—to come to a conclusion. They are very helpful, and that is why they are used so frequently. Sometimes, however, dependence on them can cause serious errors of judgment.[21] In order to make better decisions, it is important to be alert to the fallacious reasoning that can be involved.

Heuristics

Heuristics is the fancy name given to general, inferential rules used by people to make complicated decisions simpler—for example, assuming that hazards that are frequently talked about are the most important to do something about. Even statisticians and scientists when presented with risks in complex situations beyond their field of expertise use these "lay" heuristics to evaluate the situation. In most cases they are approximately accurate. But, at times, they lead to large and persistent biases with serious implications for social policy.

People view the world as deterministic, not probablistic, and schools do not teach children to learn judgment and decision strategies for dealing with a probablistic world. Individuals find this upsetting. In their minds, certainty equals security and uncertainty equals fear. Two common heuristics—representativeness and availability—are used that account for a considerable amount of errors in judgment and women need to be aware of them. By becoming informed and being able to recognize when they are falling into these "heuristic traps," women can differentiate between serious and frequent exposure to hazards and those exposures that should not be included in that category.

Representativeness depends on the similarity of the object, or event, being evaluated to a stereotype regardless of the actual probabilities. For example, people will judge a studious-looking stranger to be a librarian, rather than a farmer, even though the number of farmers is much larger than the number of librarians. Individuals react more to stereotypes than they do to the actual number of people in given occupations (base rates).

The recency of a hazard, or the frequency with which a type of hazard has had media coverage makes it seem more severe—that is, available. If something is easier to recall, it seems more hazardous than something more difficult to remember. Biased newspaper coverage of dramatic events leads to inaccurate perception and judgment. Other more serious hazards may fall into an "out of sight, out of mind" mode of thinking.[22]

Women (and men) who have not been trained to be wary have great confidence in judgments based on heuristics. They tend to overestimate the hazards that receive a great deal of media coverage and underestimate their own vulnerability.[23] Yet despite these tendencies, individuals are likely to improve their risk-estimating capabilities if presented with clear and accurate information.[24]

Once women have become alerted to the heuristic biases and have collected the information they feel is needed to make a decision, the decision they make depends on their value systems and their opportunities. Experts can only provide information and a perspective, and their perspective may be different than that of those who have to live with their decisions. What is most upsetting, though, is that hazards are often hidden. It is not until someone suffers the ill effect, whether it is a pelvic inflammatory disease from an intrauterine device or an allergic reaction to indoor air pollution, that other women learn that they too may be at risk.

This list gives an idea about how many areas of women's lives involve evaluations of hazards and estimations of risks.

A. Reproduction
   1. Infertility
   2. Birth control

    3. Birthing options (use of electronic-fetal monitor, C-sections, home births)

    4. Hysterectomies

    5. Hormone replacement therapy

B. Families

    1. Breast feeding in a polluted environment

    2. Food (nutritional content, additives, pesticides)

    3. Vaccinations

    4. Older, severely ill, parents—medical interventions

C. Lifestyle

    1. Food—dieting and binging

    2. Exercise

    3. Drug and alcohol use

    4. Sexual practices and partners

D. Home

    1. House cleaning product safety

    2. Radon and asbestos

    3. Lawn and tree care

E. Work

    1. VDT use

    2. Indoor air pollution

    3. Toxic exposure

F. Community

    1. Garbage disposal

    2. Clean air and water

    3. Toxic dumpsites

What Makes Something a Hazard and How Is It Measured?

Women should be clear about the difference between a hazard and a risk (in the statistical sense) before they become embroiled in an "outrage" controversy. While hazards and risks are often used interchangeably, they really are different concepts. Usually, the term "hazard" refers to the substance, condition, or behavior that is suspected of causing harm. First scientists identify a hazard. Then they identify the relationship between exposure to the hazard and its unhealthy effect on humans.

"Risk" refers to the probability of harm arising from the individual's exposure to a hazard, For example, having unprotected sex with an intravenous drug user with AIDS poses a hazard for a woman. The risk is the likelihood, or probability, of her contracting AIDS as a result of that particular exposure. Epidemiologists attempt to ascertain the number of people suffering ill effects and whether particular groups are at greater risk. Exposure is an important aspect to consider because, with certain chemical substances and biological or physical agents, people may be at risk only if they are subjected to high exposures or lower exposures over a long period of time.

Risks are not only associated with exposures to particular chemical substances, or biological or physical agents. Just living is a risky business. Let us look at childbirth, a point in life that has always been associated with risk, though for middle-class women this risk is now minimal. A short walk through 18th- and 19th-century cemeteries poignantly attests to that fact. Childbirth always has and always will bear some degree of risk to mother or fetus. Because of this, the introduction of new technology under the guise of reducing risk is rarely questioned and can be rapidly disseminated without being adequately studied or evaluated.

The Electronic Fetal Monitor

If you have given birth in an American hospital during the past fifteen years, you are probably familiar with the electronic fetal monitor. More than half of the births in the United States in the last decade involved the use of an electronic monitor.[25] The women at time of delivery were either monitored externally, with ultrasound and pressure-recording equipment attached around their abdomens, or internally, with electrodes attached to the fetus' scalp, and a pressure instrument placed in the uterus. Eight clinical trials have shown no indication that the use of either of these monitors improves the health of the babies. The monitors have, however, increased the number of unnecessary cesarean sections due to "false positives"—a reading showing fetal distress when there is none.[26]

Why was the use of the monitors so widespread and why are they still being used so prevalently? Were they scientifically tested on a large sample of pregnant women and the outcome contrasted with a control group before they became widely used? No! Now that research studies show no benefit from the monitors, will their use be halted? Probably not! Why not? Economics plays a part. There is a nursing shortage; it would be difficult to replace all these machines with nurses. Also, tremendous investments have been made in these machines, and hospitals need to get a return on their investments. Hospital prestige is also at stake. It is difficult to downgrade a unit from a higher technological level to a lower one, especially when the patient population has been indoctrinated into believing that advanced technology is the equivalent of better health care. Last, but not least, there is the specter of medical malpractice suits.

Even if the obstetrics group stops recommending the use of electronic monitoring, it may be risky to drop the technology, since most medical malpractice lawsuits turn on the question of whether the doctor followed the usual local practices. And obstetricians are aware that parents whose babies are born with a serious problem are apt to file malpractice suits while it is unlikely that doctors will be sued for ordering unnecessary monitoring or questionable Caesareans.

Technologies sort of appear abruptly, spread widely and then don't fade away very fast even if later research doesn't show them to be effective.[27]

In part, ... this is because there is a sales force marketing the machines, and a training process that makes doctors comfortable using them—but no counterbalancing force "unselling" machines, or retraining doctors to work without them.[28]

One counterbalancing force attacking the use of electronic fetal monitors has been the women's health movement. Advocates have been quite successful in showing that risk of harm to mother and baby is not greater for natural childbirth in hospitals, birthing centers, or even at home if proper prenatal and birthing health care is given.[29] While natural childbirth has made great strides over the past two decades, affecting the way birthing is viewed in the United States, birth technology, while maimed, still reigns.

Medical control over normal pregnancies is still a major issue. Currently, in the United States, birth is rarely a family event where the woman due to deliver can walk around, do her chores, eat, or lie in whatever position is more comfortable for her. In the medical model, she has to adhere to a hospital's schedule, lie flat on her back tied to an electronic fetal monitor, be fed intravenously, and be given anesthesia. The prone position with feet in stirrups, typical of most hospital deliveries, is convenient for the doctor. He doesn't hurt his back (when this became common practice the doctor was usually a "he"), while the woman has to deliver against the force of gravity.

Ironically, in addition to the studies showing no advantage of using the fetal monitor, one study involving premature babies, the group the monitor was originally designed for, showed a poorer outcome for those "preemies" monitored electronically than for those monitored with a stethoscope. At eighteen months of age, 20 percent of the surviving infants electronically monitored were diagnosed as having cerebral palsy, compared with 8 percent of those checked with a stethoscope.[30] The debate over the electronic fetal monitor illustrates the classic dilemma for women: uncertainty is involved, the outcome is exceedingly important, and professional opinion is skewed in favor of the technology.

What Risk Should Women Take?

Society assigns women primary responsibility for the general well-being of their families. In order to alleviate their uncertainties and fears, women need to learn how to rank hazards they face in terms of importance and decide which ones they are going to try to do something about and in what order. Without some basis for judgment, hazards they choose to avoid may not be those that do the most harm. They need to learn how to make a reasonable judgment as to which of their fears are well-founded and which are not.

Women need to become chronic question askers. Despite the gaps in available information, they can better decide how risk averse they want to be. Here are some questions that women should ask. The first set of questions deals with the issue of whether or not a specific substance or agent is considered a hazard.

1. Determine whether an agent or substance is harmful to your health?
    A. Can it damage specific organs of the body?
    B. Can it cause cancer?
    C. Can it cause a mutation or damage an embryo or fetus?
2. If it is harmful, how harmful is it?
3. If it is harmful, what is the likelihood that you are exposed to it?
4. Who may be particularly at risk?
    A. Individuals working in certain occupations
    B. Individuals living in certain communities
    C. Children
    D. Men and women contemplating having a child
    E. Pregnant women and fetuses
5. What kind of evidence was the risk assessment based on and how strong is it?
6. What were the sources of information on which the estimates were based?
7. Upon what assumptions are the estimates based and how much uncertainty is there about these estimations?
8. How do regulatory agencies evaluate the low risk of a severe hazard as compared with a high risk of a moderate hazard when making rulings?[31]

The second set of questions is aimed at helping assess whether an individual woman is at risk from being harmed from an exposure to a potential hazard.

Information Needed
1. Find out what substances and agents you are exposed to at home, in the workplace, and in the community.
2. What kind of health problems can be caused by these substances?
3. Do you breathe (inhale), swallow (ingest) or have skin contact with these substances?

4. How long have you been exposed to these substances—minutes, hours, days, months, years? Is the exposure continuous or occasional (sporadic)?

5. How high a dosage of the substance have you been exposed to?[32]

RISKS AND HAZARDS: SOME WAYS TO IMPROVE RISK COMMUNICATION

What could Kay Gaudet, the village pharmacist, do to find out why so many women in her town had miscarriages, or what can any woman do when concerned about risks and hazards in her life? In addition to asking specific questions, women can collect information, seek out organizational resources, press for research into areas of concern, and (if necessary) conduct their own research, organize themselves, and form coalitions in order to reduce known and suspected risks. These are major tasks. Most women do not have the time or inclination to undertake a major project, but they can contribute their small part. If every woman would question more, accept less on face value, judge risk communicators on their openness, their willingness to consider women's concerns and priorities, and their ability to say "I don't know" how much risk is involved rather than give false assurances, then these many small steps will have a large impact.

Trust in the accuracy of information presented is of prime importance. If trust and credibility are not ingredients, then the supposedly scientific information is suspect. Women conducting "barefoot" epidemiology (the nickname for investigations carried out by people who have been personally affected by an occupational or environmental hazard but who do not have formal epidemiological and statistical training) at Love Canal or Worcester, Massachusetts, dramatically demonstrated the validity of their suspicions.[33]

The job of risk communicator is not only to present information, but to know when to alert and when to reassure. People have been lied to so often that this latter task is nearly impossible because reassurance is no longer believed. Both women and providers of health information need to be willing to work together. This requires some "give" on both sides.

Suggestions have been made to improve communications for both senders and receivers, experts and individuals. These are particularly germane to issues of concern to women.[34] Risk communicators should:

1. Use simple, clear, and nontechnical language.

2. Provide examples and anecdotes to clarify the technical risk data they provide.

3. Acknowledge and respond to the emotions expressed by women—anger, fear, anxiety, helplessness, outrage—as being legitimate.

4. Acknowledge and respond to the concerns that women feel are important.

5. Discuss what action is being taken, what can and cannot be done, and the reasons behind these decisions.

6. Outline a procedure for monitoring risks and designating people who are accountable for the safety decisions.

Experts need to:

1. Consider ways in which human errors can affect technological systems.
2. Be aware of their overconfidence in current scientific knowledge, current risk assessments, and debatable assumptions in risk models.
3. Be more alert in detecting chronic, cumulative effects.
4. Anticipate human neglect or error in adhering to safety measures.
5. Anticipate failures that simultaneously damage systems that are designed to be independent.
6. Be more aware of their own cognitive limitations and objective data.
7. Learn what might bias judging risks.
8. Be more open to new evidence offered by business, government, and scientists. Previous misinformation from these sources should engender skepticism but not a closed mind.

There are sources of information other than the mainstream media. Women can check with large newsdealers in their communities and libraries about consumer-oriented, public-interest publications. These have their own biases—even women's and consumer's groups have their organizational and political agendas. But, at least, they are usually biased in favor of the consumer. It is wise to read articles about a potential risk that you are worried about—for example, a proposed garbage incinerator in the community, a medical procedure, or even use of a garden pesticide—in a wide range of publications in order to find out whether there is agreement in interpretation of the risk involved and the reasons behind the differences of opinion.

The National Women's Health Network in Washington, DC, is an excellent source of material reflecting the positions of the women's health movement. *Turning Things Around: A Women's Occupational and Environmental Health Resource Guide*, published by the Network, is a very useful book that lists over 400 resource organizations nationwide that can be contacted for further occupational and environmental health information. It can be bought for $9.95 from NWHN, 1325 G St., NW, Washington, DC 20005.

Women are now active in the fields of environmental, occupational, and reproductive health, exerting "woman power" and documenting women's perspectives with evidence. Furthermore, legal challenges have been made on behalf of women. The Women's Rights Project and the Women's Reproductive Rights Project of the American Civil Liberties Union have been on the forefront of this effort.

Women in the fields of environmental and occupational health and reproductive technology intend to participate actively at all stages of the risk-assessment and decision-making process. They do not consider themselves "outsiders" to the process, but rather as "insiders" because they are frequently the risk-bearers. More important, they view themselves as "insiders" who have been unethically disenfranchised and are seeking justice.

Women activists seldom accept a tool concept of technology, a concept more congenial to men. They do not see technology as being neutral, or risk as being an abstract concept. Instead they view technology as a way of life, social in origin and character. Women activists realize that participation is essential in the societal decision-making process on technology and risk. Those promoting the "technology as neutral" concept acknowledge their participation in the decision-making process, but insist that their involvement is separate from the "objective" assessment of risk.[35]

Women who support the sociocultural approach to "risk" do not denigrate the importance of scientific criteria and economic analysis. They do, however, denigrate the attempt to make statistical probability the sole basis of social acceptability. Societal questions cannot be answered by science alone. Women need to assess how to critically compare competing claims as to what constitutes a risk when their own lives are at stake. They must participate in the social process involved in the negotiating of acceptable risks. To do this, it is often helpful to form coalitions with other groups that are also interested in finding out more about a specific risk or reducing or limiting the risk. COSH (Committees for Occupational Safety and Health) and PIRGs (Public Interest Research Groups) located in many states might be useful allies. Environmental groups such as the Natural Resource Defense Council or citizen groups such as Public Citizen can also be helpful partners. Feminist health professionals and nurse midwives have also had considerable experience in fighting for power sharing.

Influencing legislators at a local, state, or national level is another way women's vices can be heard when controversial bills concerning risks and hazards are on the agenda. Some states have Women's Bureaus, which provide guidance to novices attempting to lobby on issues benefiting women. They advise that the lobbyists be extremely well-informed, knowing more than anyone else about the pertinent issues involved. Equally important is becoming politically astute—being tuned into the political climate and ascertaining what interest of the legislator is to be tapped.

To further buttress their power-sharing approach, women can use a theoretical formulation developed by Funtowicz and Ravetz[36] to support women's inclusion in "risk decision-making." These theorists distinguish a factual dimension and a value dimension in policy-related science issues. When both dimensions are not controversial, a technological solution will usually suffice. When both are contested, the approach takes the form of a dialogue between concerned groups in society on the technical and value issues. Women as risk bearers and risk decision-makers for themselves, and frequently for their families, need to demand a vital role in this societal dialogue. Women are not alone in demanding a role in deciding how risks will be assessed and managed. Workers and citizen groups are also fighting for the right to be informed about the risks they face and even to attack the legitimacy of the technologies.

It is to be hoped that, in the future, women will be treated as equal partners in the risk-evaluation dialogue and their viewpoints will be taken more seriously. Only then can they, together with scientists, regulatory officials, business leaders, physicians, and other members of the public, work together as part of an evolving social contract to make the world a safer place for all.

NOTES

1. This is true for men as well. The main difference is that men usually judge the risks for women, and they may not view them the same way.

2. From the *Washington Post*, December 1987, as quoted in National Women's Health Network, *Turning Things Around: A Women's Occupational and Environmental Health Resource Guide* (Washington, DC: NWHN, 1990), p. 44.

3. Nadine Brozan, *New York Times*, November 14, 1986, p. A18.

4. Women have gone from cooking over hand-stoked fires to popping food into microwave ovens; from doing "piece work" at home to working in a microchip processing facility; from using manure in the family vegetable garden to using chemical fertilizers and pesticides.

5. The new advance, whether it be an electronic fetal monitor or a new birth control technique like Norplant, is usually presented as an unmitigated "good." The rare woman who questions its efficacy, or refuses to use it, is considered at best an oddity, at worst, mentally unstable.

6. Marsha Hurst and Pamela Summey, "Childbirth and Social Class: The Case of Cesarean Delivery," *Social Science and Medicine* 18 (1984): 621–631. Hurst and Summey studied cesarean deliveries and showed that they followed the pattern for medical care in general: those who are most at risk get the least care and vice-versa.

An earlier British study also found that obstetrical care, like other kinds of medical care, varied inversely with the actual need for that care. See Tim Chard and Martin Richards, "Lessons for the Future," in *Benefits and Hazards of the New Obstetrics*, ed. Tim Chard and Martin Richards (Philadelphia: Lippincott, 1977).

7. A report in the *New England Journal of Medicine* on the incidence of court-ordered obstetrical procedures, including forced cesarean sections and intrauterine transfusions, showed that 81 percent of the women were black, Hispanic, or Asian and none were private patients. Veronika Kolder, Janet Gallagher, and Michael Parsons, "Court-Ordered Obstetrical Interventions," *New England Journal of Medicine*, May 7, 1987, pp. 1192–1196.

Because medical judgment, not medical certainty, is involved, in at least six cases where requests were made to have a judge order surgery, the women gave birth vaginally to healthy children. Janet Gallagher, "Fetus as Patient," in *Reproductive Laws for the 1990s*, ed. Sherill Cohen and Nadine Taub (Clifton, NJ: Humana Press, 1989).

8. Less than a month after the new, long-lasting, controversial birth control implant (Norplant) was approved for use in the United States in December 1990, a county judge in California, without seeking any medical advice, ordered a twenty-seven-year-old woman convicted of child abuse to use Norplant as a condition for receiving three years of probation after a one-year jail sentence. In November of the same year, a seventeen-year-old Florida girl who admitted that she smothered her newborn daughter in the hospital bathroom was given a two-year prison sentence and ordered to use birth control pills for ten years after her release. Tamar Lewin, *New York Times*, January 10, 1991, p. A20.

9. Deborah Stone, "Fetal Risks, Women's Rights: Showdown at Johnson Controls." *The American Prospect* 3, no. 1 (1990): 48.

10. Ibid.

11. Harry J. Otway and K. Thomas, "Reflections on Risk Perception and Policy," *Risk Analysis* 2 (1982): 7.

12. For further discussions about the cultural dimension of risk, see: Judith Bradbury, "The Policy Implications of Differing Concepts of Risk," *Science, Technology and Human Values* 14 (1986): 380–399; Mary Douglas, *Risk Acceptability According to the Social Sciences* (New York: Russell Sage, 1985); Sheldon Krimsky and Alonza Plough, *Environmental Hazards: Communicating Risks as a Social Process* (Dover, MA: Auburn House, 1988); James Short, Jr., "The Social Fabric at Risk: Toward the Social Transformation of Risk Analysis," *American Sociological Review* 49 (1984): 711–725.

13. Peter M. Sandman, *Explaining Environmental Risk*, a report for the Office of Toxic Substances of the U.S. Environmental Protection Agency, November 1986. Also see Peter M. Sandman, "Apathy versus Hysteria: Public Perception of Risk," in *Public Perception of Biotechnology*, ed. Lekh R. Batra and Waldemar Klassen (Bethesda, MD.: Agricultural Research Institute, 1987).

14. Sandman, *Explaining Environmental Risk*; and Sandman, "Apathy versus Hysteria."

15. Peter M. Sandman, "Hazard versus Outrage in the Public Perception of Risk," in *Effective Risk Communication*, ed. Vincent Covello, D. McCallum, and M. Pavlova (New York: Plenum, 1989).

16. Sandman, "Apathy versus Hysteria."

17. Philip Shabecoff, *New York Times*, July 14, 1985, sect. 4, p. 2.

18. Erik Eckholm, *New York Times*, September 2, 1986, p. C1.

19. Adapted from Regina Kenen, *Reproductive Hazards in the Workplace: Mending Jobs, Managing Pregnancies* (Binghamton, NY: Haworth Press, 1993).

20. Ibid.

21. For detailed discussions on how people perceive and understand risks, see Baruch Fischoff, "Managing Risk Perceptions," *Issues in Science and Technology*, Fall 1985, pp. 83–96; Baruch Fischoff, Sarah Lichtenstein, Paul Slovic, et al., *Acceptable Risk* (Cambridge: Cambridge University Press, 1981); and Billie Jo Hance, Caron Chess, and Peter M. Sandman, "Setting a Context for Explaining Risk," *Risk Analysis* 9 (1989): 113–117.

22. Amos Tversky and Daniel Kahneman, "Judgment Under Uncertainty: Heuristics and Biases," *Science* 185 (1974): 1124–1131.

23. Fischoff, "Managing Risk Perceptions"; Fischoff et al., *Acceptable Risk*; Hance, et al., "Setting a Context."

24. Sandman, *Explaining Environmental Risk.*

25. Tamar Lewin, *New York Times*, March 27, 1988, p. L24.

26. Kirkwood K. Shy, David Luthy, Forrest Bennet et al., "Effects of Electronic Fetal-Heart-Rate Monitoring," *New England Journal of Medicine* 322 (1990): 588–593.

27. Stephen Thacker, assistant director for the Center for Environmental Health and Injury for the Centers for Disease Control in Atlanta. Thacker is a critic of autonomic monitors. This quote is from an article by Tamar Lewin in the *New York Times*, March 27, 1988, p. L24.

28. Lewin, in ibid.

29. Barbara Rothman, "Midwives in Transition: The Structure of a Clinical Revolution," *Social Problems* 30 (1983): 262–270.

30. Shy et al., "Effects of Electronic Fetal-Heart-Rate Monitoring."

31. Kenen, *Reproductive Hazards.*

32. Ibid.

33. Beverly Paigen, "Children and Toxic Chemicals," *Journal of Pesticide Reform*, Summer 1986, pp. 2–5.

34. Fischoff, "Managing Risk Perceptions"; Fischoff et al., *Acceptable Risk*; Hance et al., "Setting a Context."

35. Bradbury, "The Policy Implications of Differing Concepts of Risk."

36. Silvio O. Funtowicz and Jerome R. Ravetz, "Three Types of Risk Assessment: A Methodological Analysis," in *Environmental Impact Assessment, Technology Assessment, and Risk Analysis*, ed. Vincent T. Covello et al. (New York: Springer-Verlag, 1985).

10

Women's Sexuality from the Inside Out

Gail Walker

Did you turn to this chapter first? Did you avoid this chapter? What words did you expect to see on these pages? Are there truths, quietly contained inside you, that you hope will be echoed? What would happen if your truths were echoed here? Would your sexuality be more yours? Is your sexuality different than you think it should be? Who told you how it should be? Take a minute to coalesce your sense of sexuality. Then read on.

Women have been asked to believe that their given roles, dictated by culture, politics, psychology, and religion, are an accurate reflection of their natural inclinations. Recent decades have seen women shift from accepting others' definitions of their nature and roles to examining and defining themselves.

The challenge to women entering the 21st century is to identify and then to articulate their sexuality without male bias. This chapter will offer questions and tentative answers to aid in this process, and to inspire further work on the subject.

Women's realities have been explained and organized in ways that don't always make sense to women but that make sense to those doing the description and analysis—predominantly men. Clusters that reflect male bias have been said to be the only valid ways to pattern data. What has been seen as key are the data that fit into the male framework.

Even the parameters of female sexuality have been male-derived. Male researchers, scholars, and psychologists historically have defined women's sexuality based on their knowledge of male sexuality. In this way, sexuality as it is known to men becomes the model for all sexuality. And what has been observed as sexuality in women is compared to male data to normalize it.

In surveys such as Kinsey's, women have been invited to fill in their own answers to questions posed about sexuality. However, the questions being asked continue to be framed by a male perspective that reflects a male understanding of sexuality. The very act of responding to these questions shapes the cognition of what sexuality is and is not. What is not surveyed is defined as not being sexuality. In this way, male-derived norms limit the ability of women to reflect freely on women's sexuality. The addition of women's own data to the existing categories is necessary but not sufficient. Adding women's data to the prescribed framework is like coloring with a Venus Paradise Coloring Set or drawing with Connect the Dots. The shapes and parameters are a given and the filling out can be only inside the lines and constructs that already exist on the page. Women need to start from scratch to define their sexuality. Thus a new model can be created that allows the articulation of a woman-defined context as well as content of sexuality.

As women define their own sexuality, some forms are likely to overlap with existing ways of ordering data. Much, however, will cluster together differently from the current organization as a result of delving inside women's ways of gathering and structuring information. Through women's eyes, bodies, and minds there may be new contexts for the information already gathered, and additional material to be included. The challenge is to articulate sexuality from inside women's reality. An inward focus is a way to return over and over to the mooring of sexuality in women's bodies and in their experiences. Women can then define their sexuality from the inside out.

This section and the one that follows, "From the Outside In: Male Definitions of Women's Sexuality," explore what we have been told and how our sexuality has been shaped by others. Then, in "Obstacles to Redefining Women's Sexuality," we examine areas such as language, traditional psychology, religion, politics, and culture to identify the problems and fears we face in this process of defining our sexuality. "Reasons to Redefine Women's Sexuality" explores the reasons for engaging in this process despite the obstacles. The next section, "From the Inside Out: A Process of Defining and Expressing Women's Sexuality," presents a working definition of female sexuality to be used throughout this chapter. It discusses how women can work to formulate the "context" and "content" of their sexuality. "Complexities in Women's Sexuality" looks at how women currently feel about their bodies, both in cycles, such as the menstrual cycle, and in different life stages, such as pregnancy. This theme is continued in the next section, "Learning to Appreciate Our Woman-Defined Sexuality: And Its Diversity

Among Us." Here we also explore the depth and range of our sexuality and the diverse ways it may be defined and expressed by individual women. "Suggestions for Growing and Healing" examines more ways that women have repressed or been denied access to their sexuality, and how to begin healing. "Suggestions for Research" emphasizes the need for "woman-derived" research and data to make this process of redefinition valid. And the concluding section, "Moving Forward: Toward Women's Embodied Sexuality," shows how we may benefit from this process with a greatly enriched sense of self and sexuality.

FROM THE OUTSIDE IN: MALE DEFINITIONS OF WOMEN'S SEXUALITY

Viewed from the outside from a male perspective, women's sexuality has been seen as goal-oriented, interactive, and other-oriented. Thus far women have accepted this way of fathoming their sexuality. In fact, many women have been introduced to their sexuality by males. The male definition of sexuality is what women have been taught from the outside in.

The goal of sexuality as perceived by males can be procreation but more often is orgasm, usually with another person, and at just the "right" time. In fact, Masters and Johnson discussed the "human sexual response" almost exclusively in terms of orgasm. When they described a process called "sensate focus" (which includes heightened body awareness, receptivity, touching, and a feeling of safety), they described it less as part of the range of sexual expression than as a tool in the service of orgasm. While orgasm is, of course, a part of the human sexual response for many people, it is not the only goal many women seek in their range of sexual expressiveness.

Freud has offered an even more specific goal, that of vaginal orgasm. Many women accepted this and spent years seeking a satisfactory vaginal orgasm. Of course, later research done on women's own bodies has revealed that there is no specific vaginal orgasm. In defining orgasm or vaginal orgasm as the goal, most of the range of female sexuality is being discounted.

Sexuality has also been regarded as interactive, as if having sex was the same thing as having sexuality. The assumption seems to be that the only point of having sexuality is having sex. Yes, sex can be a fulfilling expression of sexuality, but the act of having sex is not the same as the life process of having sexuality. Women have been denied ownership of their bodies and their experiences by being told what to like and what to hold as goals.

The sexual act has been glorified and the process of having sexuality has been ignored. The moments of "who-does-what-when-with-whom-and-with-what-result" have been seen as the whole story, when in fact they describe only an outer manifestation of a broader inner process. In this interactive and goal-oriented framework, it is as if sexuality exists only with a partner and/or an orgasm. In both these ways sexuality is defined exclusively by its outer expression or product. No attention is given to the process or the mooring of sexuality inside the body-self. Even the sex drive seems to be defined as a measure of an interactive, goal-oriented activity and not as a level of internal energy flow.

Another way sexuality has been described is in an "other-oriented" manner. A woman's sexuality is defined by who her partner is and not by who she herself is. In contrast, intellect is defined not by what particular books are read, but rather by the capacity to read and understand a certain range of books. Sexuality that is more self-defined would emphasize who you know yourself to be; awareness of your body and its sensations; how you choose whether, when, and with whom to share yourself; what to share; and how such sharing affects you and perhaps another. Since sexuality may be expressed or not expressed, may be with or without a partner, may be an authentic or compromised expression of one's nature, and may include a range of activity, an other-based process of definition is limiting.

The issue of virginity is another good example of how women's sexuality is shaped by others. Is virginity a concept that has intrinsic value to women, or has it been a significant issue for centuries because of its importance to men?

Heterosexism, the presumption of heterosexuality, is another concept that limits women's ability to define their sexuality. The assumption here is that there is only one right way for everyone to be. This is not unlike religions that preach that there is only one right type of God to worship and one right way to worship "him"; and that this religion has exclusive domain to name that God. The danger of heterosexism is not so much that it advocates heterosexuality, but that it denies the right to self-define to those who would choose to do so. Such imposed definitions affect women in particular, since women's sexuality historically has been defined from the outside in.

The given definitions of sexuality also reflect the mind-body split that is pervasive in our culture. Even though, in many ways, sexuality is about the body, it does not escape this prevalent fragmentation. The body is mistrusted and tends to be conscripted in the mind's service in order to accomplish mind-derived goals. The body is to be tamed by the mind's will. (We forget that it was the mind that evolved to serve the body.) In sexuality, the mind tries to tell the body what is or is not arousing, what is or is not acceptable to be aroused by, when the body should perform, what the body should do, and how the body should feel. Although rooted in the body, sexuality is expected to be responsive to the mind's commands. Like sexuality, other activities that seem to connect people to their bodies, such as sports, aerobics, yoga, or Lamaze, often steer the body's expression with the mind's will.

There is an alternative approach to body expression, the receptive body, in which the body would interact with the mind to inform or guide the mind through body cues, currents, and sensations. The wisdom of the body would lead. In times of such embodiment the body would be the driver of the car taking the mind on a journey, rather than being the horse carrying the mind to the destination that the mind has chosen.

Each of these ways of framing sexuality that are imposed from the outside is a layer of camouflage that obscures the essence of a woman's sexuality. An old television game show called "Camouflage" had two contestants who competed to be the first to trace accurately the pattern of an object hidden under layers of grids and squiggles. When they correctly answered a true or false question, a squiggled layer of the camouflage would be removed, after which the contestant had one chance to perceive, identify, and try to trace the hidden object. As the game progressed and additional layers were removed, the outline and definition of the object that had been embedded in the camouflage became more obvious. Finding the essence of women's sexuality will require a peeling away of the layers that camouflage it. The mind-body split, being defined by the other, the interactive view, and goal orientation are squiggled grids that have been placed over us. As we look behind these layers we come closer to a view of women's own sexuality.

Obstacles to Redefining Women's Sexuality

There are many obstacles to overcome in order for women to feel empowered to define their own sexuality. The way we use language can distance women from their understanding of themselves. It is hard to use language to capture, embrace, and describe sexuality. Language used with an objective distancing tone divides us from the directness of our experience. Women are already distanced from their inside knowledge without regarding it from an additional arm's length. Women have been accustomed to know their sexuality from the outside in, using the language of males to describe what they see. Redefining women's sexuality from women's point of view can provide the missing language that encompasses both how we look to ourselves and the words we would use to describe our experience. We can then explore how to group what we see into concepts, clusters, or organizing principles.

The language used in this chapter will attempt to reduce the distance between women's minds and their sexuality. Despite the academic standard that one must separate oneself from "the subject" in order to view it objectively, an effort will be made to be united with the subject of sexuality so that the language can match the process of getting inside women's authentic self.

Many other obstacles block redefinition. The way sexuality has been defined in the past in structure and content reflects the values of traditional psychology, religion, culture, and politics. Although these institutions are formidable, several beliefs must be challenged.

One such belief is that the female sex role is preferably one of service to others, one of harmonizing; that women should not seem overly interested in their own sexuality.

Another issue is that for decades psychological and medical experts have been telling women how they should feel. In many cases women have tried to believe them. Since many women were introduced to their sexuality by boys, we learned to expect another to teach it to us, to be our expert. This has kept women from approaching an independent definition of sexuality.

An important issue for some women is the fact that religion threatens us with a fall from grace and/or abandonment and renunciation for challenging "The Word." Some religions believe that women must comply with their self-limiting doctrines and rules or be denied participation in their group.

A related political issue is that access to the media and grants is generally difficult for topics like women-owned sexuality that challenge the status quo. Thus, even when "The Word" is challenged, it is unlikely to be heard publicly.

Another major obstacle for women in our society is the underlying threat of violence for stepping too far out of line. Specific to sexuality is the hovering threat of rape as a means of control and punishment for all women and especially for women who own their sexuality.

Finally, in the structure of some personal relationships, sexuality is used or bartered in service of emotional and economic security. In such situations sexuality would be more like a commodity, a kind of currency of exchange. This would be another source of resistance to self-definition.

Culture is another realm that has created obstacles. Women have been kept from discovery or ownership of their bodies by objectification. Advertising uses its idea of women's sexuality to sell every product imaginable. The diet and cosmetics industries launch a steady assault of prompts about how women's bodies should look, feel, smell, and be shaped as, for example, Naomi Wolf describes in her book, *The Beauty Myth*.[1] Women's appearance and sexual attractiveness are often regarded as the sole measure of their worth as a human being. Women often have to struggle to gain a positive body image in this climate. This combination of a loss of a positive body connection and the presence of the negative and judgmental distances us from the wisdom and support of our bodies as we try to define our authentic sexuality. Even worse, many women have been physically traumatized by battering, incest, abuse, and diseases such as anorexia and bulimia. Women whose bodies have been an object of disdain or violence, and women whose sexuality seems in some way spoiled, may not feel that a redefinition of sexuality is worth the effort.

A final obstacle to overcome is one shared by all oppressed groups: the struggle to feel entitled to define themselves. Like any oppressed group, women have been described by the prevailing power group according to the roles it needs us to fill. This view states: "You exist as we define you."

We must claim the authority to define ourselves in the contexts of our lives. Once we feel entitled to ask ourselves who we really are and what we really like, we will need to develop better skills at articulating, and then answering, the questions that follow. There will be confusion and disagreement among us. It may seem tempting at times to fall back into the comfort of being defined by others. But the old definitions will fade and the new ones will emerge.

Reasons to Redefine Women's Sexuality

With such obstacles confronting us, why enter this process of women's self-definition of sexuality? The task of wrestling our truths from our given roles seems daunting. We do not know in advance what we will learn from our investigation. The subject of sexuality can make us angry and shy all at once. There is discomfort in the answers we have been given and yet there is discomfort in risking new questions.

The dynamics in this stage of women's self-definition of sexuality are similar to those of adolescence. In adolescence we progress from being defined by our families to comparing identities within our peer groups and eventually to defining ourselves. After years of being told "This is who you are," the old definitions are examined as we ask, "Who am I really?" There can be anger and rebellion at being seen as someone who is not really oneself. There can be layers of confusion and intense fluctuation in solidifying an authentic sense of self. Shyness and insecurity abound. And yet the developmental tasks remain; self-definition, peer comparison, autonomy, and eventually "leaving the father's house" to begin a separate life with our own ways of relating to others.

Women may now be in a transition process, individually and as a group. Women may be saying, "No, I'm not what you say I am. I'm not the daughter you define me to be. It's time to define myself. This is who I am." These assertions can be seen by the "father" either as an act of rebellion against the correct rules and definitions or as a healthy individuation and launching into the next stage of life. Either way, as we approach the 21st century, women seem to possess the boldness and courage to search for the truth about ourselves in our own contexts, though we do not know in advance where that search might lead.

Women may start this search in a state of shyness. If we express our real truths will we be welcomed? Not knowing the answer we may mumble, avert our eyes, cringe from meeting and encountering. Gender roles have imposed shyness on women's sexuality. There are messages of invalidation, that it shouldn't exist, that it is bad, that it is a demon that will overwhelm us and get us into trouble. Unless the preexisting script for women's sexuality matches the nature of a particular woman, then women are systematically barred from relationship to their true, sexual selves. Thus women learn to be sexual chameleons, blending into the environment of imposed definitions and disappearing from their own realities.

It is not men's work to be women's mirrors. It is not men's work to research or formulate the context and content of women's sexuality. It is our work, women's work, to name what we already know, to speak with each other, and to go into the darkness of what we do not know to find the material and to sculpt our truths into a nameable, frameable form that genuinely reflects our inner selves. This is why we must redefine ourselves.

FROM THE INSIDE OUT: A PROCESS OF DEFINING AND EXPRESSING WOMEN'S SEXUALITY

In the spirit of exploration, inquiry, and synthesis of women's experience, a working definition of women's embodied sexuality will be proposed. This material is offered in hope and with room for revision and reframing. The reader is enthusiastically invited to wander in this framework and feel how it fits her history, experience, and understanding. The author's fantasy would be to leave one-half of each remaining page of this chapter completely blank. These half-empty pages would emphasize that there are huge amounts of information and truths about women's sexuality still absent from this analysis. Such a format could also visually prompt readers to see the room for their realities and to fill in these empty spaces with their stories and perceptions.

This process of self-discovery starts, for many women, from a point of nebulousness. As we search for clarity we will not refer to traditional literature on sexuality so that we may allow for the evolution of a woman-conceived framework. Some feminist analysis has expanded existing models by adding women-generated data. Other feminist analysis has sought sameness and differentness between what is given for men and what seems true for women. In both these forms of analysis the male-derived contexts remain untouched.

A female-derived context needs to be created. Contexts as discussed in this chapter are "interrelated conditions in which something exists or occurs, i.e. environment."[2] Contexts will be regarded as the skeletal structures that frame and order content, "a part element or complex of parts."[3] The distinction between content (the ideas, experiences, and sensations) and context (the framework that gives definition to these elements) is key.

Much of the feminist analysis being done in the psychology of women at the Stone Center of Wellesley College seems to proceed successfully from content to context. These researchers and clinicians examine the individual, couple, and group to see what patterns fit the observed data rather than examining how the data fit existing theories. They can then follow the observed data and the patterns emanating from the data back and forth in dynamic interplay. Speaking of the work that has been done in the psychology of women, Jean Baker Miller has said:

One way to think about it may be that some people have worked on modifications of existing bodies of work such as Freudian, Jungian, Object Relations, Behavior Modification, and others, and tried to adapt these to women's experience. Others have begun with staying very close to listening to women and finding that women's experience leads us to new visions, new values, new assumptions—assumptions different from those that underlie prior theories.[4]

Those new assumptions would be similar to new contexts. The process used in this chapter to find those new contexts is similar to Janet Surrey's internalized self-empathy, "to make known her own experience and bring her experience into her own relational context."[5] We must see women as subjects and not as objects.

We begin by examining women's experiences and concepts and allowing women to explain, in Carol Gilligan's words, "herself to herself."[6] There is likely to be tremendous diversity in our questions and answers. As we delve inside women's structuring and gathering of information, patterns may emerge that will form context.

The key to women's identifying their sexuality is that it be a process from the inside out, so that context emerges from women's ways of experiencing, seeing, and shaping sexuality. This sexuality would be embodied in women's sense (intellect), sensation (bodies), and sense-ability (emotional patterning). What is found to be indwelling could then be used to generate norms.

Sexuality emanates from the individual's body. It is a kind of life pulse, like breathing. It is a sense of aliveness that allows receptivity to stimulation from the inner or outer world. Although it can be activated by, and a source of, interpersonal contact, it is also a pulse of responsiveness to life's tides that ebbs and flows, often cyclically. It catalyzes an energy current within one's self between mind and body, and between one's self and others.

This inner pulse is a kind of body way of knowing, a kind of body-voice. By recognizing it we become embodied, rather than being exclusively mind-bodied, where the mind determines reality through its cues. If we listen, this voice gives us a different kind of knowledge of ourselves.

Sexuality as sensed by the body teaches us first about the verb side of life: the shifts, the flow, the process, and the movement; and secondarily about the noun side: the person, place, or thing. Sexuality exists in the body as a process with many potentials for content that is far more extensive, interesting, and fulfilling than simply "who does what, when, and with whom."

This life pulse may or may not result in activity. As a voice of the inner body world, it exists whether or not it is expressed or accessed. When it is named only in interpersonal terms as a feeling for another, the relation within the self between body and mind and inner and outer currents is lost. Sexuality as an inner pulse leads us to knowledge of and receptivity to our inner and outer impressions. When sexuality is linked only to external stimuli its source as a body pulse is ignored.

Like a stream, this inner pulse fluctuates in its intensity. Due to inner cycles or environmental stressors it can run dry at times, or get dammed by obstacles in its path, or freeze up during certain seasons of life. Like a stream, it can also flood us in certain circumstances. Lust can feel like a flooding, like a power surge in the energy circuit of the life pulse. Lust can surge in response to an external source such as another person. It can also surge in response to an inner source with either a known cause (such as the menstrual cycle or spring) or an unknown cause. If this lust leads to interpersonal expression such as shared sexuality, it can have a personal quality when shared with another person; or it can have an impersonal quality when it stems from an internal surge but is attached to some person who just happens to be present. That type of sexual expression is interpersonal but is more about self-expression than sharing with the other.

Thus, sexuality is a relationship with the body-self and sometimes others. Sexuality is not about object choice although it may often include an outer object. Rather, it is about creating, yielding, and joining with inner energy and perhaps with the energy of another. Outer expression may or may not follow the awareness of this life pulse but the inner current flows.

Sexuality as an energy may have a range of contents. Thus, within a particular woman and among many women there can be different forms of sexual activity that are equally expressive of authentic sexuality.

We have many choices in how we deal with this inner pulse. It can be expressed, repressed, contained, or reframed. In an embodied expression we would let our inner desires lead us. When expression is mind-bodied, the energy of the pulse is screened and modified by the mind's values regarding appropriateness. In these ways, the content of expression can be separate or different from the content of the sexual life pulse. Other choices are whether to recognize the energy or to repress it, whether to express the energy or contain it, and whether the energy expressed matches with inner currents or is reframed and directed to other activities. There can be joy in containing the energy and keeping it a secret.

As a pulse and as a process, embodied sexuality exists across the lifespan. It exists in disability, in aging, in chronic pain, in illness, and in stress. The content may change and the intensity may change but the process continues. Body trauma, emotional trauma, upheaval, and sexual wounding can create fluctuations that require a search for new forms of expression. Sometimes our sexuality lies dormant for awhile and the process seems to stop. But eventually it begins again as we seek to connect with and express our inner self. Liberated from outside forces that historically have prescribed both what sexuality can be and what sexuality should accomplish, the sexual pulse can seek different levels in a variety of inner connections and outer expressions.

In this working definition of women's sexuality the process is a communication loop inside the body that alerts us to energy shifts and to sensations that enliven us. This inner pulse leads us to be more deeply related to our own self and, if we choose, to a partner. This deeper body relatedness and enlivening is our goal rather than seeking sexual encounters as we have been led to believe we must do in order to be sexual human beings. We are affected by our sexuality regardless of outer expression or validation by another.

This working definition is still evolving. There is much unknown about the content and cultural diversity of women-named experiences, perceptions, and understandings. But one truth is universal: women themselves must define their sexuality.

Complexities in Women's Sexuality

There are complex areas of content in women's sexuality that are distinct from those embedded in models of men's sexuality. These contents are rooted in women's bodies and issues of procreation and objectification. A comprehensive view of women's sexuality must encompass these issues.

How does it influence women's sexuality that we all emerge from women's bodies, that a woman's body has been our first home? What does it mean that most people's childhood reaction to learning about the birds and the bees was to feel shocked? How does this reaction impinge on the way we see our female bodies?

What impact is made on women's sexuality by the possibility of pregnancy when that sexuality is expressed as intercourse? Many women report that during pregnancy and, in some cases, nursing they feel that they no longer own their bodies but are subjects of the child. How does this affect women's sense of body image and sexuality? Is there a permanent shift in the sense of body-self and sexual self after pregnancy? Some women feel joyfully initiated into their female bodies after pregnancy. In cases where intercourse is sexuality expressed in service of getting pregnant, how does a menstrual period that signals the death of hope for that particular conception impact feelings about sexuality? And in miscarriage, when something dead comes from the woman's body, how does this affect her sense of her sexual self? For women who wish to get pregnant but are infertile, does the lack of reproductive possibility produce a diminished sense of sexuality? Does involvement with reproductive technologies cause detachment from sexuality? Pregnancy as a possible content of sexuality seems to affect the process of sexuality for many women. Not choosing pregnancy may provoke criticism of not being a real or complete woman. What does this mean for the sexuality of lesbian, bisexual, and heterosexual women who choose not to have children?

Women's biological cycles have influenced the inner pulse of sexuality as well. Women's stages of reproductive life are signaled by menarche and menopause. In our culture some would suggest that women's sexuality exists only in tandem with reproductive possibility. Menarche has been seen as a threshold: now you are a woman. Does that make menopause a marker for no longer being a woman? For many women menstrual cycles offer awareness of the ebb and flow of their sexual pulse. Increasingly, women are honoring menopause as a transition to another chapter of life with a different body sense that may have a different sexual pulse.

Our culture projects asexuality onto women as they have children and as they age. Yet women as a group outlive men. This might challenge women to make shifts in the content of their interactive sexuality across their lifespans.

Another difficult issue in women's sexuality is the steady objectification of women's bodies by advertising, by constant harassment on the streets, and by the very real threats of sexual assault. A percentage of all women, sometimes calculated as high as 60 percent, have been or will be sexually violated in their lifetime. What does it mean that most women have been, or know friends who have been, sexually wounded? Does this cultural objectification evoke a distancing from or avoidance of our own sexuality? How are we contaminated and invaded by these threats and projections that are so constant and pervasive?

These areas of content have largely been unexplored and unintegrated into our concepts of women's sexuality. The absence both of this information and of a contextual model rooted in women's realities combines with the presence of contrived images and concepts. This combination creates uncertainty in women about their own perceptions of their sexual selves. Some women can feel forced to distance from their sexuality when it doesn't "fit" within the parameters. Women-generated theories would encapsulate women's true selves and help to protect us from the onslaught of images that present us as objects. Such theories would be more likely to mirror the images a particular woman has about her own sexuality and to make her feel blessed as she is in spite of the "should be's" she encounters.

Learning to Appreciate Our Woman-Defined Sexuality—And Its Diversity Among Us

The process of identifying the woman-rooted contexts and contents of an authentic sexuality provides many lessons. Embodied sexuality itself guides us to a deeper body connection and a more integrated sense of self. The endeavor of seeking and sharing embodied sexuality activates psychological and political growth issues.

We can be stretched psychologically while exploring unknowns. Working from the inside out requires a movement between inner search and speculation, and outer search and comparisons. This movement between sources involves confrontation with contradictory messages. There is the temptation to say either one or the other is exclusively true. For example, an inner ultimatum might be, "If you love your partner you will do this now; not doing it means you don't love your partner." The challenge of this lesson is to be able to identify and observe different themes and to be able to feel the pull of the old respond to the progress of the new. An inner dialogue might go something like this: "I know I love my partner. I know my partner wants this. I love me too. I know I don't want this now. I'll disappear. I'm so scared to say no. I'm so scared to go ahead. My body doesn't want to. My body says no. My heart wants to. My heart wants my body to say yes. My mind is confused. I know what I should want, what I want to want. I know that I don't want what I want to want. What's wrong with me? Do I have to betray one side of me to satisfy the other side? I don't know what to do. What if I say this out loud? Could we talk about this or would there be a fight or a hurt? Could my partner help? Is there another alternative for today?"

Working from our own foundation within ourselves we can acknowledge both our own needs and those of the other person and can move forward even while fluctuating back and forth. The process of embodied sexuality is not unidimensional and that may make it appear unclear. We learn in the process to invite all contents forward and to tolerate the presence of resistance so that the resistance does not accumulate to dam or divert the stream. Learning to explore ourselves with openness to the many possibilities as well as with openness to the existence of limitations is the challenge.

Finding our individual and collective voices as members of an oppressed group requires assertion and tolerance of diversity. Within an oppressed group there tend to be pressures for conformity in order to present a united front to the oppressors. This pressure can also create tension within the individuals to be clear and protected in who they are. Since the model of women's embodied sexuality describes fluidity across each woman's lifespan and diversity among women, tolerance of changes and differences becomes essential.

This model also advocates tolerance for not knowing, for understanding sexuality primarily as a process and secondarily as a content form of expression. The model challenges us to learn about our process, our inner pulse, and to accept our truths from the inside out instead of disappearing into media images or cowering in the comfort of conformity for conformity's sake.

As we have seen in recent years, there is pressure to divide women's unity along so-called sexual preference lines. "You're okay, but they're not; we can relate to your issues but not theirs," is the theme used to try to separate heterosexually defined women from their lesbian and bisexual sisters. This pressure may be applied from society in general but it may also be applied from inside the membership of women's organizations. An oppressed group can learn to oppress itself with the same mechanism that the outside oppressor uses. Repeated messages of oppression become like an automatic program operating within us, like a computer virus. They can cause us to work in ways that are not in our own interest. Sexuality certainly has been a subject so affected, and this has created obstacles against diversity within and between us.

To an oppressed group under fire it is easy to be convinced that the battle is what "they" define it to be, that the choices are what "they" say they are, and that the weapons are those "they" define as appropriate. Women's sexuality has been such a field of fire. In our culture, women-owned sexuality is as political as it is physical. How liberating it would be to find our way to stand together, to bridge our diversity and to appreciate the stir-fry, each woman comfortable within her own self, teaching and strengthening each other.

Awareness of women's sexuality as a steady life force leads us toward acceptance of the multifaceted nature of life. In life, many things can be true simultaneously. Even when we are focusing on a single subject, multiple valid facets weave through our awareness. Sexuality can be present even when circumstances seem unfavorable for it. For example, it has been observed that there is often a strong sense of sexuality in times of tragedy, catastrophe, and death. Although this seems to be more the rule than the exception, many people feel shame about themselves or their sexuality upon experiencing this. Sexuality as an underlying energy coexists with other life events.

When sexuality is experienced as a life force there are options and choices to be made about expression. Content may need to be transformed in times where there is no partner and in times of illness, pain, and disability. During such times there can be a tendency to turn away from the body and our sexuality. In the effort to escape body awareness, breathing may become shallow and skin temperature may decrease. The body can seem like an enemy. When the body changes in pregnancy and aging or is changed by mastectomy or hysterectomy, the content once chosen may no longer serve. The experience of the body may be temporarily or forever different. The sexual pulse may lead us through the process of grieving the lost content; through a time of having no form of expression; then through a time of reemerging, redefining, and experimenting with new forms; and finally to the discovery of new ways to be. These transitions show a way to stay in life even when things die. Incorporating awareness of sexuality as an inner pulse at such times can be part of reclaiming wholeness.

These areas of challenge make the process of claiming, naming, and embodying our sexuality a great learning experience. Each lesson brings us closer to ownership of ourselves. In our psyches, embodied sexuality involves a deep acceptance of our bodies as they are and of our choices in the outer world. Often our battle scars from living this life impinge on the free flow of sexuality as an inner pulse. Through wrestling with and dwelling with these challenges we can strengthen our connection with our sexuality and with our power.

SUGGESTIONS FOR GROWING AND HEALING

The concepts discussed so far can be used in healing on one's own and in clinical work. A woman can be encouraged to find her sexuality as a life pulse and to identify the physics of that pulse by using questions such as, How does it flow? How does it move? What stirs it from the inside? What evokes it from the outside? Fluctuations may occur and these can be explored in terms of cycles, stress, self-esteem, emotional shifts, seasons, and so on. Content can then be considered and expressed as a contained or interactive reflection of the inner pulse. Since choices can be made about sexual self-expression, the content of such expression can be gauged as an attempt to please others or as a self-revelation.

Couples can be asked to explore their individual sexuality; and once the individual realities have been identified, each person can share this information with the other. Then they can pioneer their sexual expression as a couple based on their individual pulses.

Some things that have been labeled sexual disorders may actually be collisions between mind-bodied sexual demands and embodied sexual truths. "Problems" with interactive sexual function, such as vaginismus and inorgasmia, could be explored using the framework of authentic sexuality. The body may not want to do what the mind wills it to do. Sexual sharing that reflects the body's will may forge different content and activity than the mind had planned.

Inhibited sexual desire may be another example of a mind-bodied label. Inherent in the definition of inhibited sexual desire is a standard, usually based on some outside source, of what sexual desire should be. An additional assumption is that, within the individual, desire should be at a constant level or in a prescribed range across time and circumstances. Healing may be approached through clarifying the body's tempo and rhythm.

Many people have dissociated from their authentic sexuality for a variety of reasons: wounds from betrayal, wounds from violence, body traumas, loss of a beloved partner, repression, fear of the true self, and fear of being overwhelmed or invaded by sexual energy. When there has been violation or wounding where sexual behavior was the weapon, then sexuality can become contaminated and associated with memories and sensations of abuse. Incest may contaminate the entire body-self and cause the victim to run from that part of her which she was told, or assumed, "caused" the betrayal and violation by a trusted adult.

Another situation that can provoke a desire to ignore the sexual pulse is when it evokes a yearning for someone no longer available. Similarly, sexual longing can cause confusion when we get attached to an inappropriate person, for example, in codependency or relationship addiction. Some people may never have found their authentic sexuality and may have been role-playing sexual behavior based on what they think, or have been told, they should feel and do.

When sexuality is known as a predominantly "other-defined" experience, then actions of harm or betrayal by an "other" can make all of sexuality seem hurtful, bad, and dangerous. When sexuality exists as an inner force, it has an underlying constancy that is larger than a harmful event. A trauma would be integrated with a wide range of other experiences. The trauma would be likely to cause a blurring or contamination of one's sexuality; but when we recognize our sexuality as a continuous life force within us, then it may overcome individual traumas and we can heal successfully.

When women's sexuality is regarded as a life pulse, it is like a country stream that has the capacity to clean itself as it moves along. Time, space, and rain can be sources of renewal. The ability of the stream to clean itself is affected by the degree of toxicity of the contaminant and by the duration and frequency of the contamination. It is as if poison had been poured into the stream or a dam erected somewhere along it. These issues may need to be dealt with in therapy. The therapy process can remove downed tree limbs in which debris has lodged and can skim the floating debris to help the stream flow clean through the damming obstacles. In most cases the stream did exist before the contamination and does exist somewhere beyond it. Dry times might mean the stream will run low but usually will be followed by times of fullness again. The nature of the stream is to be self-cleansing and replenishing.

As sexuality is integrated into the self-image, it becomes a channel of self-awareness, energy, self-healing, sharing, joy, and celebration. Embodied sexuality enlivens, informs, and enriches us.

SUGGESTIONS FOR RESEARCH

The most important task for future research is to fill in the missing half that is symbolically blank on each page of this chapter. The attempt made here to frame a new context that regards sexuality as a process and to offer a women-generated ordering of contents is a preliminary mapping. Clearly the old model given from the outside does not mesh with most women's sense of sexuality. Whether the model offered here is congruent with the reader's concepts is open for evaluation.

As future research and contemplation define more of the process and articulate more of the content of women's sexuality, some interesting comparisons could be made. What data would emerge from the exploration of diversity between women within one culture, between women of different cultures, and between women and men? (Before we compare women with men we need to have two equally developed, comprehensive bodies of work on context and content.) If categories of discrete "sexual identity" continue to exist, what could we learn by exploring the diversity between lesbian, bisexual, and heterosexual women and the similarities and contrasts between lesbians and gay men?

The research already conducted on traits such as intelligence, shyness, musical ability, athletic ability, and thrill-seeking behavior has shown that people begin life with innate tendencies. They seem to have a predisposition to attain certain levels in these areas, which is then affected by their experiences and the environment in which they live. These predispositions tend to be arranged over a bell-shaped curve with a normal distribution. In such a curve 34.13 percent of the population would fall in the first grouping on either side of the midpoint and would comprise the (+) and (−) first standard deviation. The second standard deviation would be 13.59 percent on each side of the first standard deviation, and the third standard deviation would be the remaining 2.2 percent of the population to either side of the second. A full 68 percent of the population would fall (+) or (−) within the first standard deviation.

It is appealing to conceptualize a similar predisposition in sexuality because it would explain a broad spectrum of what is seen clinically. The exploration of people's fantasies, dream material, and behaviors would seem to support a bisexual potential in the template of the psyche of many, but certainly not all, people. Such a distribution would explain why some people, the third standard deviation, could not fathom the opposite end of the continuum; why some people appear to be ambisexual (because they are at the mean and are 50/50 by nature); why some people pass through one sexual identity as a "developmental stage" yet arrive at another; and why, in cases of trauma, some but not all people cross over to a different sexual identity but return to their original identity after completion of a healing process. Since this innate predisposition would also be shaped by environment, experience, culture, and convention, the reported behavior would not always be an index of the distribution of innate potential.

It may be that there is an innate curve with an environmental curve superimposed over it. The expression of innate predisposition would be affected by environmental factors such as oppression, lack of modeling, suppression, trauma, and social trends. Thus the population reporting itself to be heterosexual would be comprised both of the 50 percent on that side of the midpoint plus the 34 percent on the homosexual side who, by nature, are 60/40 gay but who identify as straight due to environmental factors and pressures to "fit in." This would yield the 84 percent of the population that

appears to be heterosexual in current surveys. Those who express homosexual experimentation only as a phase most likely would be those from
the first gay standard deviation but may include some people from the first
straight standard deviation who are influenced in some way by environmental factors. The 10–15 percent of the population that surveys as gay
would be likely to be the second and third standard deviations whose given
nature is 75/25 to 95/5.

Because of the predominant heterosexism in our society it would be difficult at this time to test directly the existence of such an innate curve because
environmental "shoulds" would obscure it. However, testing this hypothesis
indirectly through the use of correlation studies is possible. A sampling
technique such as those used in political science to measure trends of liberalism and conservatism could be employed. If we were to predict that
times of more liberal trends would correlate with times of greater tolerance
and expression of diversity, and that more conservative times would correlate with suppression of diversity, then comparing results from the liberal/
conservative scale with results from a range of sexual behavior sampling
might be a way to look at the movement of the bell-shaped curve as an
entity.

At five- to ten-year intervals a representative sample matched for age,
race, gender, and class could be surveyed about range of sexual expressions
and impressions. This hypothesis would predict that if American culture
continues its growth toward tolerance and acceptance of diversity, the data
would cluster progressively closer to the bell-shaped curve at each sampling.
Conversely, and perversely, if the culture becomes more conservative and
repressive, the data would pull the bell-shaped curve toward the heterosexual domain. Thus we could explore how the social change of the past thirty
years will evolve in the 21st century in the area of sexuality.

An additional research project could be done following a sample in a
longitudinal study. It would be especially interesting to draw one sample
from a liberal decade and one from a conservative decade and follow both
samples across the life span. Such investigation could clarify what shifts
might be a natural fluctuation of content expression across a life span. Such
a longitudinal study could also explore within what range of variation these
shifts occur and perhaps identify a maximum range of variation for any
individual given their predisposition. There may well be a maximum fluctuation of plus or minus 10 percent from an individual's mean point across
a lifetime. A comparison between the subjects drawn from the conservative
and liberal samples could explore whether the average center point or mean
seems different and whether the range of fluctuation is the same, greater,
or lesser.

Such research could provide a quantitative basis for the diversity that is
already observed in clinical practice and in society. In addition, this proposed

research may transform the way sexuality is viewed from a static, goal-oriented, other-focused domain to a more fluid intrapersonal life force.

MOVING FORWARD: TOWARD WOMEN'S EMBODIED SEXUALITY

As women in this society we may approach our sexuality with some shyness and perhaps mystery. Like social shyness, sexual shyness would cause us to avert our eyes, feel awkward, cringe from meeting and encountering others, swallow ourselves up, and put out signals of our own uneasiness that could make others perceive the uneasiness and become less likely to offer welcome and acceptance. Sexual shyness would keep us from interrupting what seems to be an important conversation already in progress in day-to-day life—for instance, obligations, chores, deadlines, and schedules; it would seem like an unwelcome interruption. Sexual shyness would make us unlikely to initiate sexual expression and we would be slow to feel its stirrings, shifts, and pulses. Then we might become unfriendly, reclusive, unreceptive, unaware, and unlikely to strike up relationships. After years of repetition, this pattern of shyness could seem to be our true nature, but most likely it is not.

Many of us start one step removed in our search for embodied sexuality. Here is one way to begin to approach this part of us. To start, we need to acknowledge with our minds that a sexual pulse exists and that it is beating somewhere within.

Next, we would begin to search for this sexual pulse with the senses. This is a bit like the process of anticipating spring; of knowing from the calendar that spring is near, and looking and waiting to see buds swell; of lifting the mulch to check for sprouts of crocus; of smelling the air in search of the one February day of thawing; of listening for the return of the songbirds; of watching the scrub growth along the highway get a reddish haze. As enough of these signs of spring accumulate, there is evidence that spring is happening. In some ways though, the sense of spring may still be known in the mind only. You have not yet felt its quickening inside you. So you keep observing the manifestation of spring, bearing witness to its being out there. The separation between you and spring may be frustrating. You know it exists, but it hasn't reached you inside or made your own sap bubble up.

Then one day it happens. The smell of the onion grass, the sun on your skin, a warm breeze enwrapping you, the almost alarming brightness of early morning light through the not-yet-leafed trees, make something quicken inside you—and so spring arrives. You may feel a quicker tempo, a boost of energy, a lightness, a richness. The posture of bearing witness is now transformed, and you are inside the seam of spring and spring is streaming inside you.

That process, the progression from knowing, to seeking, to observing, to reflecting, to embodying, is much like the process of grasping the inner sexual pulse. Once that pulse is found, it becomes a source of life's movement in and through you. Life-giving and energizing, women's embodied sexuality enlivens us from the inside out.[7]

NOTES

1. Naomi Wolf, *The Beauty Myth* (New York: William Morrow, 1991).

2. *Webster's Ninth New Collegiate Dictionary* (Springfield, MA: Merriam Webster, Inc., 1983).

3. Ibid.

4. Jean Baker Miller, "Women's Psychological Development: Connections, Disconnections, and Violations." Rockville Communications, Track 2 Taping, 1991.

5. Janet Surrey, "The 'Self-in-Relation': A Theory of Women's Development," work in progress publication no. 13 (Wellesley, MA: The Stone Center, Wellesley College, 1985).

6. Carol Gilligan. *In a Different Voice* (Cambridge, MA: Harvard University Press, 1982), p. 173.

7. With gratitude to my first mentor, Jane Kettering of Summemann West, who taught me to see with the body's eyes and speak with the body's voice.

Bibliography

WOMEN'S ECONOMIC ROLE

Adelman, Clifford. *Women at Thirtysomething: Paradoxes of Attainment.* A special study prepared for the U.S. Department of Education, Office of Educational Research and Improvement, June 1991.

American Scholar Forum. "Women on Women." *The American Scholar* 41 (Autumn 1972): 599–627.

Becker, Gary. *Human Capital,* 2d ed. Chicago: University of Chicago Press, 1975.

Bergmann, Barbara R. *The Economic Emergence of Women.* New York: Basic Books, 1986.

Burtless, Gary, ed. *A Future of Lousy Jobs?* Washington, DC: Brookings Institution, 1990.

Carnevale, Anthony Patrick. *America and the New Economy.* Alexandria, VA: The American Society for Training and Development and the U.S. Department of Labor, Employment and Training Administration, 1991.

Evans, Sara M., and Barbara J. Nelson. *Wage Justice, Comparable Worth and the Paradox of Technocratic Reform.* Chicago: University of Chicago Press, 1989.

Faludi, Susan. *Backlash: The Undeclared War Against American Women.* New York: Crown Publishers, 1991.

Fuchs, Victor R. *Women's Quest for Economic Equality.* Cambridge, MA: Harvard University Press, 1988.

Galbraith, John Kenneth. *Economics and the Public Purpose.* Boston: Houghton Mifflin, 1973.

Goldin, Claudia. *Understanding the Gender Gap*. New York: Oxford University Press, 1990.

Hutner, Frances C. *Equal Pay for Comparable Worth*. New York: Praeger, 1986.

Institute for Women's Policy Research. "Women's Work, Family Diversity, and Employment Instability: Public Policy Responses to New Realities." Testimony by Heidi Hartmann, director, before the Committee on Labor and Human Resources, U.S. Senate, January 7, 1991, revised January 31, 1991, Washington, DC.

———. Spalter-Roth, Roberta M., Heidi I. Hartmann, and Linda M. Andrews. "Mothers, Children, and Low-Wage Work: The Ability to Earn a Family Wage." Washington, DC: IWPR, revised September 1990.

———. Spalter-Roth, Roberta, and Heidi Hartmann. "Women and the Workplace: Looking Toward the Future." Testimony before the Subcommittee on Employment and Productivity, Committee on Labor and Human Resources, U.S. Senate, July 18, 1991.

Keynes, John Maynard. "Obituary, Mary Paley Marshall." *Economic Journal*, 54 (June–September 1944): 268–284.

Marshall, Alfred. *Principles of Economics*, 8th ed. 1920. London: Macmillan, reprinted 1938.

Mill, John Stuart. *Principles of Political Economy*. London: Longmans, Green, 1909.

National Committee on Pay Equity. "Pay Equity Activity in the Public Sector, 1979–1989." Executive Summary. Washington, DC: October 1989.

Paglia, Camille. *Sexual Personae: Art and Decadence from Nefertiti to Emily Dickinson*. New Haven, CT: Yale University Press, 1990.

Pigou, A. C. *The Economics of Welfare*, 4th ed. London: Macmillan, 1932.

Pujol, Michele A. *Feminism and Anti-Feminism in Early Economic Thought*. Aldershot, England: Edward Elgar Publishing, 1992.

Reskin, Barbara F., and Patricia A. Roos. *Job Queues. Gender Queues: Explaining Women's Inroads into Male Occupations*. Philadelphia: Temple University Press, 1990.

Schor, Juliet B. *The Overworked American*. New York: Basic Books, 1991.

Smith, Adam. *The Wealth of Nations*. New York: The Modern Library, 1937.

Stone, Lawrence. *Road to Divorce, England, 1530–1987*. New York: Oxford University Press, 1990.

U.S. Department of Labor, Bureau of Labor Statistics. *Working Women: A Chartbook*. Washington, DC, August 1991.

U.S. General Accounting Office. "A Changing Work Force: Demographic Issues Facing the Federal Government," GGD-92-38, Washington, DC, March 24, 1992.

U.S. Joint Economic Committee, *Hearings on the Economic Problems of Women*, 93rd Congress, 1st session, Part 1, July 10, 11, and 12, 1973.

Veblen, Thorstein. "The Barbarian Status of Women." In *Essays in Our Changing Order*, 50–64. New York: Viking Press, 1943.

———. *The Theory of the Leisure Class*. New York: B. W. Huebsch, 1918.

Wellesley College Center for Research on Women, Susan McGee Bailey, Director. *How Schools Shortchange Girls: A Study of Major Findings on Girls and Education*. Washington, DC: American Association of University Women Educational Foundation and National Education Association, 1992.

WOMEN IN LEADERSHIP

Baxter, Sandra, and Marjorie Lansing. *Women and Politics: The Visible Majority.* Ann Arbor: University of Michigan Press, 1983.

Bunch, Charlotte. *Passionate Politics.* New York: St. Martin's Press, 1987.

Burrell, Barbara. "The Political Opportunity of Women Candidates for the U.S. House of Representatives in 1984." *Women and Politics* 8 (1988): 51–68.

———. "Women's and Men's Campaigns for the U.S. House of Representatives, 1972–1982: A Finance Gap?" *American Politics Quarterly* 13 (1985): 251–272.

Cantor, Dorothy, and Toni Bernay, with Jean Stoess. *Women in Power: The Secrets of Leadership.* Boston: Houghton Mifflin, 1992.

Carroll, Susan J. "Feminist Scholarship on Political Leadership." In *Leadership: Multidisciplinary Perspectives,* ed. Barbara Kellerman. Englewood Cliffs, NJ: Prentice-Hall, 1984.

———. "The Personal Is Political: The Intersection of Private Lives and Public Roles Among Women and Men in Elective and Appointive Office." *Women and Politics* 9 (1989): 51–67.

———. *Women as Candidates in American Politics.* Bloomington: Indiana University Press, 1985.

Carroll, Susan J., Debra L. Dodson, and Ruth B. Mandel. *The Impact of Women in Public Office: An Overview.* New Brunswick, NJ: Center for the American Woman and Politics, Eagleton Institute of Politics, Rutgers University, 1991.

Darcy, R., Susan Welch, and Janet Clark. *Women, Elections, and Representation.* New York: Longman, 1987.

Dodson, Debra L., ed. *Gender and Policy Making: Studies of Women in Office.* New Brunswick, NJ: Center for the American Woman and Politics, Eagleton Institute of Politics, Rutgers University, 1991.

Dodson, Debra L., and Susan J. Carroll. *Reshaping the Agenda: Women in State Legislatures.* New Brunswick, NJ: Center for the American Woman and Politics, Eagleton Institute of Politics, Rutgers University, 1991.

Flammang, Janet A. *Political Women: Current Roles in State and Local Government.* Beverly Hills, CA: Sage Publications, 1984.

Gertzog, Irwin N. *Congressional Women: Their Recruitment, Treatment, and Behavior.* New York: Praeger, 1984.

Hartmann, Susan M. *From Margin to Mainstream: American Women and Politics Since 1960.* New York: Alfred A. Knopf, 1989.

Helgesen, Sally. *The Female Advantage: Women's Ways of Leadership.* New York: Doubleday, 1990.

Kelly, Rita Mae, and Mary Boutilier. *The Making of Political Women: A Study of Socialization and Role Conflict.* Chicago: Nelson-Hall, 1978.

Kirkpatrick, Jeane J. *Political Woman.* New York: Basic Books, 1974.

Klein, Ethel. *Gender Politics.* Cambridge, MA: Harvard University Press, 1984.

Lake, Celinda, and Vincent J. Breglio. "Different Voices, Different Views: The Politics of Gender." In *The American Woman 1992–93,* ed. Paula Ries and Anne J. Stone. New York: W. W. Norton, 1992.

Le Veness, Frank P., and Jane P. Sweeney, eds. *Women Leaders in Contemporary U.S. Politics.* Boulder, CO: Lynne Rienner Publishers, 1987.

Mandel, Ruth B. *In the Running: The New Woman Candidate*. New York: Ticknor and Fields, 1981; Boston: Beacon Press, 1983.

———. "The Political Woman." In *The American Woman 1988–89*, ed. Sara E. Rix. New York: W. W. Norton, 1988.

Mandel, Ruth B., and Debra L. Dodson. "Do Women Officeholders Make a Difference?" In *The American Woman 1992–93*, edited by Paula Ries and Anne J. Stone. New York: W. W. Norton, 1992.

Morris, Celia. "Changing the Rules and the Roles: Five Women in Public Office." In *The American Woman 1992–93*, edited by Paula Ries and Anne J. Stone. New York: W. W. Norton, 1992.

———. *Storming the Statehouse: Running for Governor with Ann Richards and Dianne Feinstein*. New York: Charles Scribner's Sons, 1992.

Mueller, Carol M., ed. *The Politics of the Gender Gap: The Social Construction of Political Influence*. Newbury Park, CA: Sage Publications, 1988.

Natividad, Irene. "Women of Color and the Campaign Trail." In *The American Woman 1992–93*, ed. Paula Ries and Anne J. Stone. New York: W. W. Norton, 1992.

Sapiro, Virginia. "Private Costs of Public Commitments or Public Costs of Private Commitments? Family Roles versus Political Ambition." *American Journal of Political Science* 26 (1982): 265–279.

Schwartz, Felice N. "Management Women and the New Facts of Life." *Harvard Business Review*, No. 1 (January–February 1989).

Sivard, Ruth Leger. *Women: A World Survey*. Washington, DC: World Priorities, 1985.

Stanwick, Kathy A., and Katherine E. Kleeman. *Women Make a Difference*. New Brunswick, NJ: Center for the American Woman and Politics, Eagleton Institute of Politics, Rutgers University, 1983.

The World's Women, 1970–1990. New York: United Nations, 1991.

WOMEN'S SPIRITUALITY

Allen, Paula Gunn. *The Sacred Hoop: Recovering the Feminine in American Indian Traditions*. Boston: Beacon Press, 1986.

Anima: The Journal of Human Experience. Chambersburg, PA.

Austen, Hallie Inglehart. *The Heart of the Goddess*. Berkeley, CA: Wingbow Press, 1990.

Bennetts, Leslie. "Marianne's Faithful." *Vanity Fair* 54, no. 6 (June 1991).

Brown, Peter. *The Body and Society: Men, Women, and Sexual Renunciation in Early Christianity*. New York: Columbia University Press, 1988.

Budapest, Z. *The Holy Book of Women's Mysteries*, 2 vols. Berkeley, CA: Wingbow Press, 1986.

Callahan, Sydney. "Person and Gender, Quelle Difference?" *Church Magazine* 6, no. 2 (Summer 1990).

Cameron, Anne. *Daughters of Copper Woman*. Vancouver, BC: Press Gang Publishers, 1981.

Christ, Carol P. *Laughter of Aphrodite: Reflections on a Journey to the Goddess*. San Francisco: Harper & Row, 1987.

Christ, Carol P., and Judith Plaskow. *Womanspirit Rising: A Feminist Reader in Religion.* San Francisco: Harper & Row, 1979.

"The Cologne Declaration." *The Tablet,* 4 (February 1989).

Craighead, Meinrad. *The Mother's Songs: Images of God the Mother.* Mahwah, NJ: Paulist Press, 1986.

Daly, Mary. *Beyond God the Father: Toward a Philosophy of Women's Liberation.* Boston: Beacon Press, 1973.

———. *Pure Lust: Elemental Feminist Philosophy.* Boston: Beacon Press, 1984.

Davis, Flora. *Moving the Mountain: The Woman's Movement in America Since 1960.* New York: Simon and Schuster, 1991.

Diaz, Adriana. *Freeing the Creative Spirit: Drawing on the Power of Art to Tap the Magic and Wisdom Within.* San Francisco: HarperSanFrancisco, 1992.

Dulles, Avery. *The Reshaping of Catholicism: Current Challenges in the Theology of the Church.* San Francisco: Harper & Row, 1988.

Ehrenreich, Barbara, and Deirde English. *Witches, Midwives and Nurses.* New York: The Feminist Press, 1973.

Eisler, Riane. *The Chalice and the Blade: Our History, Our Future.* San Francisco: Harper & Row, 1987.

Estes, Clarissa Pinkola. *Women Who Run With the Wolves.* New York: Ballantine Books, 1992.

Faludi, Susan. *Backlash: The Undeclared War Against American Women.* New York: Crown Publishers, 1991.

Feldman, Christina. *Woman Awake: A Celebration of Women's Wisdom.* London: Arkana/Penguin, 1990.

Fisher, Elizabeth. *Rise Up and Call Her Name: A Woman Honoring Journey into Global Earth-Based Spirituality.* Boston: Unitarian Universalist Women's Federation, scheduled for publication late 1993/early 1994.

Friedan, Betty. *The Second Stage.* New York: Summit Books, 1981.

Gadon, Elinor W. *The Once and Future Goddess.* San Francisco: Harper & Row, 1989.

Gallup, George, Jr., and Sarah Jones. *100 Questions and Answers: Religion in America.* Princeton, NJ: Princeton Religious Research Center, 1989.

Garvey, John. "Women's Ordination: Another Go at the Arguments." *Commonweal* 57, no. 2 (January 26, 1990).

Gilligan, Carol. *In a Different Voice: Psychological Theory and Women's Development.* Cambridge, MA: Harvard University Press, 1982.

Gimbutas, Marija. *The Goddesses and Gods of Old Europe.* Berkeley: University of California Press, 1982.

———. *The Language of the Goddess.* San Francisco: Harper & Row, 1989.

Goldenberg, Naomi R. *Changing of the Gods.* Boston: Beacon Press, 1979.

Greeley, Andrew. *American Catholics Since the Council: An Unauthorized Report.* Chicago: Thomas More Press, 1985.

Griffin, Susan. *Woman and Nature: The Roaring Inside Her.* New York: Harper & Row, 1978.

Harris, Maria. *Dance of the Spirit: The Seven Steps of Women's Spirituality.* New York: Bantam Books, 1989.

Heresies: The Great Goddess. Issue 5, revised. New York: Heresies Collective, 1982.

Journal of Feminist Studies in Religion. Atlanta: Scholars Press.

Libana, Inc. *A Circle Is Cast.* Cambridge, MA: Spinning Records, 1986.
———. *Fire Within.* Durham, NC: Ladyslipper, Inc., 1990.
Marty, Martin E. *Protestantism: Its Churches and Cultures, Rituals and Doctrines, Yesterday and Today.* New York: Holt, Rinehart, and Winston, 1972.
McCrickard, Janet. "Born Again Moon: Fundamentalism in Christianity and the Feminist Spirituality Movement." *Feminist Review*, No. 37 (Spring 1991): 65.
Miller, Judith Baker. *Toward a New Psychology of Women.* Boston: Beacon Press, 1986.
New York Times. Editorial: "The Ultimate Mother." May 12, 1991, Section E, p. 16.
Noble, Vicki. *Motherpeace: A Way to the Goddess through Myth, Art, and Tarot.* San Francisco: Harper & Row, 1983.
Orenstein, Gloria Feman. *The Reflowering of the Goddess.* New York: Pergamon Press, The Athene Series, 1990.
Pagels, Elaine. *Adam, Eve, and the Serpent.* New York: Vintage Books, 1989.
People Active in the Ministry. "Luzern Statement." *ARCC Light, Newsletter of the Association for the Rights of Catholics in the Church* 13, no. 2 (March/April 1991).
Plaskow, Judith. *Standing Again at Sinai: Judaism from a Feminist Perspective.* San Francisco: Harper & Row, 1990.
Plaskow, Judith, and Carol P. Christ. *Weaving the Visions: New Patterns in Feminist Spirituality.* San Francisco: Harper & Row, 1989.
Ranck, Shirley Ann. *Cakes for the Queen of Heaven.* Boston: Unitarian Universalist Association, 1986.
Ranke-Heinemann, Uta. *Eunuchs for the Kingdom of Heaven.* New York: Penguin, 1990.
Ruether, Rosemary Radford. *Sexism and God-talk: Toward a Feminist Theology.* Boston: Beacon Press, 1983.
Sagewoman: A Quarterly Magazine of Women's Spirituality. Point Arena, CA: Arena Press.
Schussler-Fiorenza, Elizabeth. *In Memory of Her: A Feminist Theological Reconstruction of Christian Origins.* New York: Crossroads, 1985.
Sjoo, Monica, and Barbara Mor. *The Great Cosmic Mother: Rediscovering the Religion of the Earth.* San Francisco: Harper & Row, 1987.
Spretnak, Charlene. *The Politics of Women's Spirituality.* New York: Anchor/Doubleday, 1982.
———. *States of Grace.* San Francisco: Harper & Row, 1991.
Starhawk. *Dreaming the Dark: Magic, Sex and Politics.* Boston: Beacon Press, 1982.
———. *The Spiral Dance*, rev. ed. San Francisco: Harper & Row, 1989.
———. *Truth or Dare.* San Francisco: Harper & Row, 1987.
Steinfels, Peter. "Idyllic Theory of Goddesses Creates Storm." *New York Times*, February 13, 1990, p. C1.
Stone, Merlin. *Ancient Mirrors of Womanhood.* Boston: Beacon Press, 1979.
———. *When God Was a Woman.* New York: Harcourt Brace Jovanovich, 1976.
Teish, Luisah. *Jambalaya.* San Francisco: HarperCollins, 1985.
Walker, Barbara G. *The Crone: Woman of Age, Wisdom and Power.* San Francisco: Harper & Row, 1985.

———. *The Woman's Encyclopedia of Myths and Secrets.* San Francisco: Harper & Row, 1983.

———. *Women's Rituals.* San Francisco: Harper & Row, 1990.

Weaver, Mary Jo. *New Catholic Women: A Contemporary Challenge to Traditional Religious Authority.* San Francisco: Harper & Row, 1985.

Wilkes, Paul. "The Hands That Would Shape Our Souls." *Atlantic Monthly,* December 1990.

woman of power, a magazine of feminism, spirituality and politics. Orleans, MA.

Wynne, Patrice. *The Womanspirit Sourcebook.* San Francisco: Harper & Row, 1988.

FEMINIST THERAPY

Brodsky, Annette M., and Rachel Hare-Mustin, eds. *Women and Psychotherapy: An Assessment of Research and Practice.* New York: The Guilford Press, 1980.

Broverman, I. K., D. M. Broverman, F. E. Clarkson, P. S. Rosenkrantz, and S. R. Vogel. "Sex Role Stereotypes and Clinical Judgments of Mental Health." *Journal of Consulting and Clinical Psychology* 34 (1970): 1–7.

Chesler, Phyllis. *Women and Madness.* Garden City, NY: Doubleday, 1972.

Dornbusch, Sanford M., and Myra H. Strober, eds. *Feminism, Children and the New Families.* New York: The Guilford Press, 1988.

Dutton-Douglas, Mary Ann, and Lenore E. Walker, eds. *Feminist Psychotherapies: Integration of Therapeutic and Feminist Systems.* Norwood, NJ: Ablex, 1988.

Faludi, Susan. *Backlash: The Undeclared War Against American Women.* New York: Crown Publishers, 1991.

Franks, Violet, and Vasanti Burtle, eds. *Women and Therapy.* New York: Brunner/Mazel, 1974.

Franks, Violet, and Esther D. Rothblum, eds. *The Stereotyping of Women: Its Effects on Mental Health.* New York: Springer, 1983.

Goodrich, Thelma J., Cheryl Rampage, Barbara Ellman, and Kris Halstead, eds. *Feminist Family Therapy: A Casebook.* New York: W. W. Norton, 1988.

Lerman, Hannah, and Natalie Porter, eds. *Feminist Ethics in Psychotherapy.* New York: Springer, 1990.

Masson, Jeffrey M. *The Assault on Truth: Freud's Suppression of the Seduction Theory.* New York: Farrar, Strauss and Giroux, 1984.

McGoldrick, Monica, Carol M. Anderson, and Froma Walsh, eds. *Women in Families: A Framework for Family Therapy.* New York: W. W. Norton, 1989.

Norwood, Robin. *Women Who Love Too Much.* New York: J. P. Tarcher (distributed by St. Martin's Press), 1985.

Rosewater, Lynne B., and Lenore E. Walker, eds. *Handbook of Feminist Therapy: Women's Issues in Psychotherapy.* New York: Springer, 1985.

Sturdivant, Susan. *Therapy with Women: A Feminist Philosophy of Treatment.* New York: Springer, 1980.

LITERARY CRITICISM AND LANGUAGE

Baron, Dennis. *Grammar and Gender.* New Haven, CT: Yale University Press, 1986.

Baym, Nina. "Melodramas of Beset Manhood: How Theories of American Fiction

Exclude Women Authors." In *The New Feminist Criticism: Essays on Women, Literature, and Theory*, ed. Elaine Showalter. New York: Pantheon Books, 1985.

Benson, Morton. "A Note on the Elimination of Sexism in Dictionaries." *Women and Language* 13, no. 1 (Fall 1990): 51.

Bernstein, Richard. "Nonsexist Dictionary Spells Out Rudeness." *New York Times*, June 11, 1991.

Blaubergs, Maija S. "Changing the Sexist Language: The Theory behind the Practice." *Psychology of Women Quarterly* 2 (Spring 1978): 244–261.

Bruss, Elizabeth W. *Beautiful Theories: The Spectacle of Discourse in Contemporary Criticism*. Baltimore: The Johns Hopkins University Press, 1982.

Butler, Matilda, and William Paisley. *Women and the Mass Media*. New York: Human Sciences Press, 1980.

Cannon, Garland, and Susan Roberson. "Sexism in Present-Day English: Is It Diminishing?" *Word* 36 (April 1985): 23–34.

Capek, Mary Ellen, ed. *A Women's Thesaurus: An Index of Language Used to Describe and Locate Information by and about Women*. New York: Harper & Row, 1987.

Frank, Francine Wattman, and Paula A. Treichler. *Language, Gender, and Professional Writing*. New York: The Modern Language Association of America, 1989.

Froula, Christine. "When Eve Reads Milton: Undoing the Canonical Economy." *Critical Inquiry* 10 (December 1983).

Galfand, Elissa D., and Virginia Thorndike Hules, eds. *French Feminist Criticism: An Annotated Bibliography*. New York: Garland, 1985.

Gallop, Jane. *Reading Lacan*. Ithaca, NY: Cornell University Press, 1985.

———. "Reading the Mother Tongue: Psychoanalytic Feminist Criticism." *Critical Inquiry* 13 (Winter 1987): 314–329.

Gilbert, Sandra. "Life's Empty Pack: Notes toward a Literary Daughteronomy." *Critical Inquiry*, 11 (March 1985).

Gilbert, Sandra, and Susan Gubar. *The Madwoman in the Attic*. New Haven, CT: Yale University Press, 1979.

Greene, Gayle, and Coppelia Kahn, eds. *Making a Difference: Feminist Literary Criticism*. London: Methuen, 1985.

Henley, Nancy M. "This New Species That Seeks a New Language: On Sexism in Language and Language Change." In *Women and Language in Transition*, ed. Joyce Penfield. Albany: State University of New York Press, 1987.

Jehlen, Myra. "Archimedes and the Paradox of Feminist Criticism." *Signs* 6, no. 4 (Summer 1981): 575–601.

Kanfer, Stefan. "Sispeak: A Misguided Attempt to Change Herstory." *Time*, October 23, 1972, p. 79.

Kramarae, Chris, and Paula A. Treichler. *A Feminist Dictionary*. London: Pandora Press, 1985.

Little, Judy. "The Discourses of Feminist Theory and Literary Criticism: Introductory Notes and Selected Bibliography with Annotations." Unpublished, 1989.

Maggio, Rosalie. *Nonsexist Word Finder: A Dictionary of Gender-Free Usage*. Phoenix: The Oryx Press, 1987.

Marks, Elaine, and Isabelle de Courtvron, eds. *New French Feminisms*. New York: Schocken Books, 1981.

————. "Women and Literature in France." *Signs* 3 (1978): 832–842.

Martyna, Wendy. "Beyond the He/Man Approach: The Case for Nonsexist Language." In *Language, Gender and Society*, ed. Barrie Thorne, Cheris Kramarae, and Nancy Henley. Rowley, MA: Newbury House, 1983.

McKay, Donald. "Prescriptive Grammar and the Pronoun Problem." In *Language, Gender and Society*, ed. Barrie Thorne, Cheris Kramarae, and Nancy Henley. Rowley, MA: Newbury House, 1983.

Miller, Casey, and Kate Swift. *The Handbook of Nonsexist Writing*. New York: Lippincott and Crowell, 1980.

Moi, Toril. *Sexual/Textual Politics*. London: Methuen, 1985.

Newmeyer, Frederick J. *The Politics of Linguistics*. Chicago: University of Chicago Press, 1986.

Penelope, Julia. *Speaking Freely: Unlearning the Lies of the Fathers' Tongues*. Elmsford, NY: Pergamon Press, 1990.

Rackin, Phyllis. "Androgyny, Mimesis, and the Marriage of the Boy Heroine on the English Reinaissance Stage." In *The New Feminist Criticism: Essays on Women, Literature, and Theory*, ed. Elaine Showalter. New York: Pantheon Books, 1985.

Ruthven, K. K. *Feminist Literary Studies: An Introduction*. Cambridge: Cambridge University Press, 1984.

Schneider, Michael J., and Karen A. Foss. "Thought, Sex, and Language: The Sapir-Whorf Hypothesis in the American's Woman's Movement." *ORWAC Bulletin* 1 (Spring 1977): 1–7.

Shaw, Peter. "Feminist Literary Criticism: A Report from the Academy." *The American Scholar* Autumn 1988, pp. 495–513.

Showalter, Elaine. *A Literature of Their Own*. Princeton, NJ: Princeton University Press, 1988.

Showalter, Elaine, ed. *The New Feminist Criticism: Essays on Women, Literature, and Theory*. New York: Pantheon Books, 1985.

————., ed. *Speaking of Gender*. New York: Routledge, 1989.

Smith, Barbara. "Toward a Black Feminist Criticism." In *The New Feminist Criticism: Essays on Women, Literature, and Theory*, ed. Elaine Showalter. New York: Pantheon Books, 1985.

Snitow, Ann. "Pages from a Gender Diary." *Dissent*, Spring 1989, pp. 205–224.

Spender, Dale. *Man Made Language*. London: Routledge and Kegan Paul, 1980.

————., ed. *Men's Studies Modified: The Impact of Feminism on the Academic Disciplines*. Oxford: Pergamon Press, 1981.

Steinem, Gloria. "Sex, Lies and Advertising." *Ms.*, premier issue (1990): 18–28.

Thorne, Barrie, Cheris Kramarae, and Nancy Henley, eds. *Language Gender and Society*. Rowley, MA: Newbury House, 1983.

Todd, Janet. *Feminist Literary History: A Defence*. Cambridge: Cambridge University Press, 1988.

U.S. Commission on Civil Rights. *Characters in Textbooks: A Review of the Literature*. Clearinghouse Publication 62, May 1980.

Women and Language. Vols. 1–14, 1976–91.

Wright, Elizabeth. *Psychoanalytic Criticism: Theory in Practice*. London: Methuen, 1984.

Zimmerman, Bonnie. "What Never Has Been: An Overview of Lesbian Feminist Literary Criticism." *Feminist Studies* 7 (1981): 451–475.

WOMEN AND RISK

Bradbury, Judith. "The Policy Implications of Differing Concepts of Risk." *Science, Technology and Human Values*, 14 (1986): 380–399.

Chard, Tim, and Martin Richards. "Lessons for the Future." In *Benefits and Hazards of the New Obstetrics*, ed. Tim Chard and Martin Richards. Philadelphia: Lippincott, 1977.

Douglas, Mary. *Risk Acceptability According to the Social Sciences*. New York: Russell Sage, 1985.

Fischoff, Baruch. "Managing Risk Perceptions." *Issues in Science and Technology*, Fall 1985, pp. 83–96.

Fischoff, Baruch, Sarah Lichtenstein, Paul Slovic, S. Derby, and R. Keeney. *Acceptable Risk*. Cambridge: Cambridge University Press, 1981.

Funtowicz, Silvio O., and Jerome R. Ravetz. "Three Types of Risk Assessment: A Methodological Analysis." In *Environmental Impact Assessment, Technology Assessment, and Risk Analysis*, ed. Vincent T. Covello, J. L. Mumpower, P.J.M. Stallen, and V.R.R. Uppuluri. New York: Springer-Verlag, 1985.

Gallagher, Janet. "Fetus as Patient." In *Reproductive Laws for the 1990s*, ed. Sherrill Cohen and Nadine Taub. Clifton, NJ: Humana Press, 1989.

Hance, Billie Jo, Caron Chess, and Peter M. Sandman. "Setting a Context for Explaining Risk." *Risk Analysis* 9 (1989): 113–117.

Hurst, Marsha, and Pamela Summey. "Childbirth and Social Class: The Case of Cesarean Delivery." *Social Science and Medicine* 18 (1984): 621–631.

Kenen, Regina. *Reproductive Hazards in the Workplace: Mending Jobs, Managing Pregnancies*. Binghamton, NY: Haworth Press, 1993.

Kolder, Veronika, Janet Gallagher, and Michael Parsons. "Court-Ordered Obstetrical Interventions." *New England Journal of Medicine*, May 7, 1987, pp. 1192–1196.

Krimsky, Sheldon, and Alonzo Plough. *Environmental Hazards: Communicating Risks as a Social Process*. Dover, MA: Auburn House, 1988.

National Women's Health Network. *Turning Things Around: A Women's Occupational and Environmental Health Guide*. Washington, DC: NWHN, 1990.

Otway, Harry J., and K. Thomas. "Reflections on Risk Perception and Policy." *Risk Analysis*, 2 (1982): 69–82.

Paigen, Beverly. "Children and Toxic Chemicals." *Journal of Pesticide Reform*, Summer 1986, pp. 2–5.

Rothman, Barbara. "Midwives in Transition: The Structure of a Clinical Revolution." *Social Problems* 30 (1983): 262–270.

Sandman, Peter M. "Apathy versus Hysteria: Public Perception of Risk." In *Public Perception of Biotechnology*, ed. Lekh R. Batra and Waldemar Klassen. Bethesda, MD: Agricultural Research Institute, 1987.

———. *Explaining Environmental Risk*. Report for the Office of Toxic Substances of the U.S. Environmental Protection Agency, November 1986.

————. "Hazard versus Outrage in the Public Perception of Risk." In *Effective Risk Communication*, ed. Vincent Covello, D. McCallum, and M. Pavlova. New York: Plenum, 1989.

Short, James Jr. "The Social Fabric at Risk: Toward the Social Transformation of Risk Analysis." *American Sociological Review* 49 (1984): 711–725.

Shy, Kirkwood K., David Luthy, Forrest Bennet et al. "Effects of Electronic Fetal-Heart-Rate Monitoring." *New England Journal of Medicine* 322 (1990): 588–593.

Stone, Deborah. "Fetal Risks, Women's Rights: Showdown at Johnson Controls." *The American Prospect* 3, no. 1 (1990): 43–53.

Tversky, Amos, and Daniel Kahneman. "Judgment Under Uncertainty: Heuristics and Biases." *Science* 185 (1974): 1124–1131.

WOMEN'S SEXUALITY

Belensky, Mary Field, Blythe McVicker Clinchy, Nancy Rule Goldberger, and Jill Mattuck Tarule. *Women's Ways of Knowing.* New York: Basic Books, 1986.

Gilligan, Carol. *In a Different Voice: Psychological Theory and Women's Development.* Cambridge, MA: Harvard University Press, 1982.

Jordan, Judith V., Alexandra G. Kaplan, Jean Baker Miller, Irene P. Stiver, and Janet L. Surrey. *Women's Growth in Connection.* New York: Guilford Press, 1991.

Wolf, Naomi. *The Beauty Myth.* New York: William Morrow, 1991.

Index

About the Editor and Contributors

FRANCES C. HUTNER is an economist with a special interest in women's issues. Her book, *Equal Pay for Comparable Worth*, was published by Praeger in 1986. Dr. Hutner is currently a trustee of Green Mountain College, director of an investment counseling firm in New York City, and a member of the board of directors' advisory committee of a New England public utility. She has taught economics at Smith College, Stevens Institute of Technology, Rutgers University, and Rider College.

FRANCESCA BENSON is an educational consultant and writer. She is a remedial reading specialist and co-founder of a school for children with learning difficulties. She is the author of *Famous Mathematicians*. In recent years, she has become active in feminist spirituality, and she organizes workshops and conferences in feminist spirituality and the creative arts.

LAURA CURTIS was a lecturer at Princeton University, where she taught literature. She was the author of *The Versatile Defoe* and *The Elusive Daniel Defoe*, and of several articles. She taught college from 1970 until her death in September 1993.

VIOLET FRANKS is director of psychology at the Carrier Foundation. She is past president of the American Psychological Association's section dealing with clinical psychology and women and is currently representing this section on the board of directors of the clinical division. Dr. Franks is on the adjunct faculty of Rutgers University, where she gives graduate courses on women and therapy. She is series editor of the Springer Series, *Focus on Women*, and has published three books in the area of the psychology of women.

HANNA FOX is program officer of the New Jersey Children's Trust Fund to prevent child abuse. She has written extensively about mental health, social issues, and women's issues and teaches writing at Mercer County Community College. She was the founder and director of "Parent to Parent," a pilot peer counseling program for parents of children with birth defects, sponsored by the National Foundation/March of Dimes of Mercer County.

REGINA KENEN is a professor of sociology at Trenton State College. She has done extensive research, writing, and consulting on risks in the home and workplace, on health issues, and on questions involving medical ethics and practice. Dr. Kenen's latest book is *Reproductive Hazards in the Workplace: Mending Jobs, Managing Pregnancies* (1993).

RUTH B. MANDEL is a professor at the Eagleton Institute of Politics at Rutgers University and has been the director of Eagleton's Center for the American Woman and Politics (CAWP) since 1971. Her book, *In the Running: The New Woman Candidate* (1983), describes women's experiences campaigning for political office. CAWP's most recent research examines whether women officials make a difference. Findings are summarized in Susan J. Carroll, Debra L. Dodson, and Ruth B. Mandel, *The Impact of Women in Public Office: An Overview* (1991).

JENNIFER S. MACLEOD is a social psychologist with her own firm, Jennifer Macleod Associates, which provides corporations, educational institutions, and nonprofit organizations with consulting, research, and training services on attitudes, behavior, organizational effectiveness, and equal opportunity (with special emphasis on equal opportunity for women and girls). Dr. Macleod was formerly chief psychologist for Opinion Research Corporation and was the first director of Rutgers University's Eagleton Center for the American Woman and Politics.

ROSEMARY O'BRIEN is a free-lance journalist who writes regularly for the Princeton Packet newspapers under her own byline. She has done extensive research on issues of women's spirituality.

GAIL WALKER is a psychotherapist in private practice who draws from movement therapy, feminist psychology, and Jungian theory in her work as a therapist. She has organized workshops for business and professional groups on issues related to sexuality, dreamwork, body image, internalized oppression, and mind/body/psyche connections. She has also published articles exploring the links between women's bodies, psychology, and spirituality and is currently writing a book about "the feminine." She is a member of the Feminist Therapy Institute.